STAR WARS ☼ HAN SOLO

IMPERIAL CADET

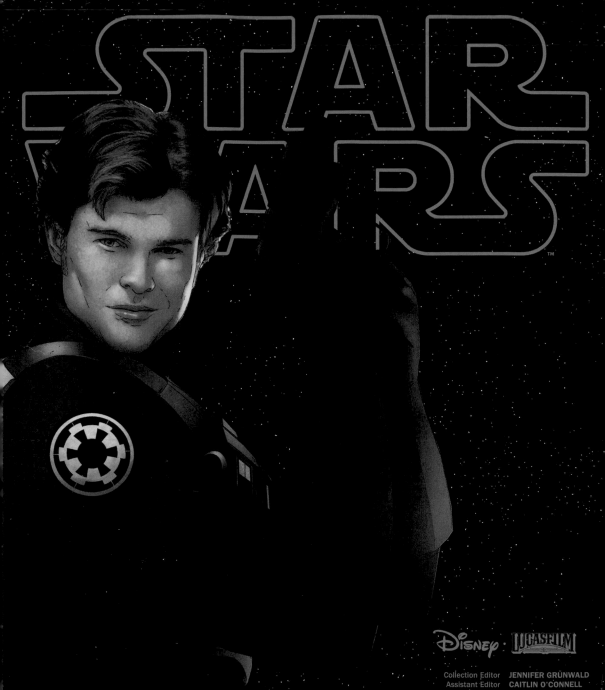

STAR WARS

Collection Editor   **JENNIFER GRÜNWALD**
Assistant Editor   **CAITLIN O'CONNELL**
Associate Managing Editor   **KATERI WOODY**
Editor, Special Projects   **MARK D. BEAZLEY**
VP Production & Special Projects   **JEFF YOUNGQUIST**
SVP Print, Sales & Marketing   **DAVID GABRIEL**
Book Designer   **ADAM DEL RE**

STAR WARS: HAN SOLO — IMPERIAL CADET. Contains material originally published in magazine form as STAR WARS: HAN SOLO - IMPERIAL CADET #1-5 and STAR WARS: BECKETT #1. First printing 2019. ISBN 978-1-302-91500-1. Published by MARVEL WORLDWIDE, INC., a subsidiary of MARVEL ENTERTAINMENT, LLC. OFFICE OF PUBLICATION: 135 West 50th Street, New York, NY 10020. STAR WARS and related text and illustrations are trademarks and/or copyrights, in the United States and other countries, of Lucasfilm Ltd. and/or its affiliates. © & TM Lucasfilm Ltd. No similarity between any of the names, characters, persons, and/or institutions in this magazine with those of any living or dead person or institution is intended, and any such similarity which may exist is purely coincidental. Marvel and its logos are TM Marvel Characters, Inc. **Printed in Canada.** DAN BUCKLEY, President, Marvel Entertainment; JOHN NEE, Publisher; JOE QUESADA, Chief Creative Officer; TOM BREVOORT, SVP of Publishing; DAVID BOGART, Associate Publisher & SVP of Talent Affairs; DAVID GABRIEL, SVP of Sales & Marketing, Publishing; JEFF YOUNGQUIST, VP of Production & Special Projects; DAN CARR, Executive Director of Publishing Technology; ALEX MORALES, Director of Publishing Operations; DAN EDINGTON, Managing Editor; SUSAN CRESPI, Production Manager; STAN LEE, Chairman Emeritus. For information regarding advertising in Marvel Comics or on Marvel.com, please contact Vit DeBellis, Custom Solutions & Integrated Advertising Manager, at vdebellis@marvel.com. For Marvel subscription inquiries, please call 888-511-5480. **Manufactured between 3/8/2019 and 4/9/2019 by SOLISCO PRINTERS, SCOTT, QC, CANADA.**

10 9 8 7 6 5 4 3 2 1

Assistant Editor	**NICHOLAS MARTINO**
Senior Editor	**ROBERT SIMPSON**
Executive Editor	**JENNIFER HEDDLE**
Creative Director	**MICHAEL SIGLAIN**
Lucasfilm Story Group	**JAMES WAUGH, LELAND CHEE, MATT MARTIN**

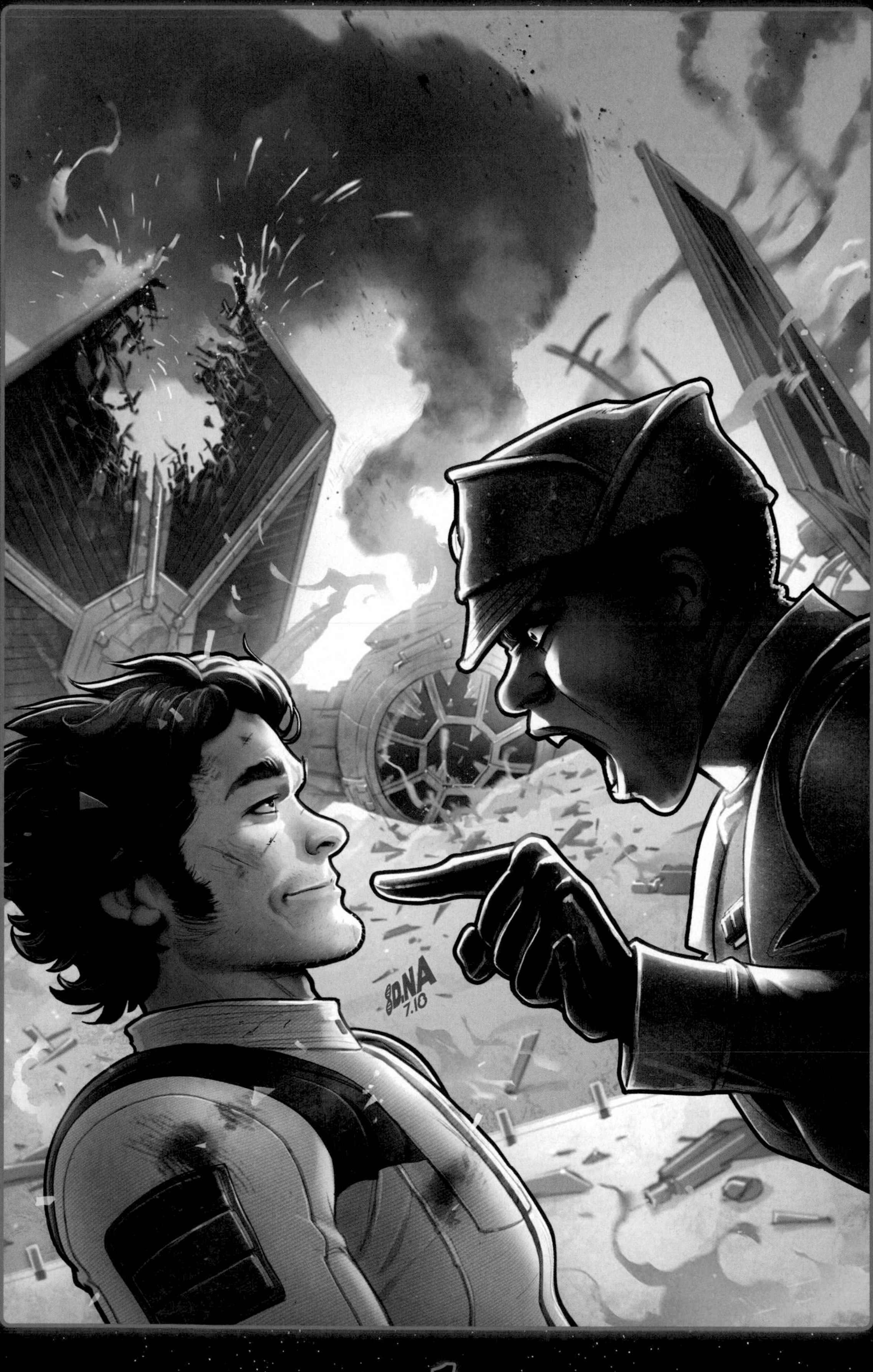

1

**HAN
SOLO**

CADET 124-329

**TRIOSA
BROOG**

TRAINING OFFICER

**HANINA
NICO**

CADET 803-308

**LYTTAN
DREE**

CADET 541-145

**TAMU
DREE**

CADET 542-146

CARIDA ACADEMY

*THE EMPIRE REQUIRES INNUMERABLE
RECRUITS TO FILL THE VAST RANKS OF OUR
ARMED FORCES.*

*NAVAL CADETS: SHOULD YOU SURVIVE BASIC
TRAINING AND EARN YOUR WINGS IN FLIGHT
SCHOOL, YOU WILL HAVE EARNED THE HONOR
OF DISPENSING THE EMPEROR'S JUSTICE UPON
COUNTLESS SYSTEMS ACROSS THE GALAXY
— AS TIE FIGHTER PILOTS!*

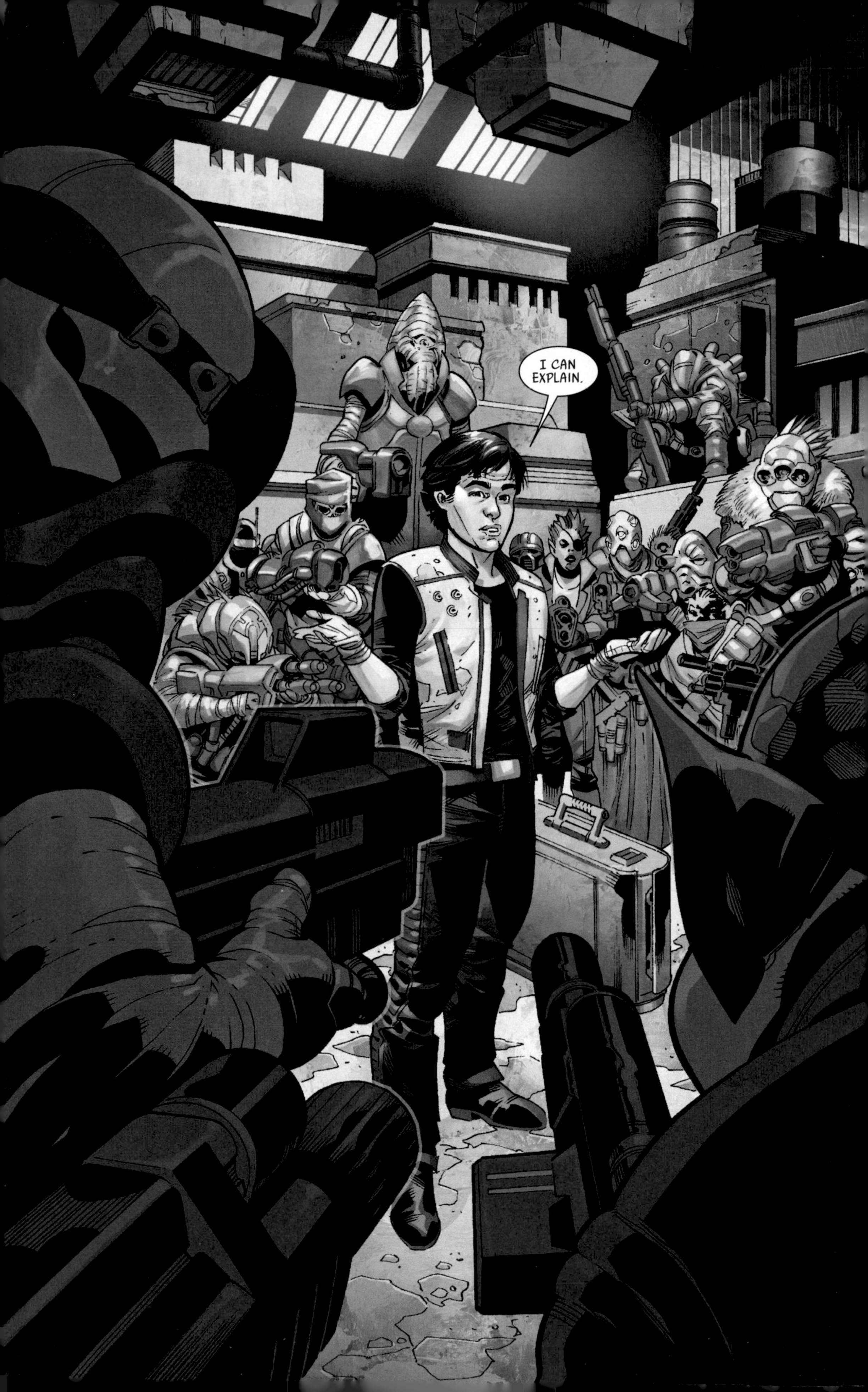
I CAN EXPLAIN.

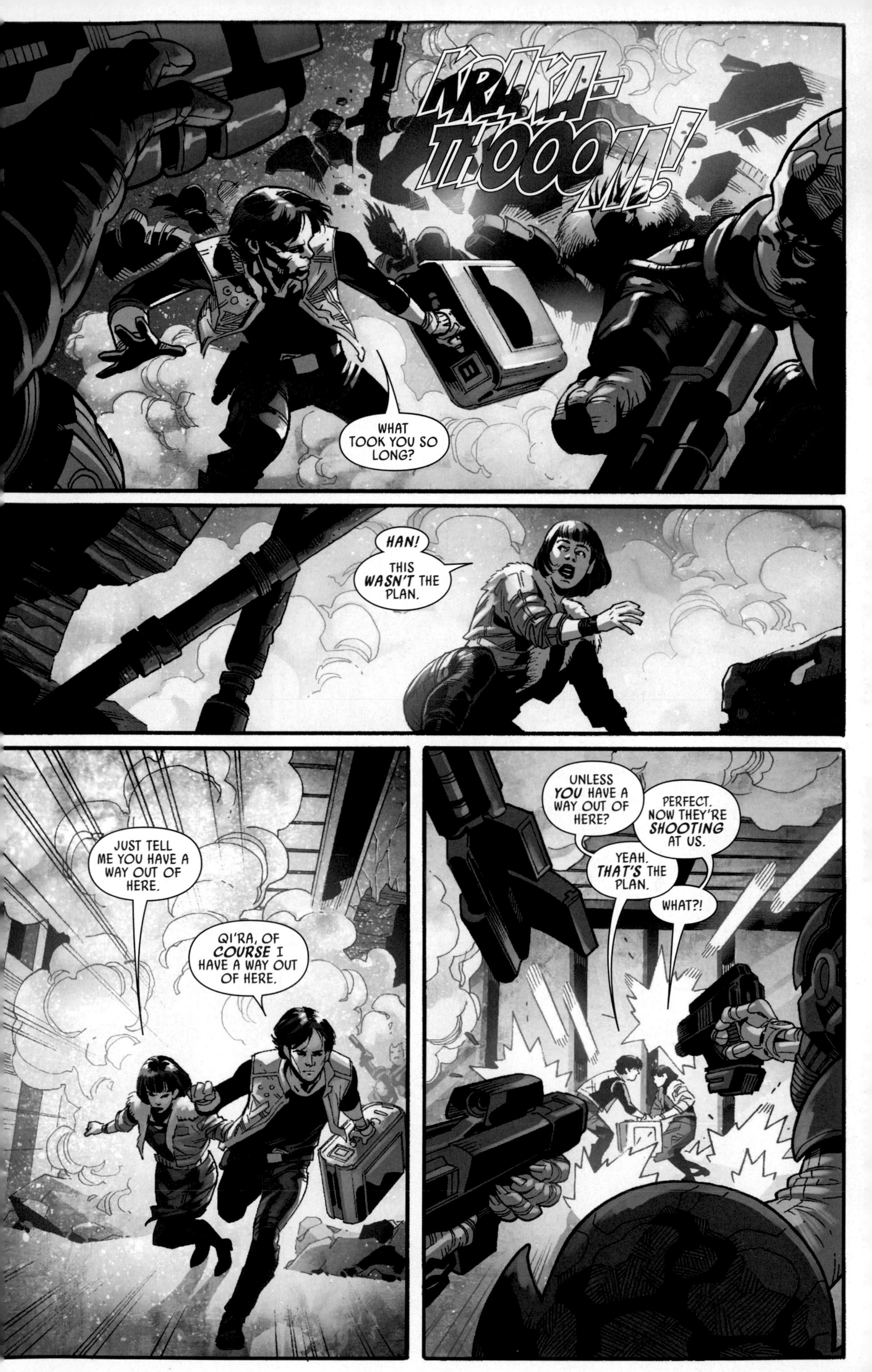
KRAKA-THOOOM!
WHAT TOOK YOU SO LONG?
HAN!
THIS WASN'T THE PLAN.
JUST TELL ME YOU HAVE A WAY OUT OF HERE.
QI'RA, OF COURSE I HAVE A WAY OUT OF HERE.
UNLESS YOU HAVE A WAY OUT OF HERE?
PERFECT. NOW THEY'RE SHOOTING AT US.
YEAH. THAT'S THE PLAN.
WHAT?!

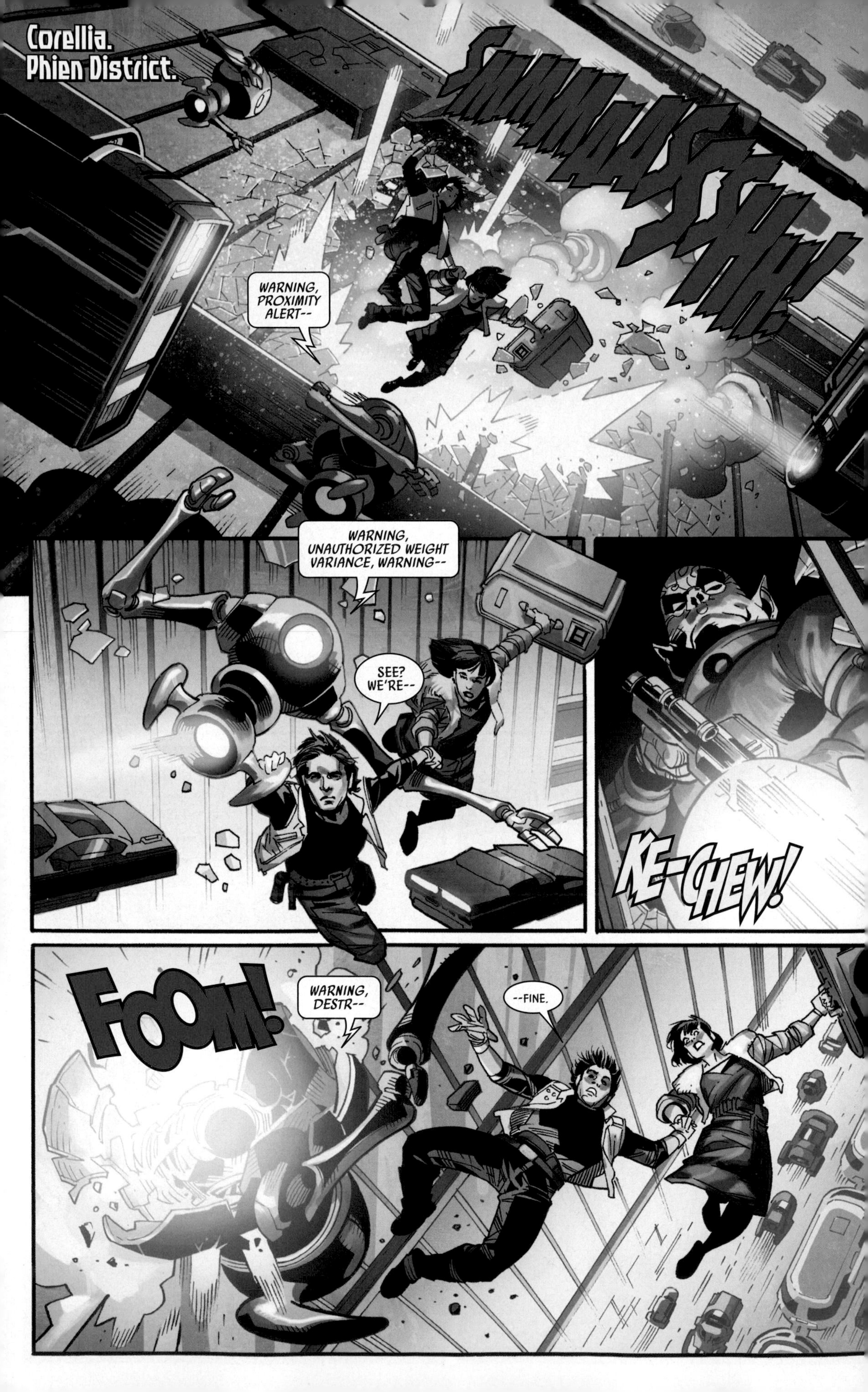
Corellia.
Phien District.
SHHMMMAASSHH!
WARNING, PROXIMITY ALERT--
WARNING, UNAUTHORIZED WEIGHT VARIANCE, WARNING--
SEE? WE'RE--
KE-CHEW!
FOOM!
WARNING, DESTR--
--FINE.

OOF!

AAAH!

BLAST THEM OFF THAT FREIGHTER TRAIN!

ONE OF THESE DAYS YOUR LUCK'S GONNA RUN OUT.

BZZT. BZZT.

EMERGENCY TURN NOW IN PROGRESS--

SCCCRRREEEEE!

AAGHH!

BOOOM

NOT AS LONG AS I'VE GOT THESE.

IF WE'D SPENT MORE TIME STEALING THAN RUNNING, WE COULD HAVE STOLEN MORE FOOD PORTIONS.

C'MON, PROXIMA'S GONNA BE THRILLED.

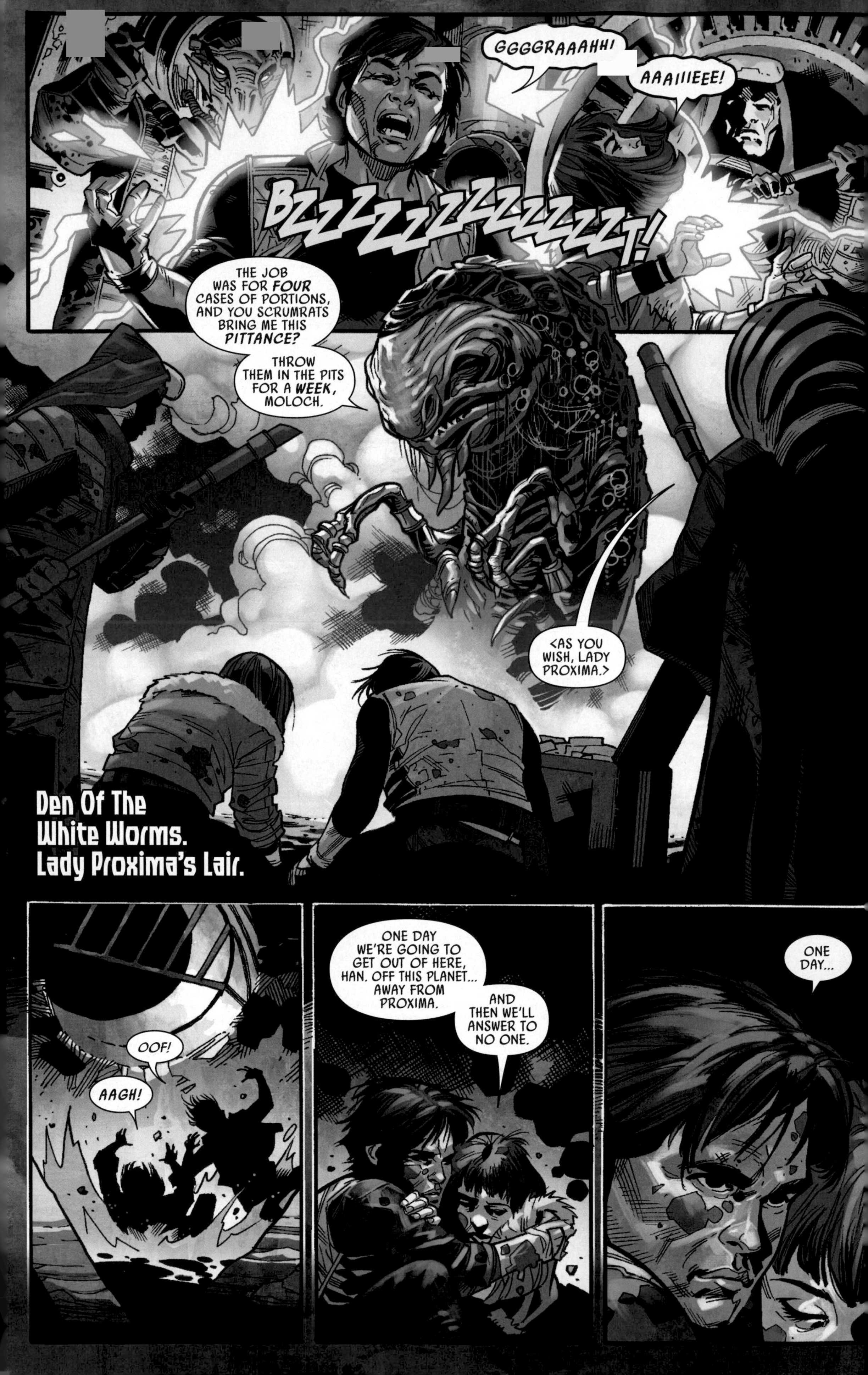
GGGGRAAAHH!
AAAIIIEEE!
BZZZZZZZZZZZZZZT!
THE JOB WAS FOR FOUR CASES OF PORTIONS, AND YOU SCRUMRATS BRING ME THIS PITTANCE?
THROW THEM IN THE PITS FOR A WEEK, MOLOCH.
<AS YOU WISH, LADY PROXIMA.>
Den Of The White Worms. Lady Proxima's Lair.
OOF!
AAGH!
ONE DAY WE'RE GOING TO GET OUT OF HERE, HAN. OFF THIS PLANET... AWAY FROM PROXIMA.
AND THEN WE'LL ANSWER TO NO ONE.
ONE DAY...

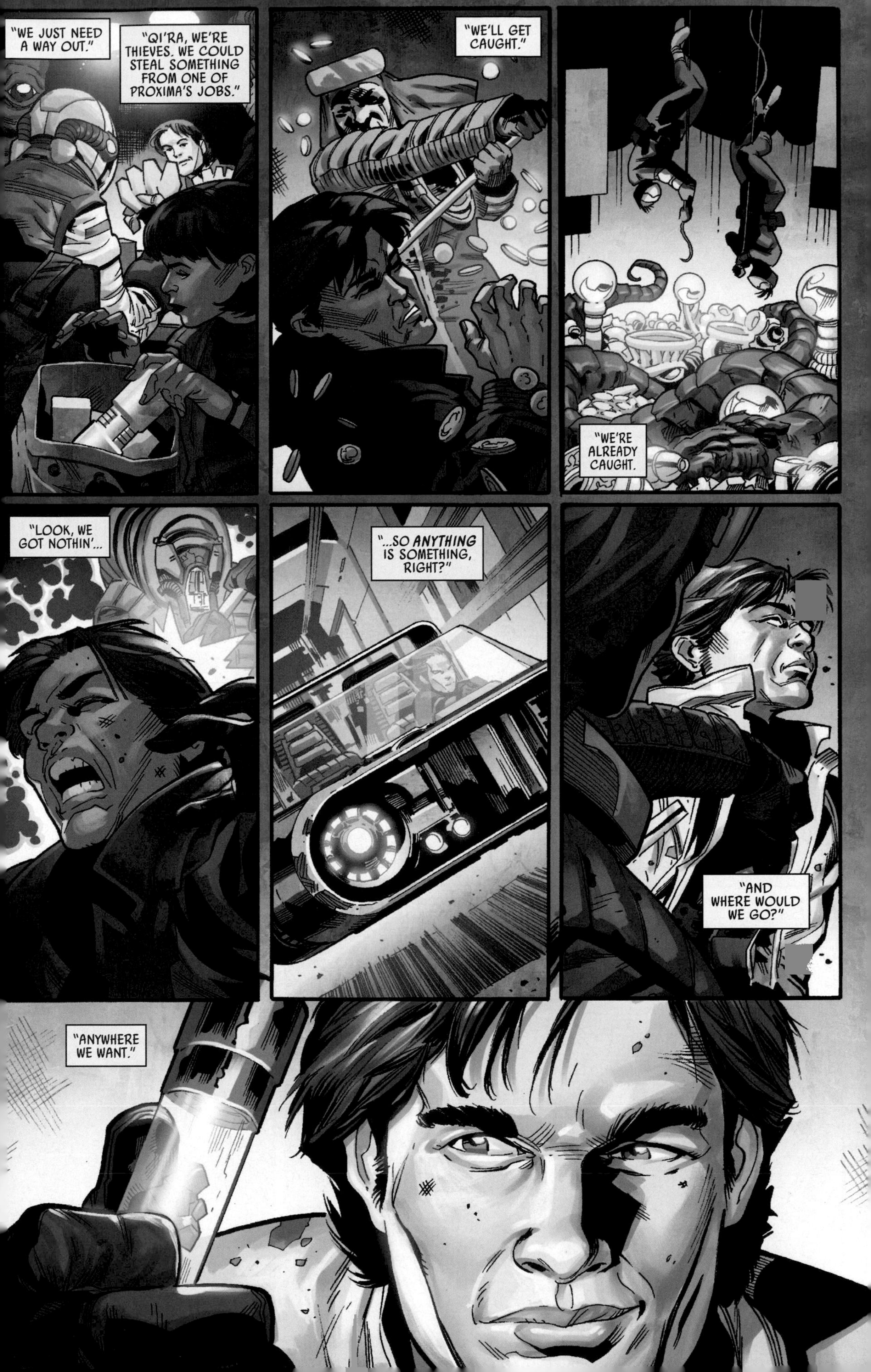
"WE JUST NEED A WAY OUT."
"QI'RA, WE'RE THIEVES. WE COULD STEAL SOMETHING FROM ONE OF PROXIMA'S JOBS."
"WE'LL GET CAUGHT."
"WE'RE ALREADY CAUGHT.
"LOOK, WE GOT NOTHIN'...
"...SO ANYTHING IS SOMETHING, RIGHT?"
"AND WHERE WOULD WE GO?"
"ANYWHERE WE WANT."

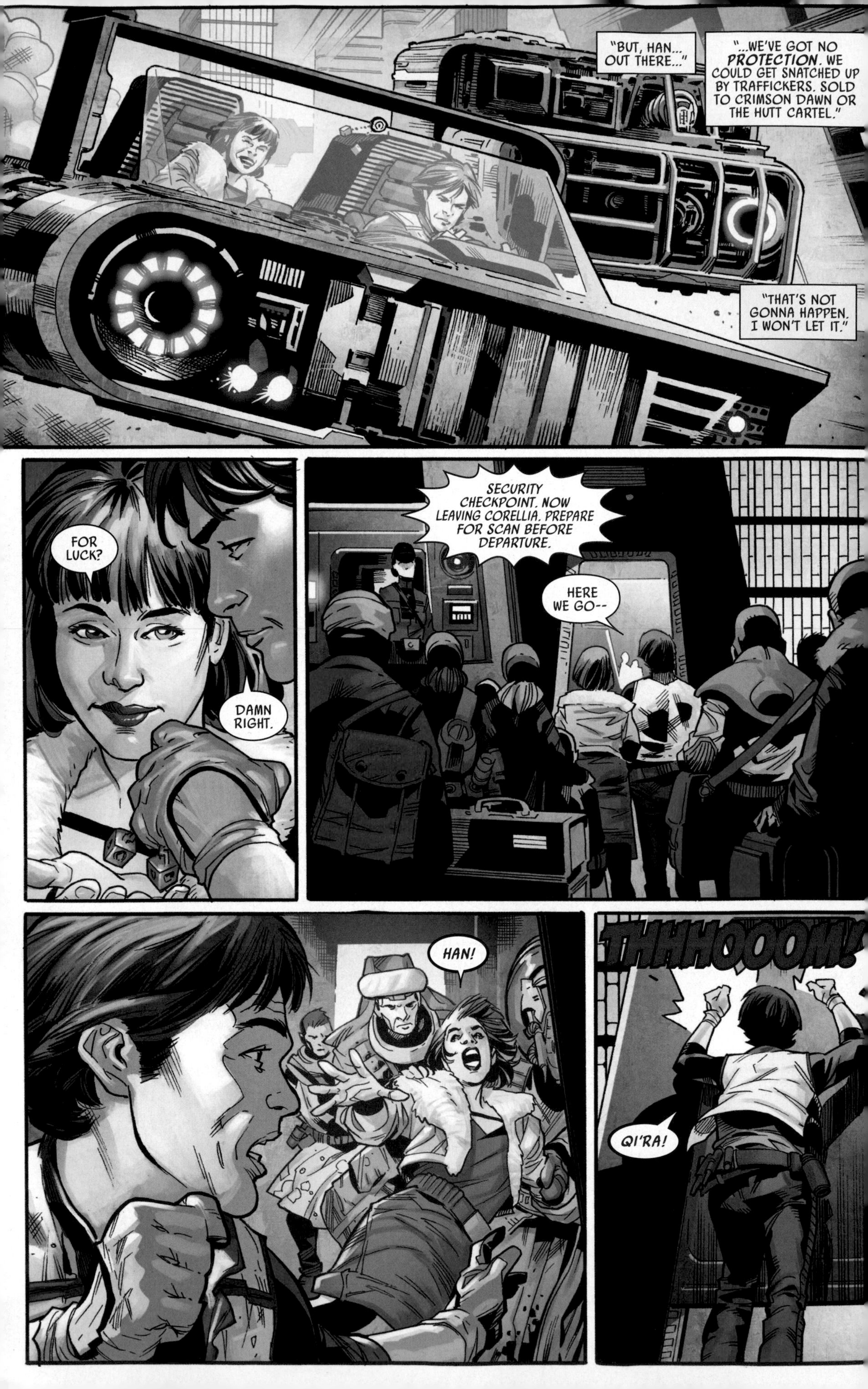
"BUT, HAN... OUT THERE..."
"...WE'VE GOT NO **PROTECTION**. WE COULD GET SNATCHED UP BY TRAFFICKERS. SOLD TO CRIMSON DAWN OR THE HUTT CARTEL."
"THAT'S NOT GONNA HAPPEN. I WON'T LET IT."
FOR LUCK?
DAMN RIGHT.
SECURITY CHECKPOINT. NOW LEAVING CORELLIA. PREPARE FOR SCAN BEFORE DEPARTURE.
HERE WE GO--
HAN!
THHHOOOM!
QI'RA!

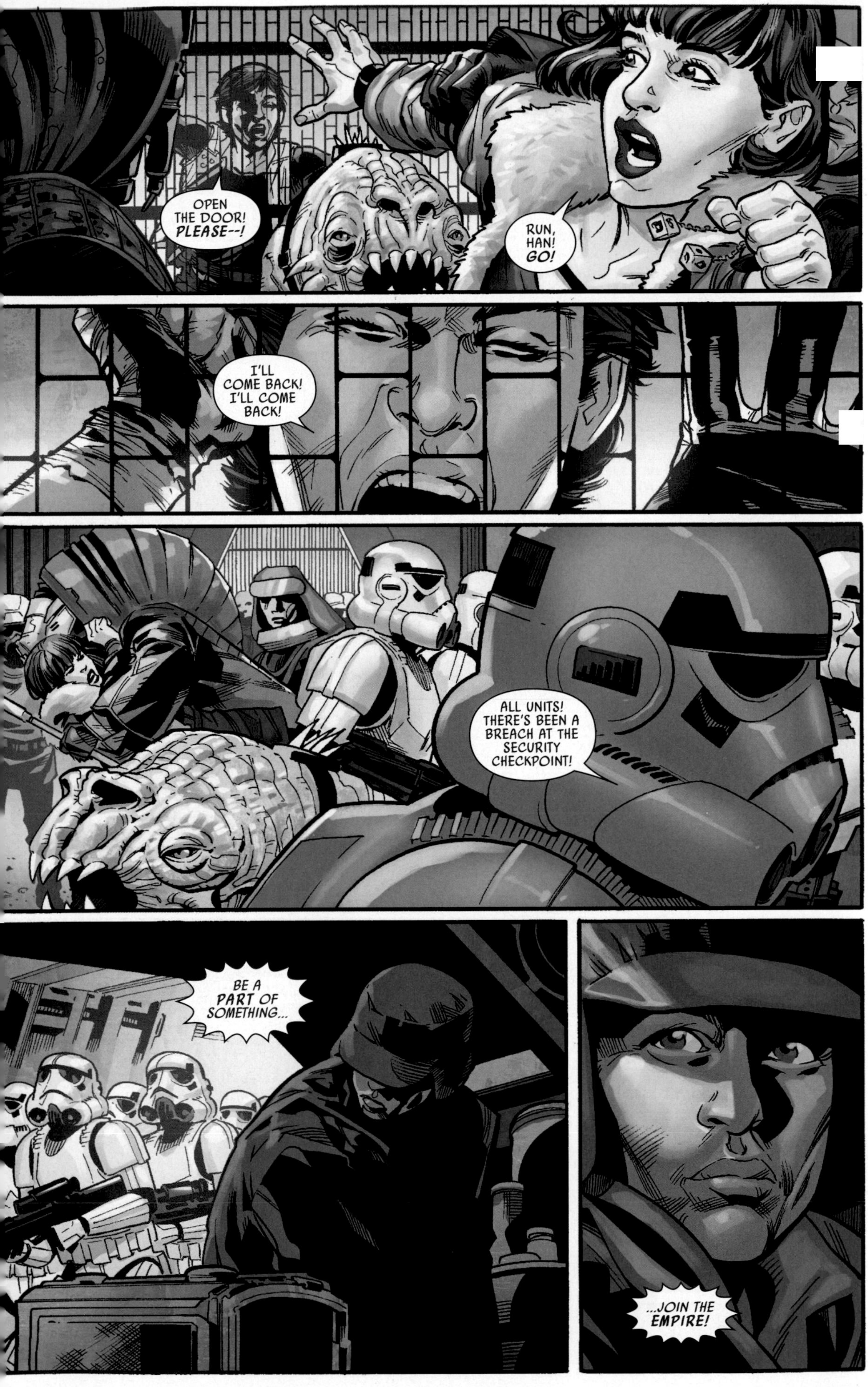
OPEN THE DOOR! PLEASE--!
RUN, HAN! GO!
I'LL COME BACK! I'LL COME BACK!
ALL UNITS! THERE'S BEEN A BREACH AT THE SECURITY CHECKPOINT!
BE A PART OF SOMETHING...
...JOIN THE EMPIRE!

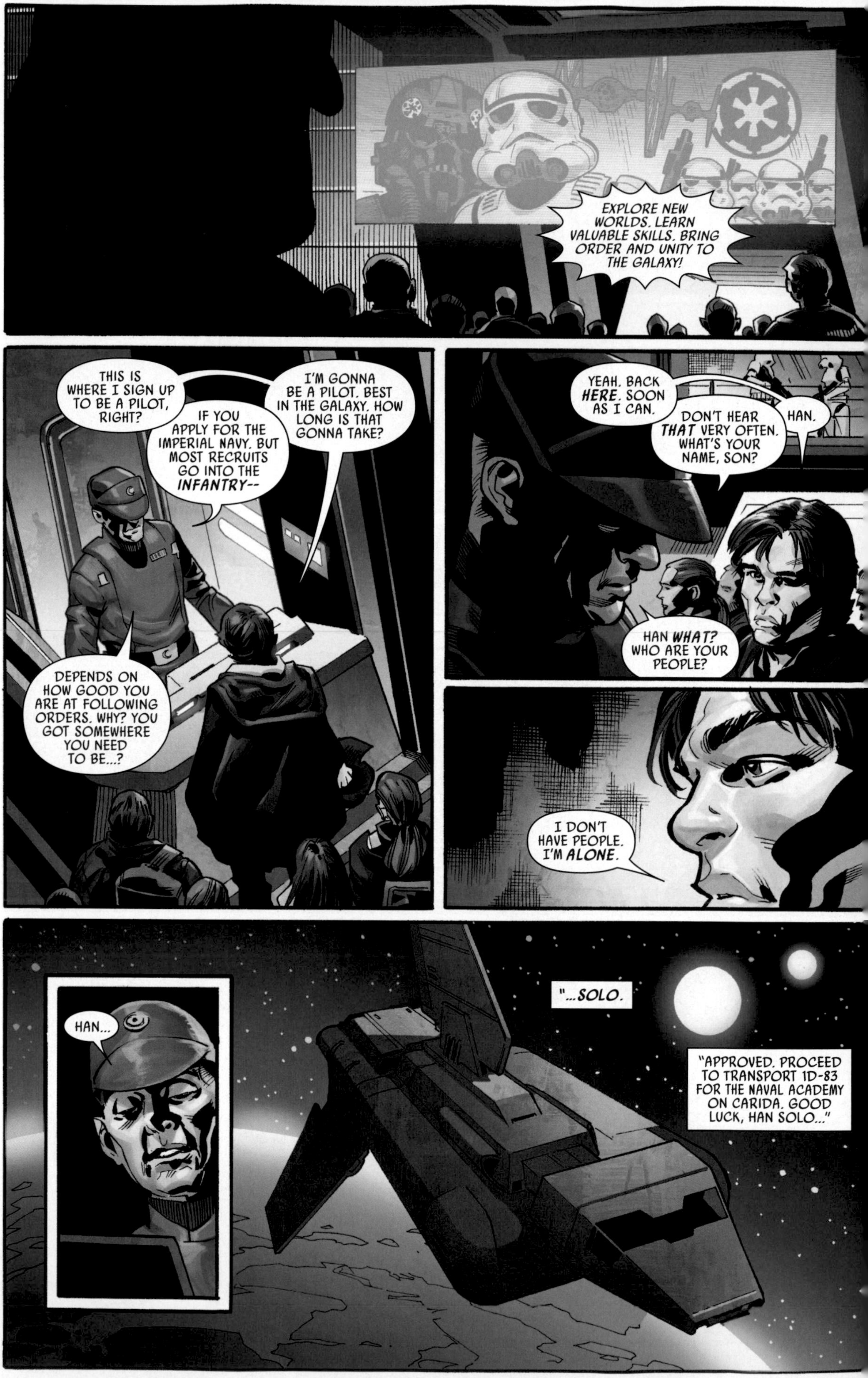
EXPLORE NEW WORLDS. LEARN VALUABLE SKILLS. BRING ORDER AND UNITY TO THE GALAXY!
THIS IS WHERE I SIGN UP TO BE A PILOT, RIGHT?
IF YOU APPLY FOR THE IMPERIAL NAVY. BUT MOST RECRUITS GO INTO THE INFANTRY--
I'M GONNA BE A PILOT. BEST IN THE GALAXY. HOW LONG IS THAT GONNA TAKE?
DEPENDS ON HOW GOOD YOU ARE AT FOLLOWING ORDERS. WHY? YOU GOT SOMEWHERE YOU NEED TO BE...?
YEAH. BACK HERE. SOON AS I CAN.
DON'T HEAR THAT VERY OFTEN. WHAT'S YOUR NAME, SON?
HAN.
HAN WHAT? WHO ARE YOUR PEOPLE?
I DON'T HAVE PEOPLE. I'M ALONE.
HAN...
"...SOLO.
"APPROVED. PROCEED TO TRANSPORT 1D-83 FOR THE NAVAL ACADEMY ON CARIDA. GOOD LUCK, HAN SOLO..."

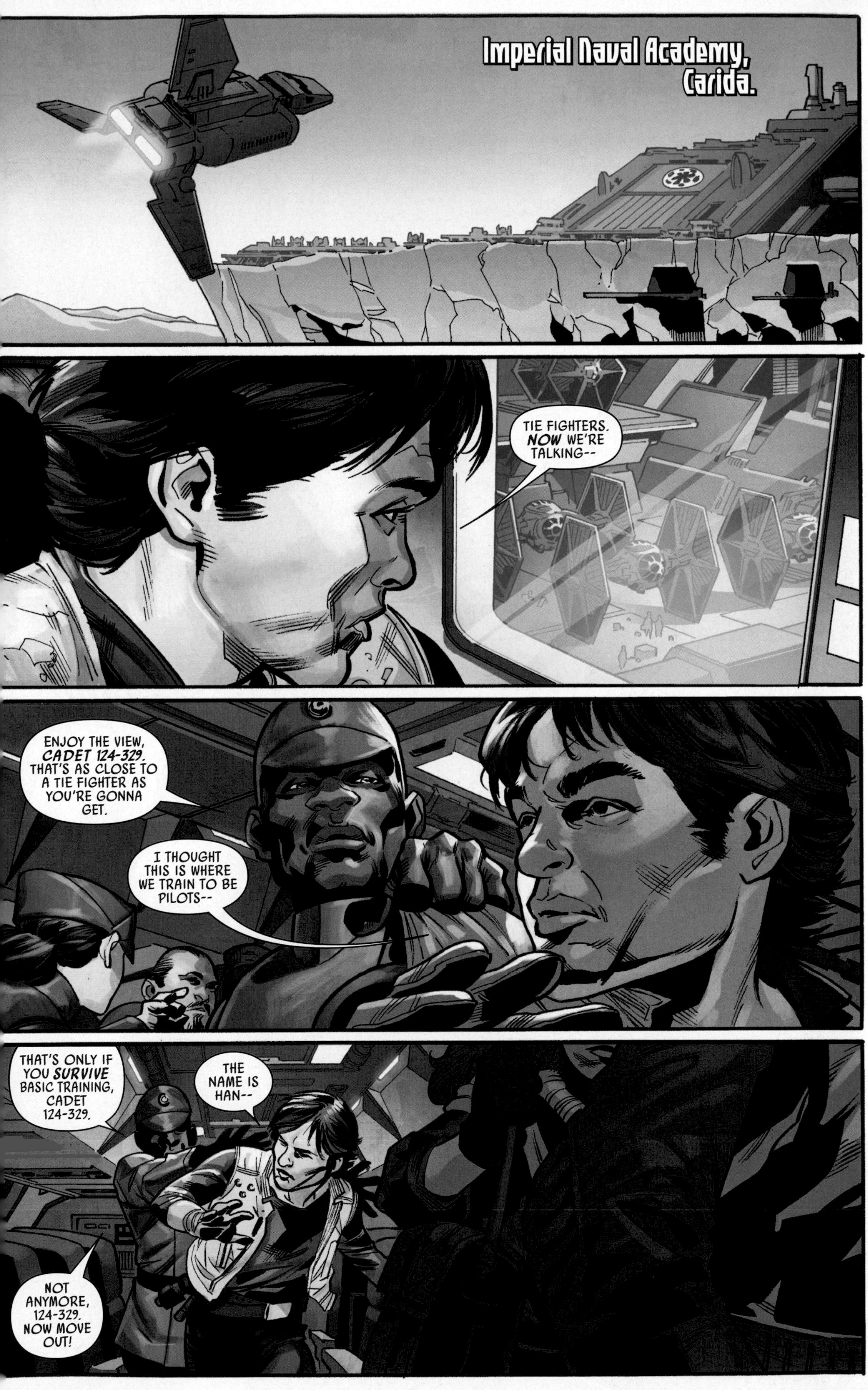
Imperial Naval Academy, Carida.
TIE FIGHTERS. NOW WE'RE TALKING--
ENJOY THE VIEW, CADET 124-329. THAT'S AS CLOSE TO A TIE FIGHTER AS YOU'RE GONNA GET.
I THOUGHT THIS IS WHERE WE TRAIN TO BE PILOTS--
THAT'S ONLY IF YOU SURVIVE BASIC TRAINING, CADET 124-329.
THE NAME IS HAN--
NOT ANYMORE, 124-329. NOW MOVE OUT!

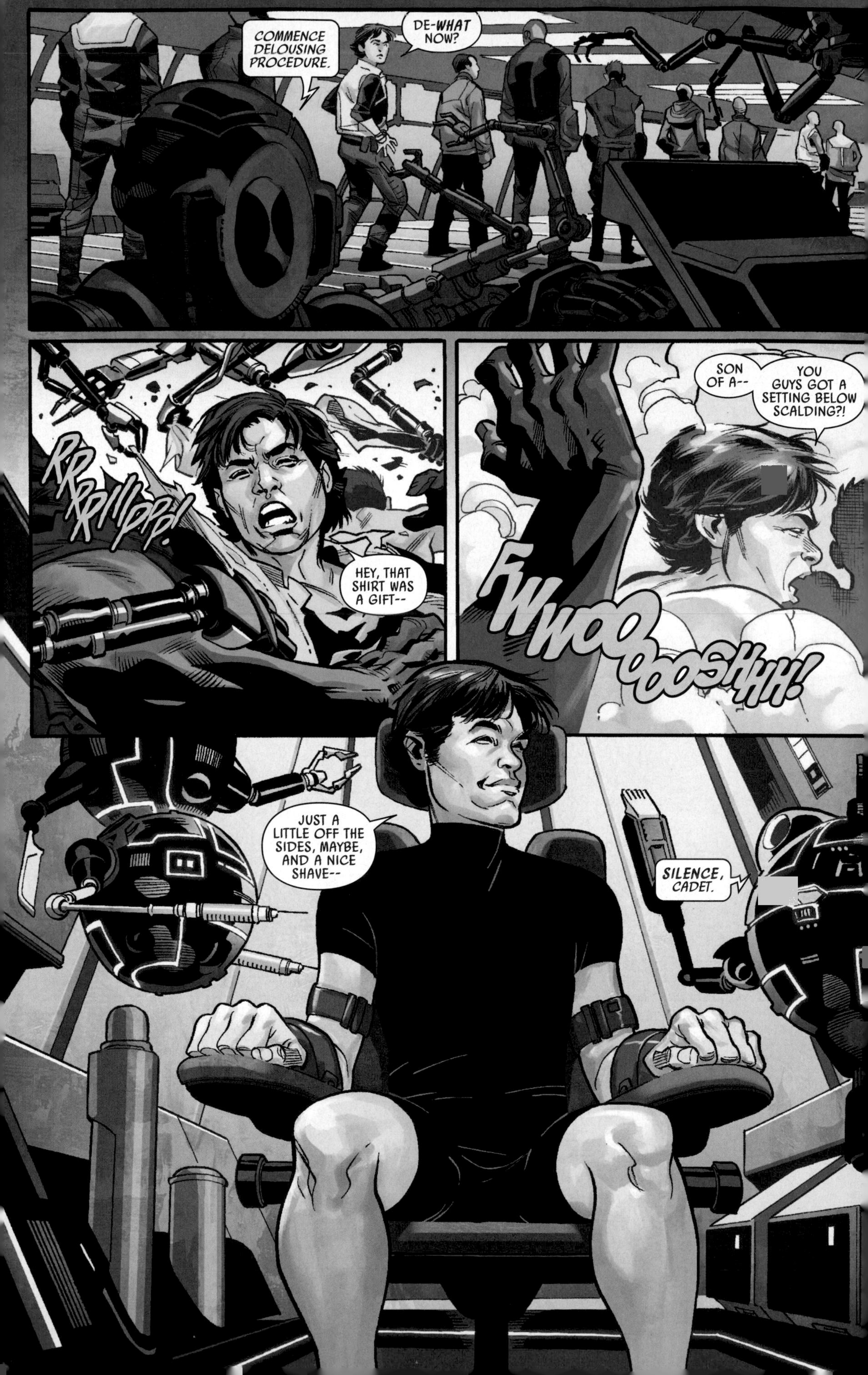
COMMENCE DELOUSING PROCEDURE.
DE-WHAT NOW?
HEY, THAT SHIRT WAS A GIFT--
SON OF A--
YOU GUYS GOT A SETTING BELOW SCALDING?!
JUST A LITTLE OFF THE SIDES, MAYBE, AND A NICE SHAVE--
SILENCE, CADET.

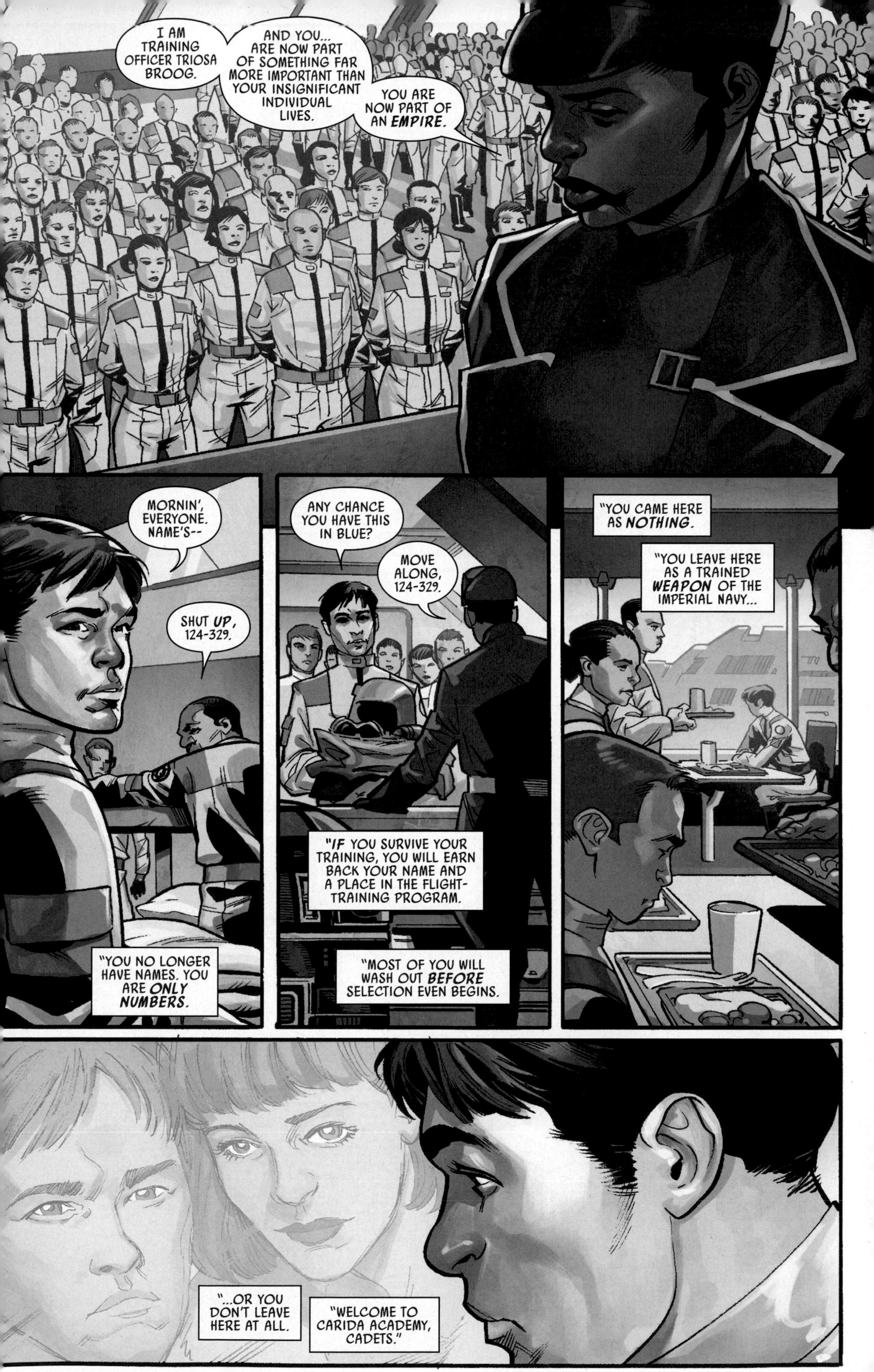
I AM TRAINING OFFICER TRIOSA BROOG.
AND YOU... ARE NOW PART OF SOMETHING FAR MORE IMPORTANT THAN YOUR INSIGNIFICANT INDIVIDUAL LIVES.
YOU ARE NOW PART OF AN *EMPIRE*.
MORNIN', EVERYONE. NAME'S--
SHUT *UP*, 124-329.
"YOU NO LONGER HAVE NAMES. YOU ARE *ONLY NUMBERS*.
ANY CHANCE YOU HAVE THIS IN BLUE?
MOVE ALONG, 124-329.
"*IF* YOU SURVIVE YOUR TRAINING, YOU WILL EARN BACK YOUR NAME AND A PLACE IN THE FLIGHT-TRAINING PROGRAM.
"MOST OF YOU WILL WASH OUT *BEFORE* SELECTION EVEN BEGINS.
"YOU CAME HERE AS *NOTHING*.
"YOU LEAVE HERE AS A TRAINED *WEAPON* OF THE IMPERIAL NAVY...
"...OR YOU DON'T LEAVE HERE AT ALL.
"WELCOME TO CARIDA ACADEMY, CADETS."

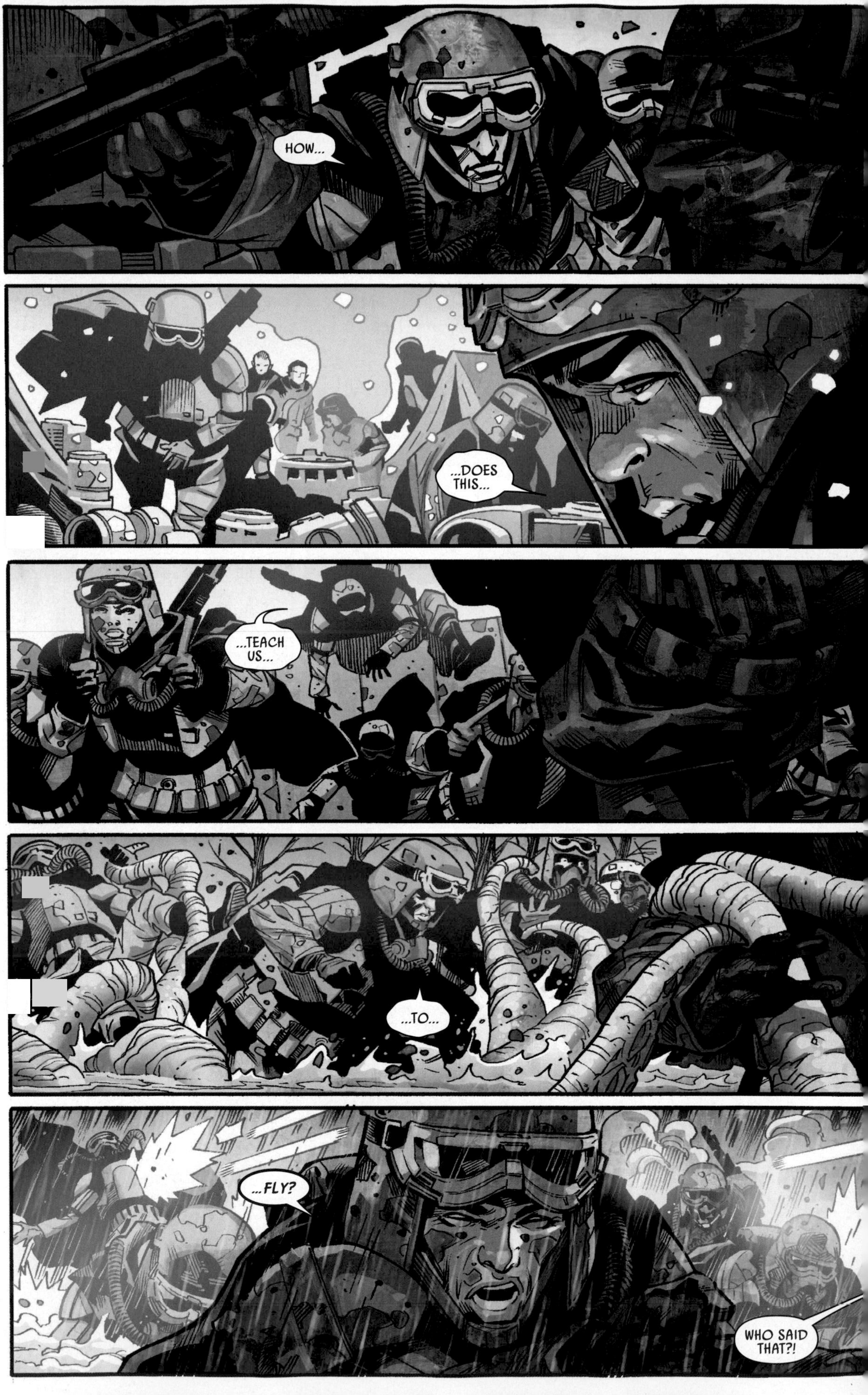
HOW...
...DOES THIS...
...TEACH US...
...TO...
...FLY?
WHO SAID THAT?!

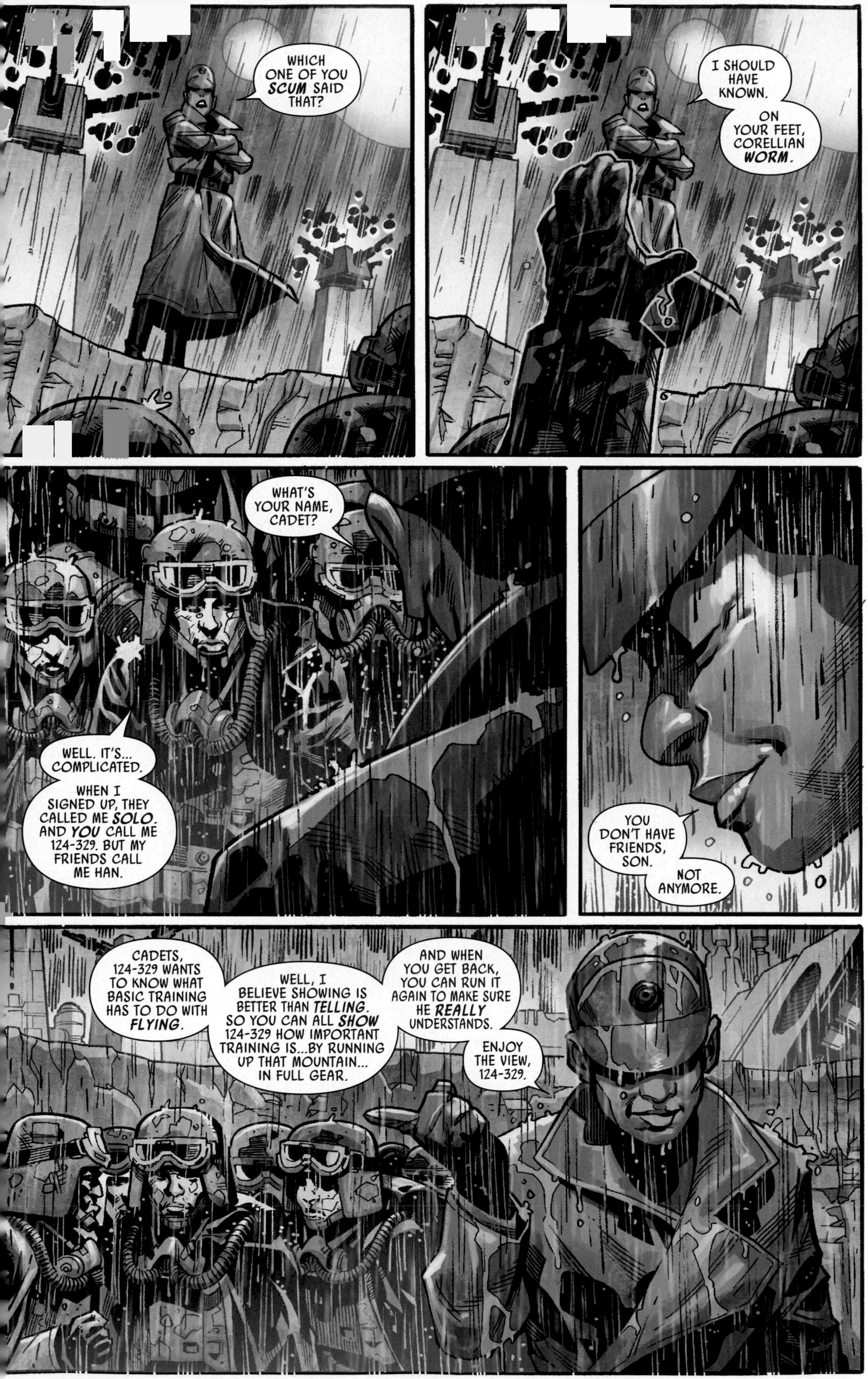
WHICH ONE OF YOU SCUM SAID THAT?
I SHOULD HAVE KNOWN.
ON YOUR FEET, CORELLIAN WORM.
WHAT'S YOUR NAME, CADET?
WELL. IT'S... COMPLICATED.
WHEN I SIGNED UP, THEY CALLED ME SOLO. AND YOU CALL ME 124-329. BUT MY FRIENDS CALL ME HAN.
YOU DON'T HAVE FRIENDS, SON.
NOT ANYMORE.
CADETS, 124-329 WANTS TO KNOW WHAT BASIC TRAINING HAS TO DO WITH FLYING.
WELL, I BELIEVE SHOWING IS BETTER THAN TELLING. SO YOU CAN ALL SHOW 124-329 HOW IMPORTANT TRAINING IS...BY RUNNING UP THAT MOUNTAIN... IN FULL GEAR.
AND WHEN YOU GET BACK, YOU CAN RUN IT AGAIN TO MAKE SURE HE REALLY UNDERSTANDS.
ENJOY THE VIEW, 124-329.

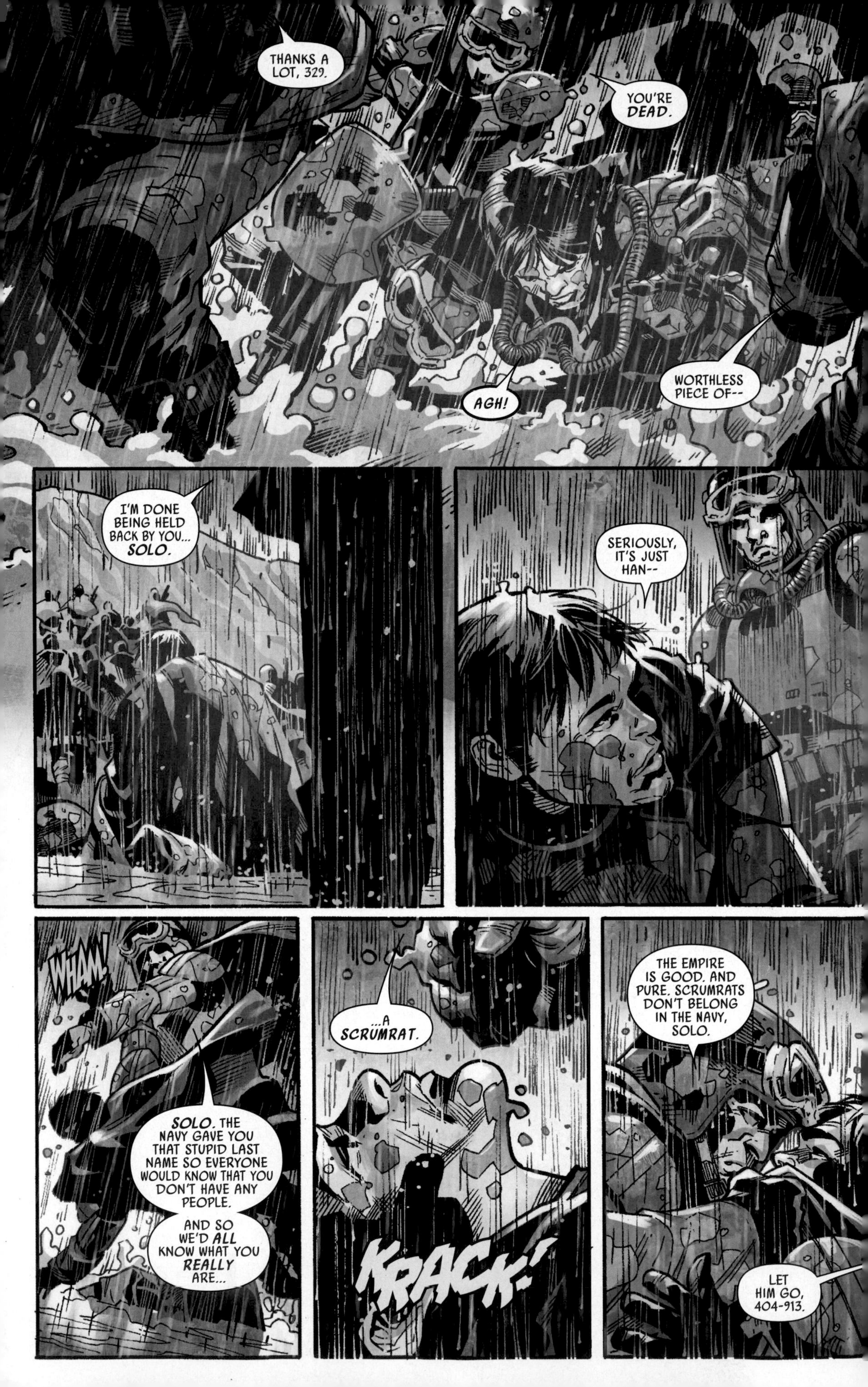
THANKS A LOT, 329.
YOU'RE DEAD.
AGH!
WORTHLESS PIECE OF--
I'M DONE BEING HELD BACK BY YOU... SOLO.
SERIOUSLY, IT'S JUST HAN--
WHAM!
SOLO. THE NAVY GAVE YOU THAT STUPID LAST NAME SO EVERYONE WOULD KNOW THAT YOU DON'T HAVE ANY PEOPLE.
AND SO WE'D ALL KNOW WHAT YOU REALLY ARE...
...A SCRUMRAT.
KRACK!
THE EMPIRE IS GOOD. AND PURE. SCRUMRATS DON'T BELONG IN THE NAVY, SOLO.
LET HIM GO, 404-913.

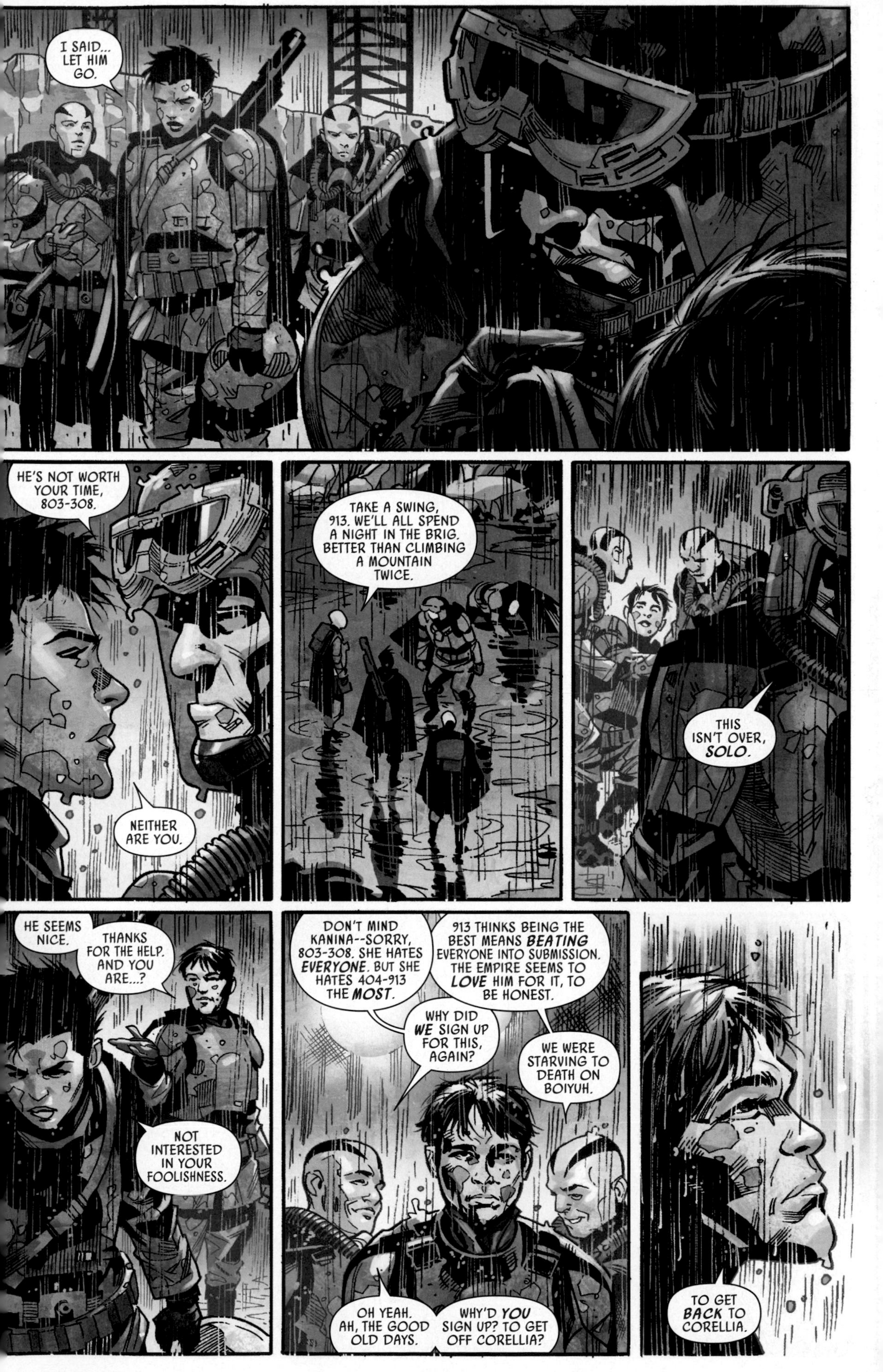
I SAID... LET HIM GO.
HE'S NOT WORTH YOUR TIME, 803-308.
NEITHER ARE YOU.
TAKE A SWING, 913. WE'LL ALL SPEND A NIGHT IN THE BRIG. BETTER THAN CLIMBING A MOUNTAIN TWICE.
THIS ISN'T OVER, SOLO.
HE SEEMS NICE.
THANKS FOR THE HELP. AND YOU ARE...?
NOT INTERESTED IN YOUR FOOLISHNESS.
DON'T MIND KANINA--SORRY, 803-308. SHE HATES EVERYONE. BUT SHE HATES 404-913 THE MOST.
913 THINKS BEING THE BEST MEANS BEATING EVERYONE INTO SUBMISSION. THE EMPIRE SEEMS TO LOVE HIM FOR IT, TO BE HONEST.
WHY DID WE SIGN UP FOR THIS, AGAIN?
WE WERE STARVING TO DEATH ON BOIYUH.
OH YEAH. AH, THE GOOD OLD DAYS.
WHY'D YOU SIGN UP? TO GET OFF CORELLIA?
TO GET BACK TO CORELLIA.

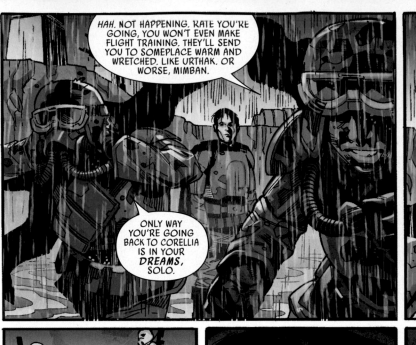

HAH. NOT HAPPENING. KATE YOU'RE GOING, YOU WON'T EVEN MAKE FLIGHT TRAINING. THEY'LL SEND YOU TO SOMEPLACE WARM AND WRETCHED. LIKE URTHAK. OR WORSE, MIMBAN.

ONLY WAY YOU'RE GOING BACK TO CORELLIA IS IN YOUR *DREAMS*, SOLO.

OR UNLESS I DO SOMETHING DEEPLY STUPID...

...WHICH SOUNDS LIKE ME.

I GUESS THE TRAINING *DID* PAY OFF.

BZZZT BZZZT

NOBODY'S GONNA MISS ONE OF THESE THINGS.

AND THEY CERTAINLY WON'T MISS *ME*.

WHOA, EASY...

BUMP!

THERE WE GO. ALL RIGHT. NO PROBLEM.

SO LONG, CARIDA.

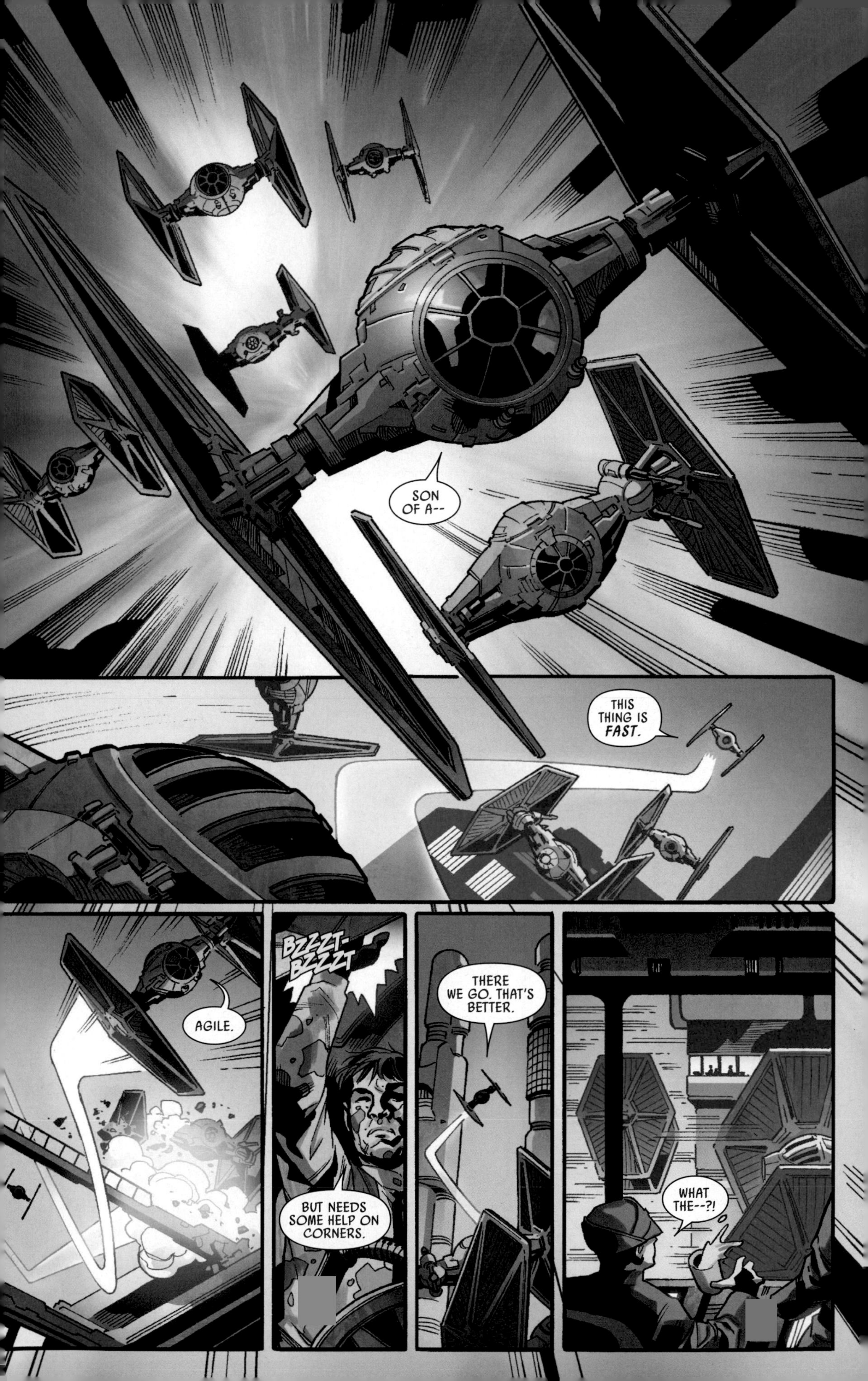
SON OF A--
THIS THING IS FAST.
AGILE.
BZZZT-BZZZT
BUT NEEDS SOME HELP ON CORNERS.
THERE WE GO. THAT'S BETTER.
WHAT THE--?!

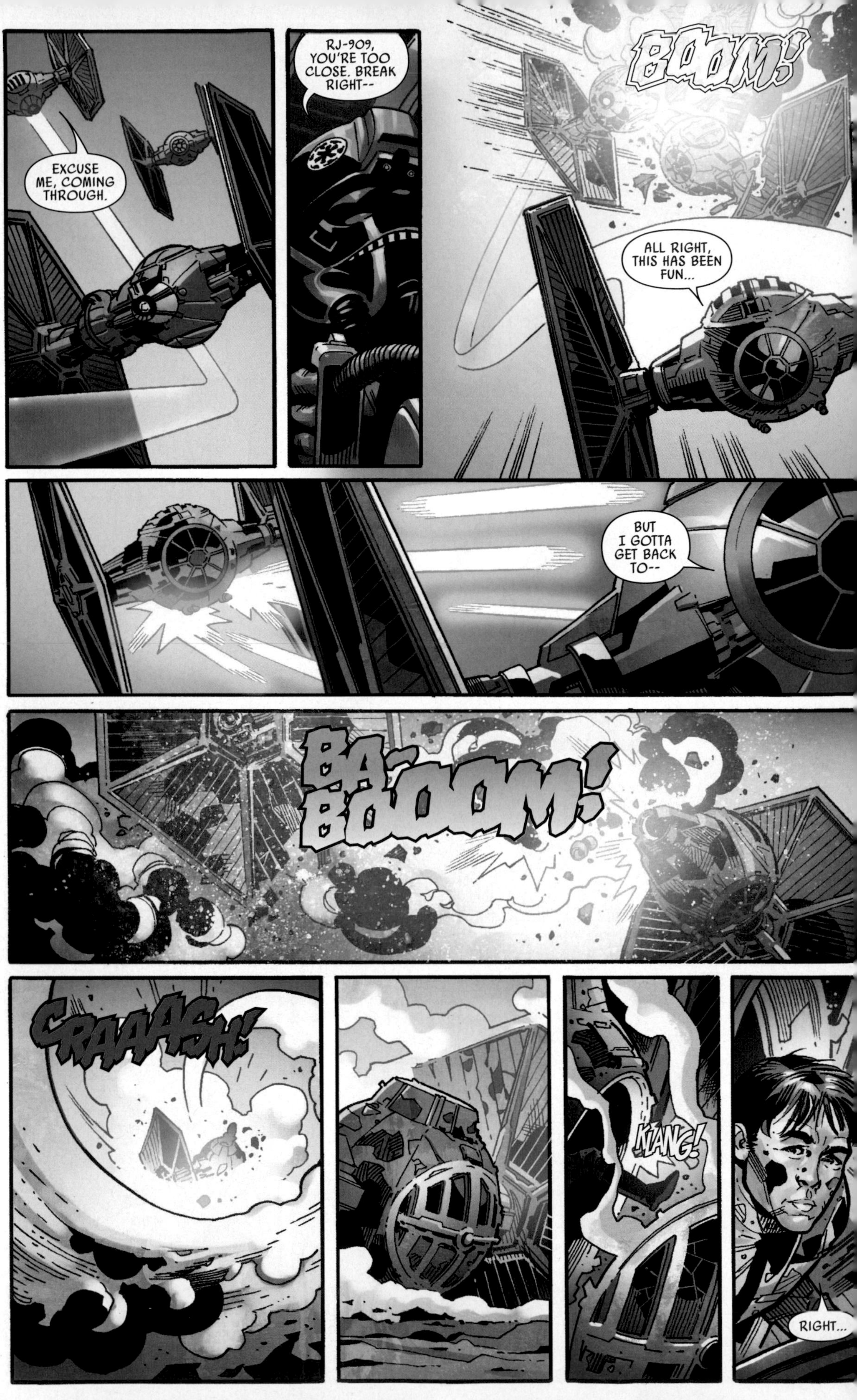
EXCUSE ME, COMING THROUGH.
RJ-909, YOU'RE TOO CLOSE. BREAK RIGHT--
BOOM!
ALL RIGHT, THIS HAS BEEN FUN...
BUT I GOTTA GET BACK TO--
BA-BOOOM!
CRAAASH!
KLANG!
RIGHT...

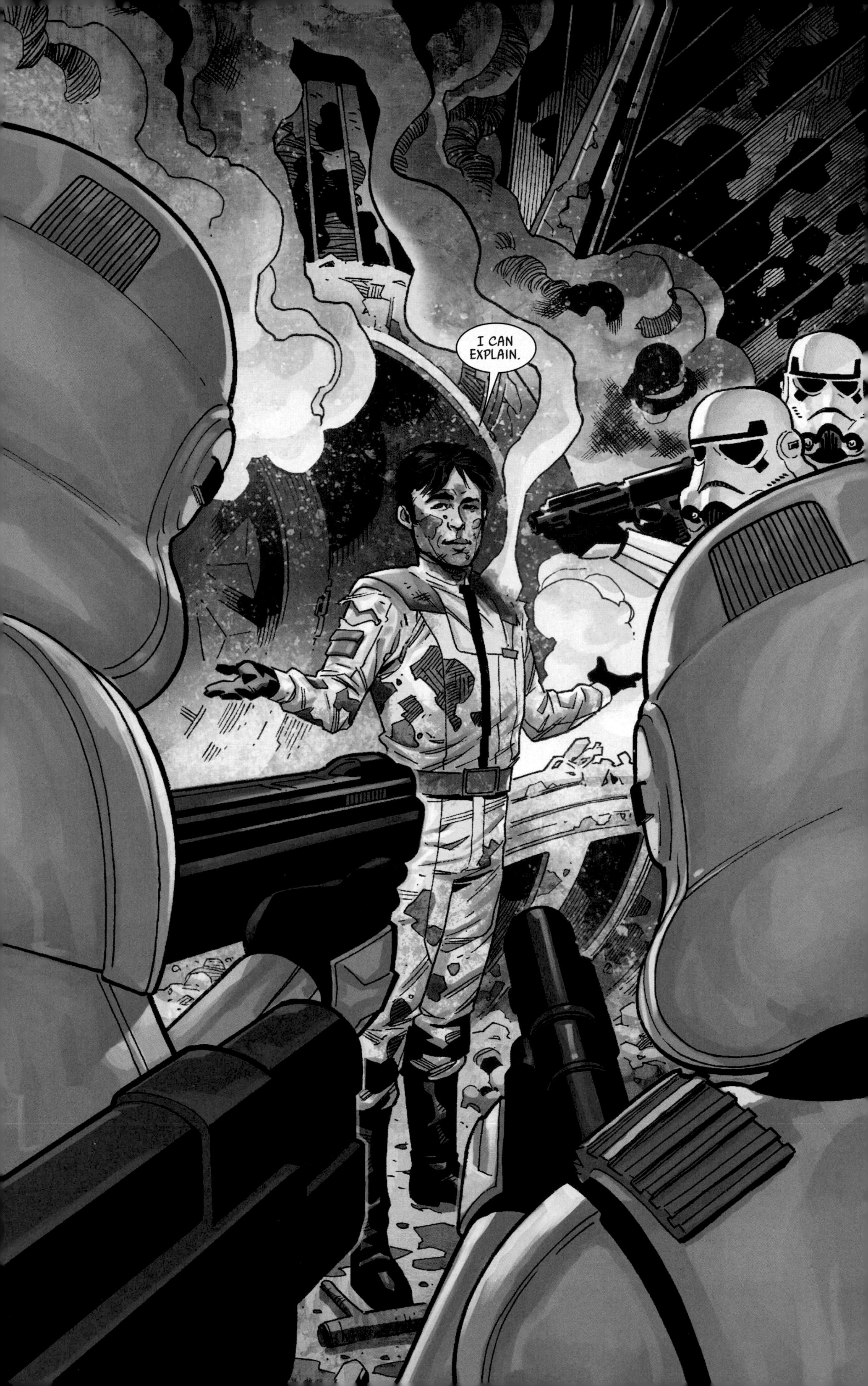
I CAN EXPLAIN.

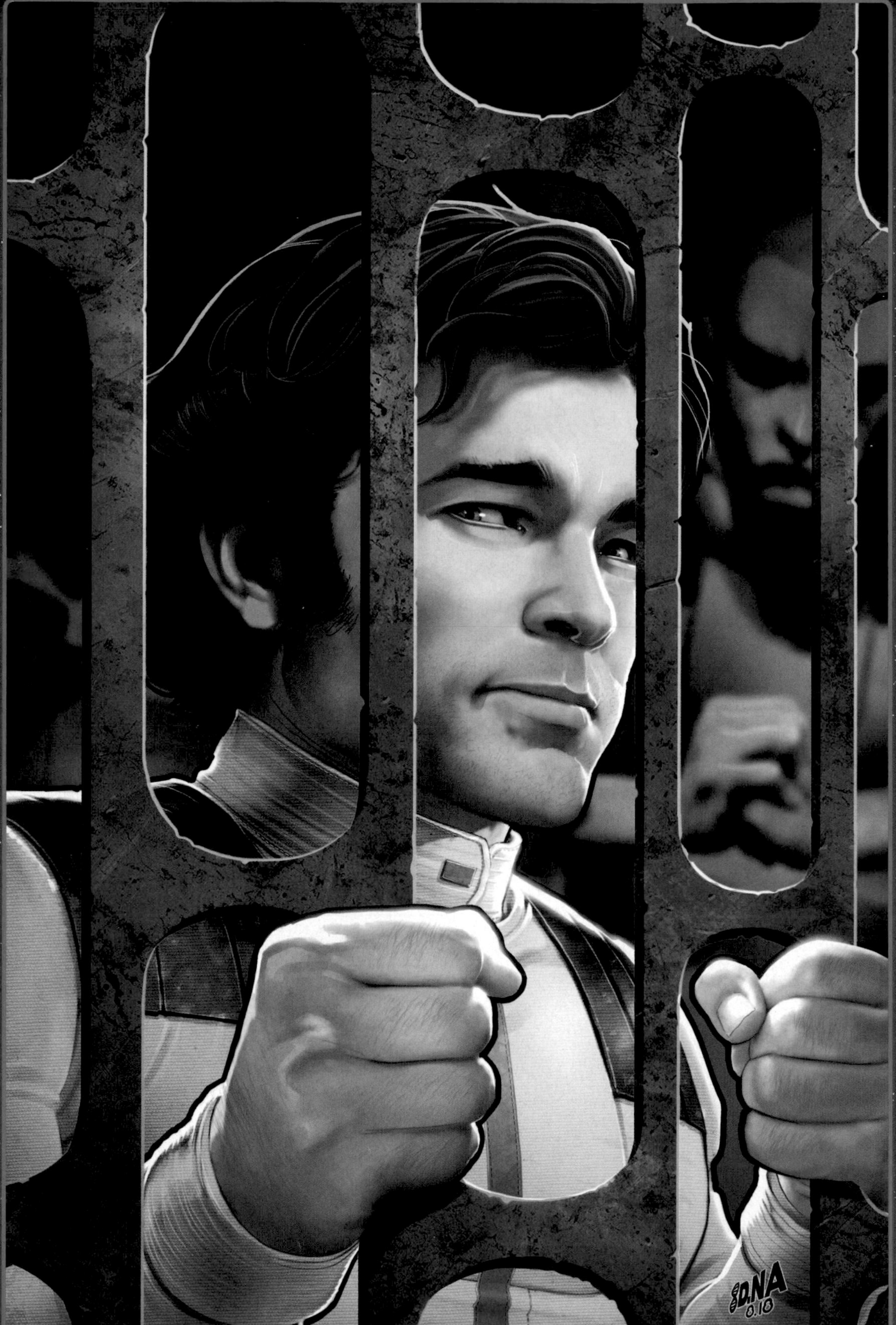

2

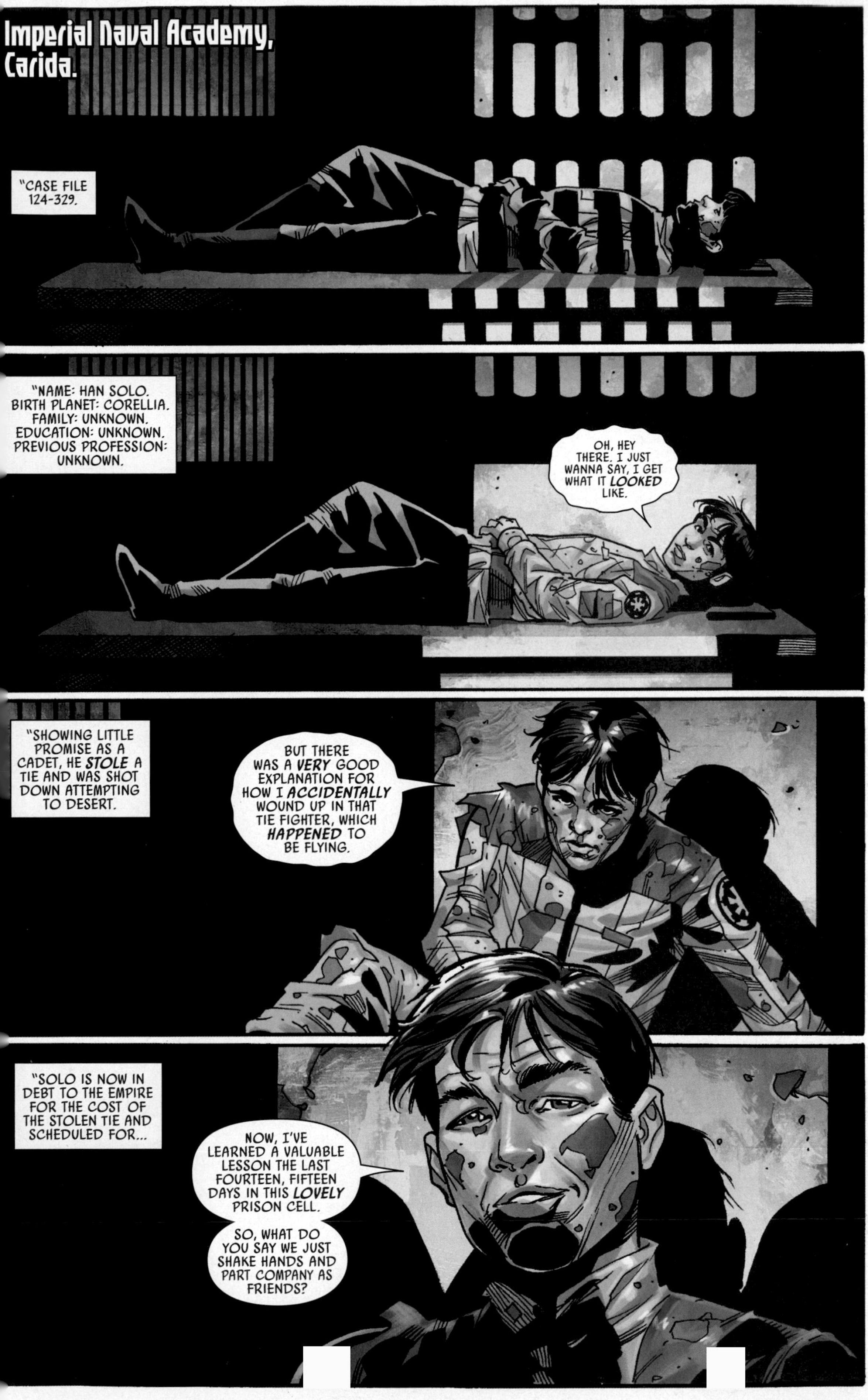
Imperial Naval Academy, Carida.
"CASE FILE 124-329.
"NAME: HAN SOLO. BIRTH PLANET: CORELLIA. FAMILY: UNKNOWN. EDUCATION: UNKNOWN. PREVIOUS PROFESSION: UNKNOWN.
OH, HEY THERE. I JUST WANNA SAY, I GET WHAT IT LOOKED LIKE.
"SHOWING LITTLE PROMISE AS A CADET, HE STOLE A TIE AND WAS SHOT DOWN ATTEMPTING TO DESERT.
BUT THERE WAS A VERY GOOD EXPLANATION FOR HOW I ACCIDENTALLY WOUND UP IN THAT TIE FIGHTER, WHICH HAPPENED TO BE FLYING.
"SOLO IS NOW IN DEBT TO THE EMPIRE FOR THE COST OF THE STOLEN TIE AND SCHEDULED FOR...
NOW, I'VE LEARNED A VALUABLE LESSON THE LAST FOURTEEN, FIFTEEN DAYS IN THIS LOVELY PRISON CELL.
SO, WHAT DO YOU SAY WE JUST SHAKE HANDS AND PART COMPANY AS FRIENDS?

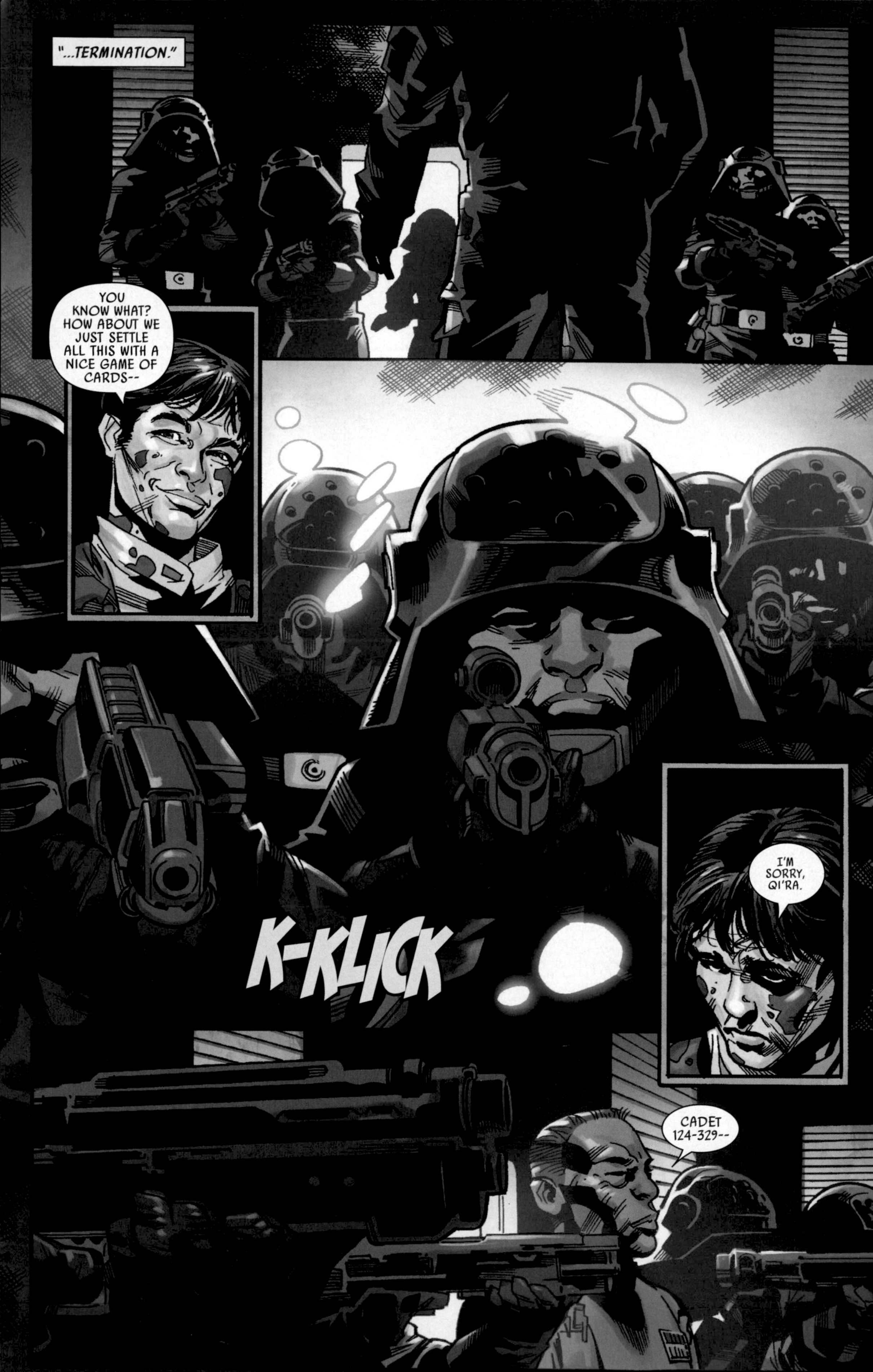
"...TERMINATION."
YOU KNOW WHAT? HOW ABOUT WE JUST SETTLE ALL THIS WITH A NICE GAME OF CARDS--
K-KLICK
I'M SORRY, QI'RA.
CADET 124-329--

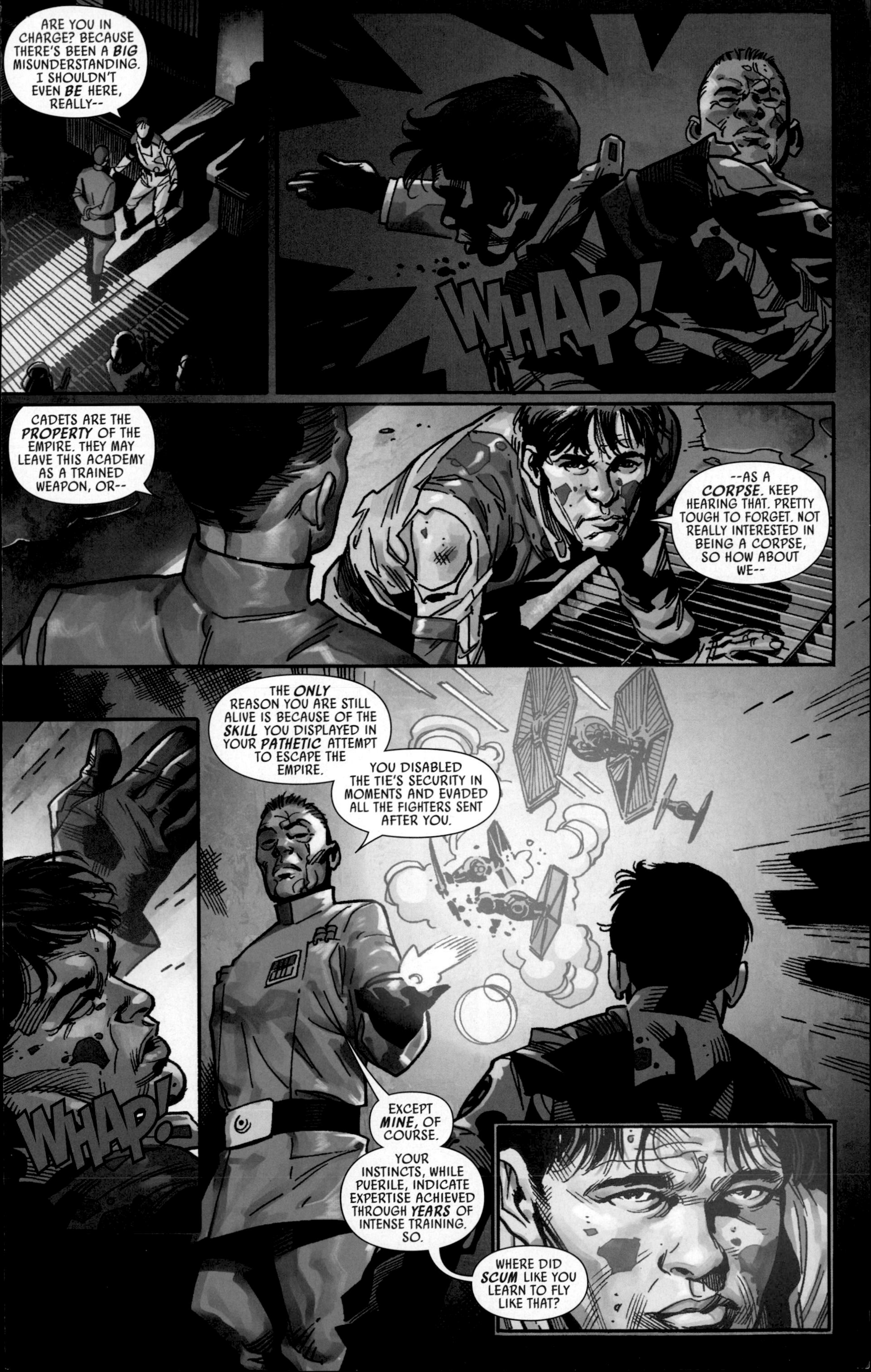
ARE YOU IN CHARGE? BECAUSE THERE'S BEEN A BIG MISUNDERSTANDING. I SHOULDN'T EVEN BE HERE, REALLY--
WHAP!
CADETS ARE THE PROPERTY OF THE EMPIRE. THEY MAY LEAVE THIS ACADEMY AS A TRAINED WEAPON, OR--
--AS A CORPSE. KEEP HEARING THAT. PRETTY TOUGH TO FORGET. NOT REALLY INTERESTED IN BEING A CORPSE, SO HOW ABOUT WE--
WHAP!
THE ONLY REASON YOU ARE STILL ALIVE IS BECAUSE OF THE SKILL YOU DISPLAYED IN YOUR PATHETIC ATTEMPT TO ESCAPE THE EMPIRE.
YOU DISABLED THE TIE'S SECURITY IN MOMENTS AND EVADED ALL THE FIGHTERS SENT AFTER YOU.
EXCEPT MINE, OF COURSE.
YOUR INSTINCTS, WHILE PUERILE, INDICATE EXPERTISE ACHIEVED THROUGH YEARS OF INTENSE TRAINING. SO.
WHERE DID SCUM LIKE YOU LEARN TO FLY LIKE THAT?

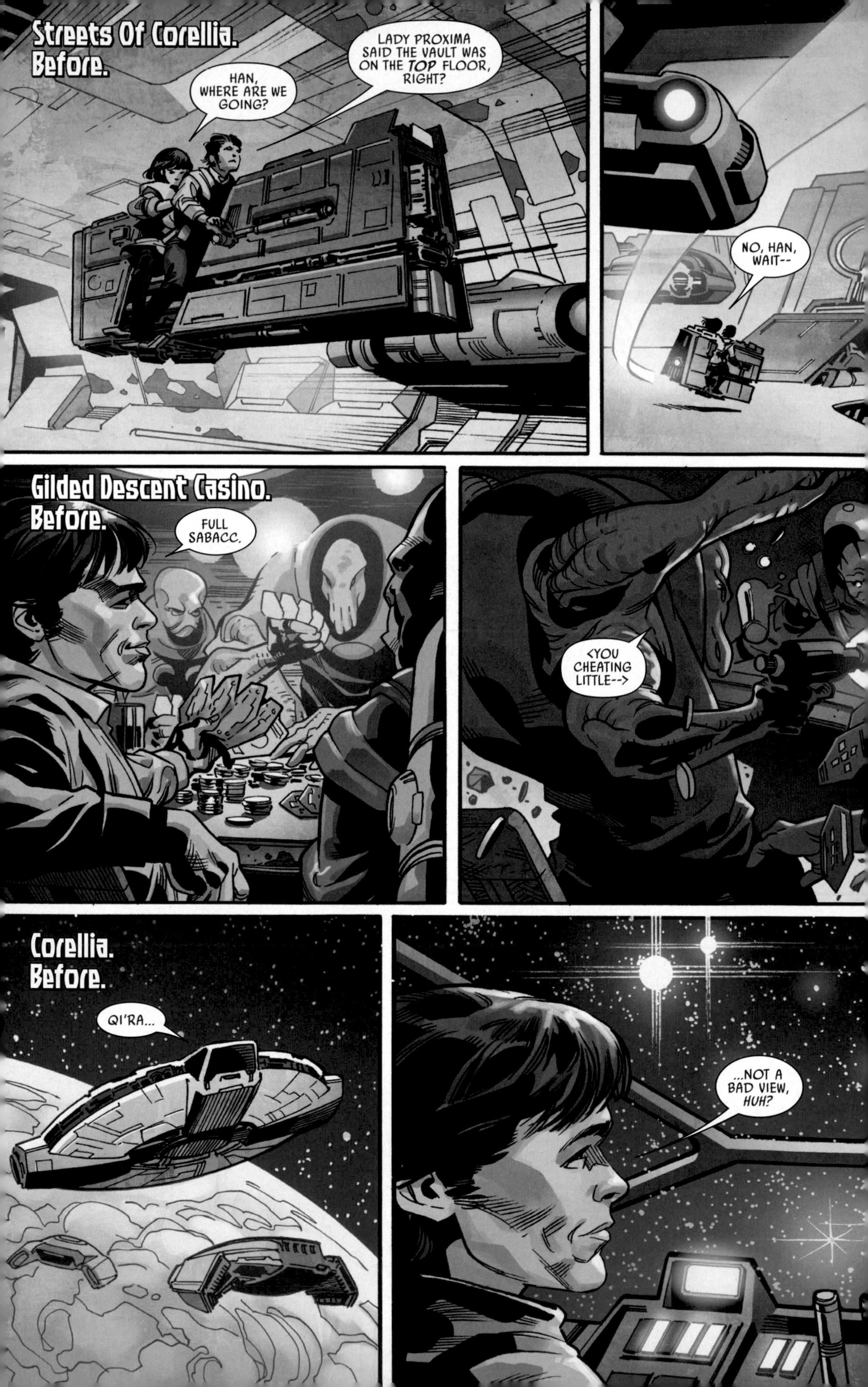
Streets Of Corellia. Before.
HAN, WHERE ARE WE GOING?
LADY PROXIMA SAID THE VAULT WAS ON THE TOP FLOOR, RIGHT?
NO, HAN, WAIT--
Gilded Descent Casino. Before.
FULL SABACC.
<YOU CHEATING LITTLE-->
Corellia. Before.
QI'RA...
...NOT A BAD VIEW, HUH?

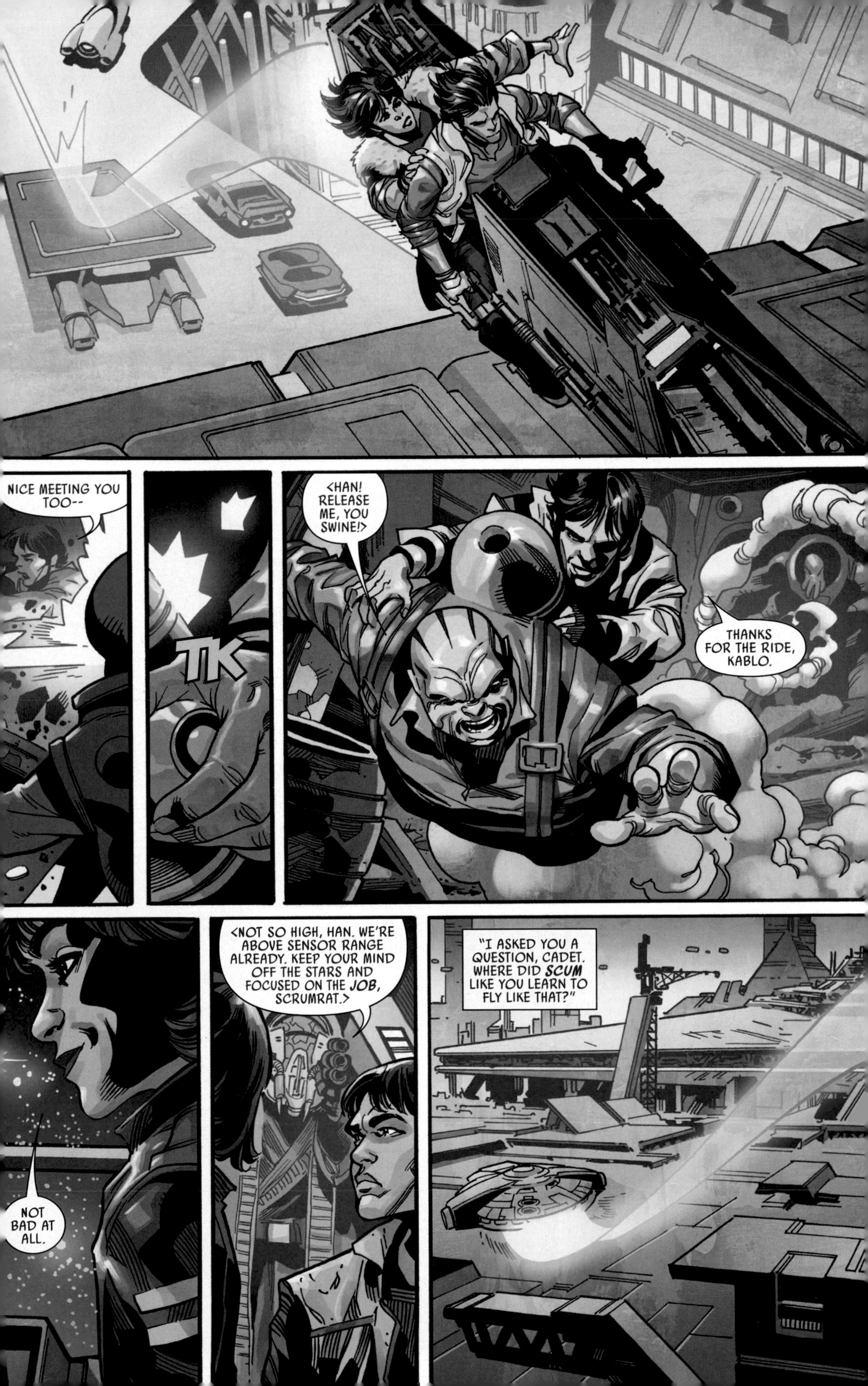
NICE MEETING YOU TOO--
TK
<HAN! RELEASE ME, YOU SWINE!>
THANKS FOR THE RIDE, KABLO.
NOT BAD AT ALL.
<NOT SO HIGH, HAN. WE'RE ABOVE SENSOR RANGE ALREADY. KEEP YOUR MIND OFF THE STARS AND FOCUSED ON THE JOB, SCRUMRAT.>
"I ASKED YOU A QUESTION, CADET. WHERE DID SCUM LIKE YOU LEARN TO FLY LIKE THAT?"

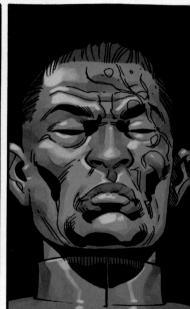

JUST COMES NATURALLY, I GUESS.

A THIEF **AND** A LIAR. PITY.

BECAUSE OF YOUR UNIQUE SKILL SET, I HAVE DECIDED TO COMMUTE YOUR SENTENCE. BUT KNOW THIS...

...YOU HAVE **ONE** MORE CHANCE, SOLO.

DO NOT DISAPPOINT ME, OR DEATH SHALL BE THE LEAST OF YOUR WORRIES.

WHAT DO YOU SEE IN SOLO, YURIB?

MYSELF, UNFORTUNATELY.

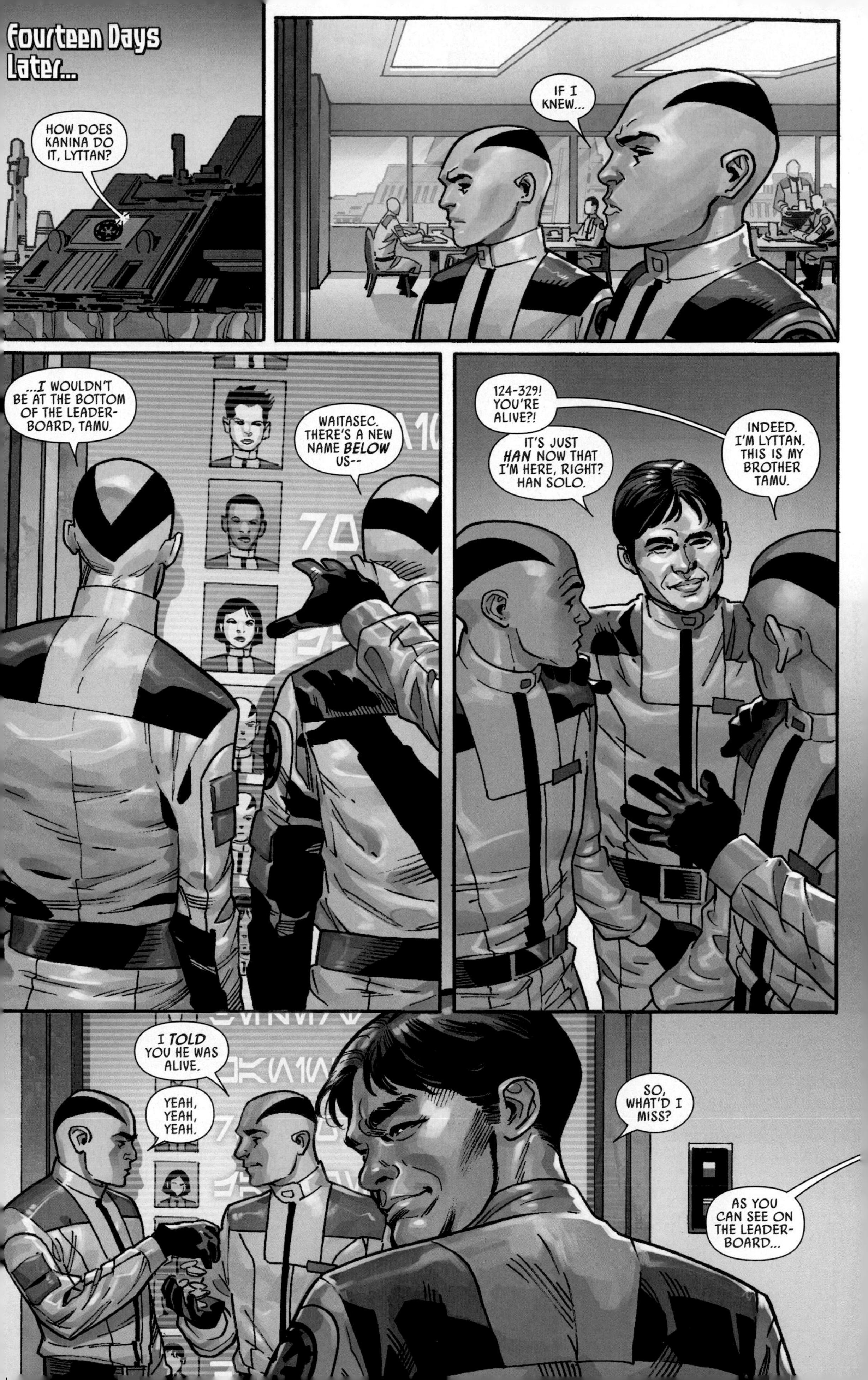
Fourteen Days Later...
HOW DOES KANINA DO IT, LYTTAN?
IF I KNEW...
...I WOULDN'T BE AT THE BOTTOM OF THE LEADER-BOARD, TAMU.
WAITASEC. THERE'S A NEW NAME BELOW US--
124-329! YOU'RE ALIVE?!
IT'S JUST HAN NOW THAT I'M HERE, RIGHT? HAN SOLO.
INDEED. I'M LYTTAN. THIS IS MY BROTHER TAMU.
I TOLD YOU HE WAS ALIVE.
YEAH, YEAH, YEAH.
SO, WHAT'D I MISS?
AS YOU CAN SEE ON THE LEADER-BOARD...

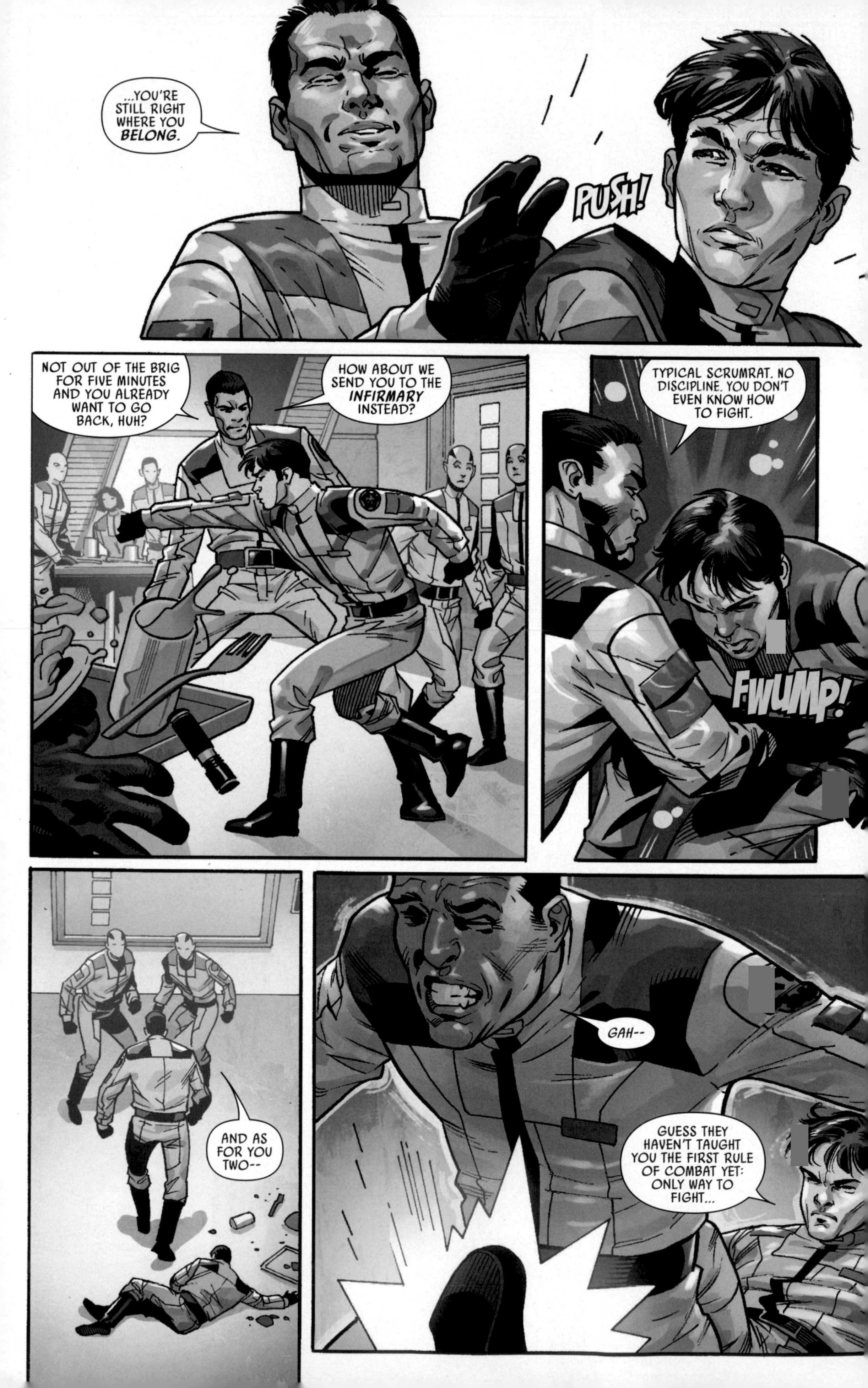
...YOU'RE STILL RIGHT WHERE YOU BELONG.
PUSH!
NOT OUT OF THE BRIG FOR FIVE MINUTES AND YOU ALREADY WANT TO GO BACK, HUH?
HOW ABOUT WE SEND YOU TO THE INFIRMARY INSTEAD?
TYPICAL SCRUMRAT. NO DISCIPLINE. YOU DON'T EVEN KNOW HOW TO FIGHT.
FWUMP!
AND AS FOR YOU TWO--
GAH--
GUESS THEY HAVEN'T TAUGHT YOU THE FIRST RULE OF COMBAT YET: ONLY WAY TO FIGHT...

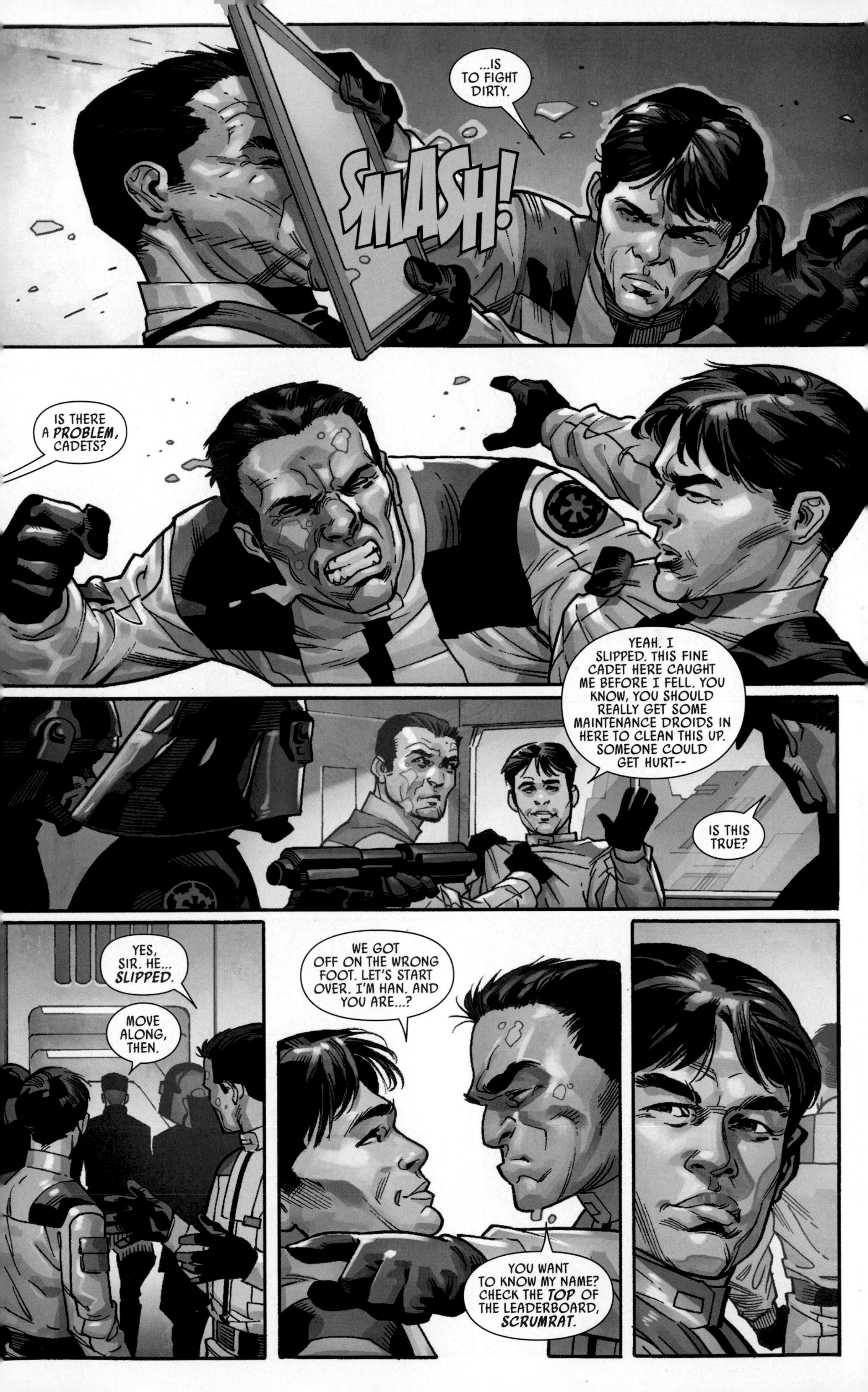

...IS TO FIGHT DIRTY.
SMASH!
IS THERE A PROBLEM, CADETS?
YEAH. I SLIPPED. THIS FINE CADET HERE CAUGHT ME BEFORE I FELL. YOU KNOW, YOU SHOULD REALLY GET SOME MAINTENANCE DROIDS IN HERE TO CLEAN THIS UP. SOMEONE COULD GET HURT--
IS THIS TRUE?
YES, SIR. HE... SLIPPED.
MOVE ALONG, THEN.
WE GOT OFF ON THE WRONG FOOT. LET'S START OVER. I'M HAN. AND YOU ARE...?
YOU WANT TO KNOW MY NAME? CHECK THE TOP OF THE LEADERBOARD, SCRUMRAT.

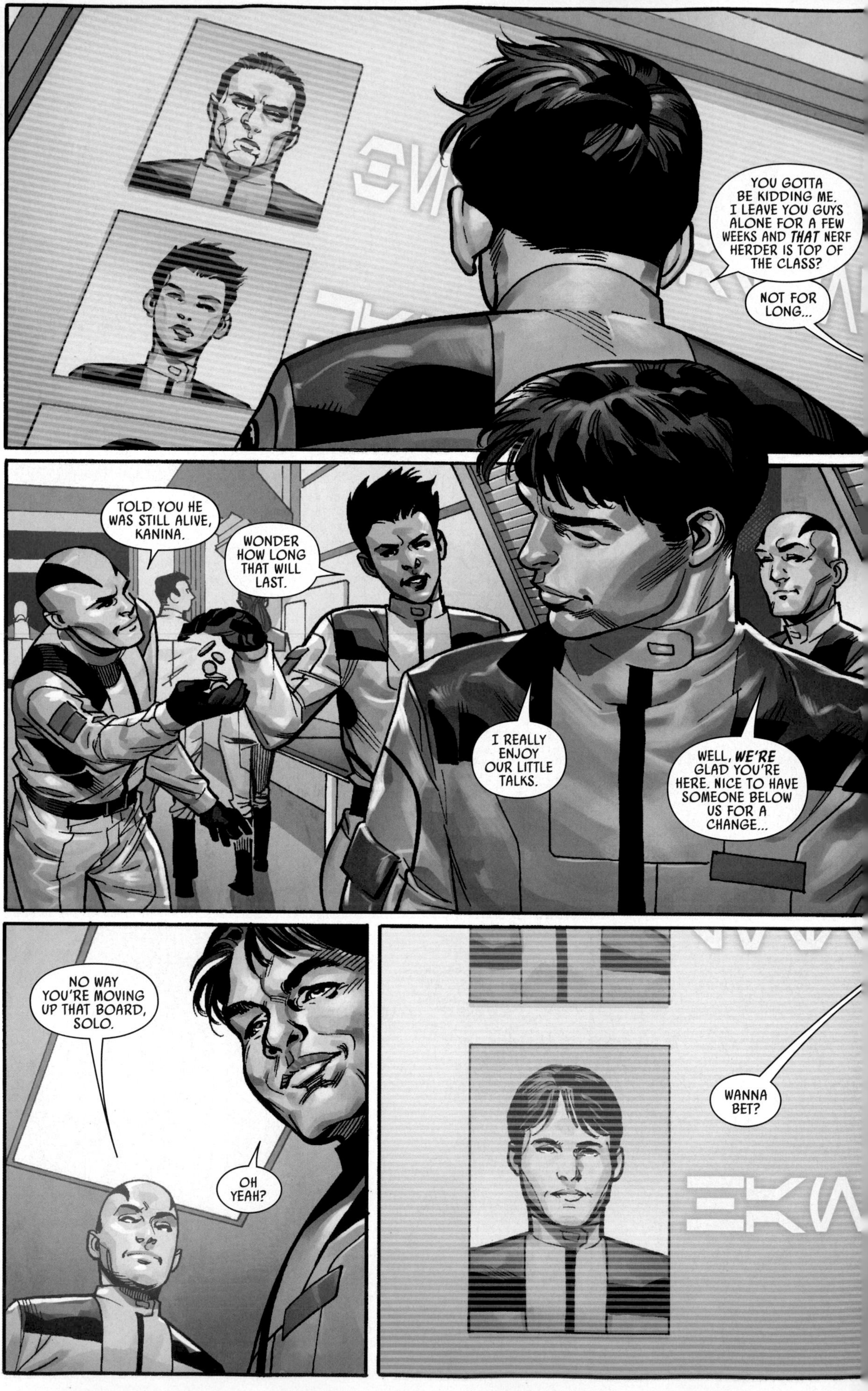
YOU GOTTA BE KIDDING ME. I LEAVE YOU GUYS ALONE FOR A FEW WEEKS AND *THAT* NERF HERDER IS TOP OF THE CLASS?
NOT FOR LONG...
TOLD YOU HE WAS STILL ALIVE, KANINA.
WONDER HOW LONG THAT WILL LAST.
I REALLY ENJOY OUR LITTLE TALKS.
WELL, *WE'RE* GLAD YOU'RE HERE. NICE TO HAVE SOMEONE BELOW US FOR A CHANGE...
NO WAY YOU'RE MOVING UP THAT BOARD, SOLO.
OH YEAH?
WANNA BET?

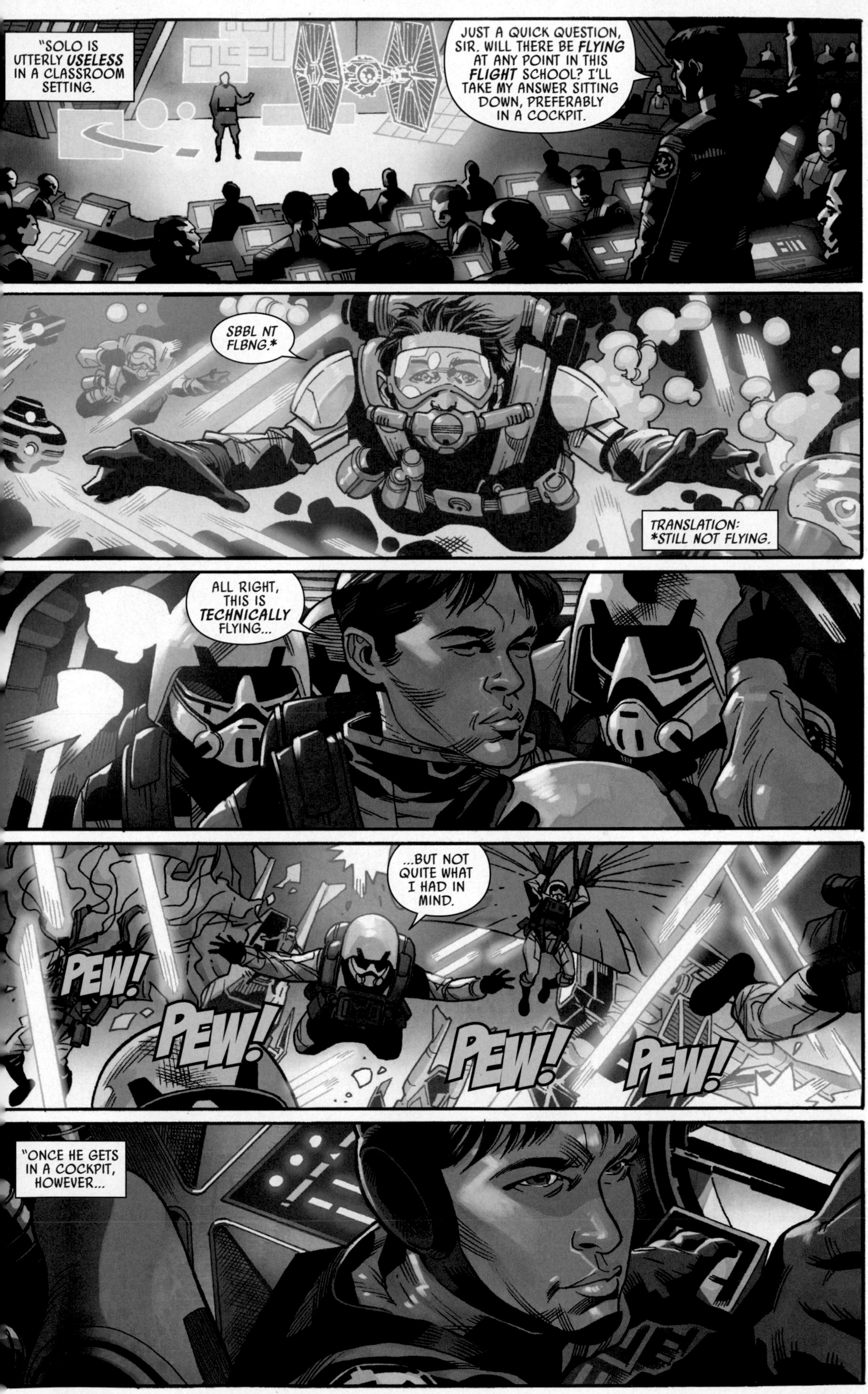
"SOLO IS UTTERLY USELESS IN A CLASSROOM SETTING.
JUST A QUICK QUESTION, SIR. WILL THERE BE FLYING AT ANY POINT IN THIS FLIGHT SCHOOL? I'LL TAKE MY ANSWER SITTING DOWN, PREFERABLY IN A COCKPIT.
SBBL NT FLBNG.*
TRANSLATION: *STILL NOT FLYING.
ALL RIGHT, THIS IS TECHNICALLY FLYING...
...BUT NOT QUITE WHAT I HAD IN MIND.
PEW!
PEW!
PEW!
PEW!
"ONCE HE GETS IN A COCKPIT, HOWEVER...

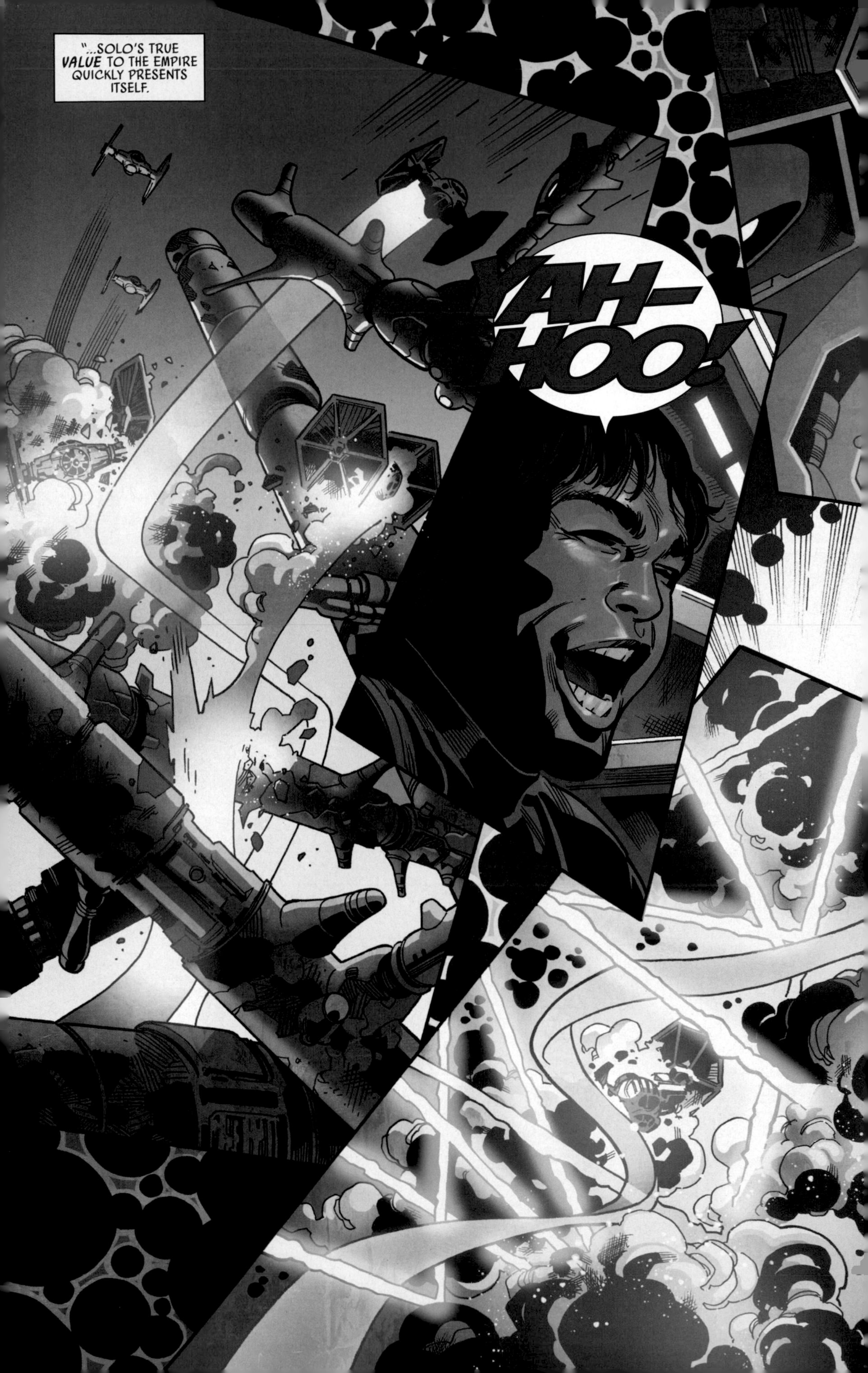
"...SOLO'S TRUE VALUE TO THE EMPIRE QUICKLY PRESENTS ITSELF.
YAH-HOO!

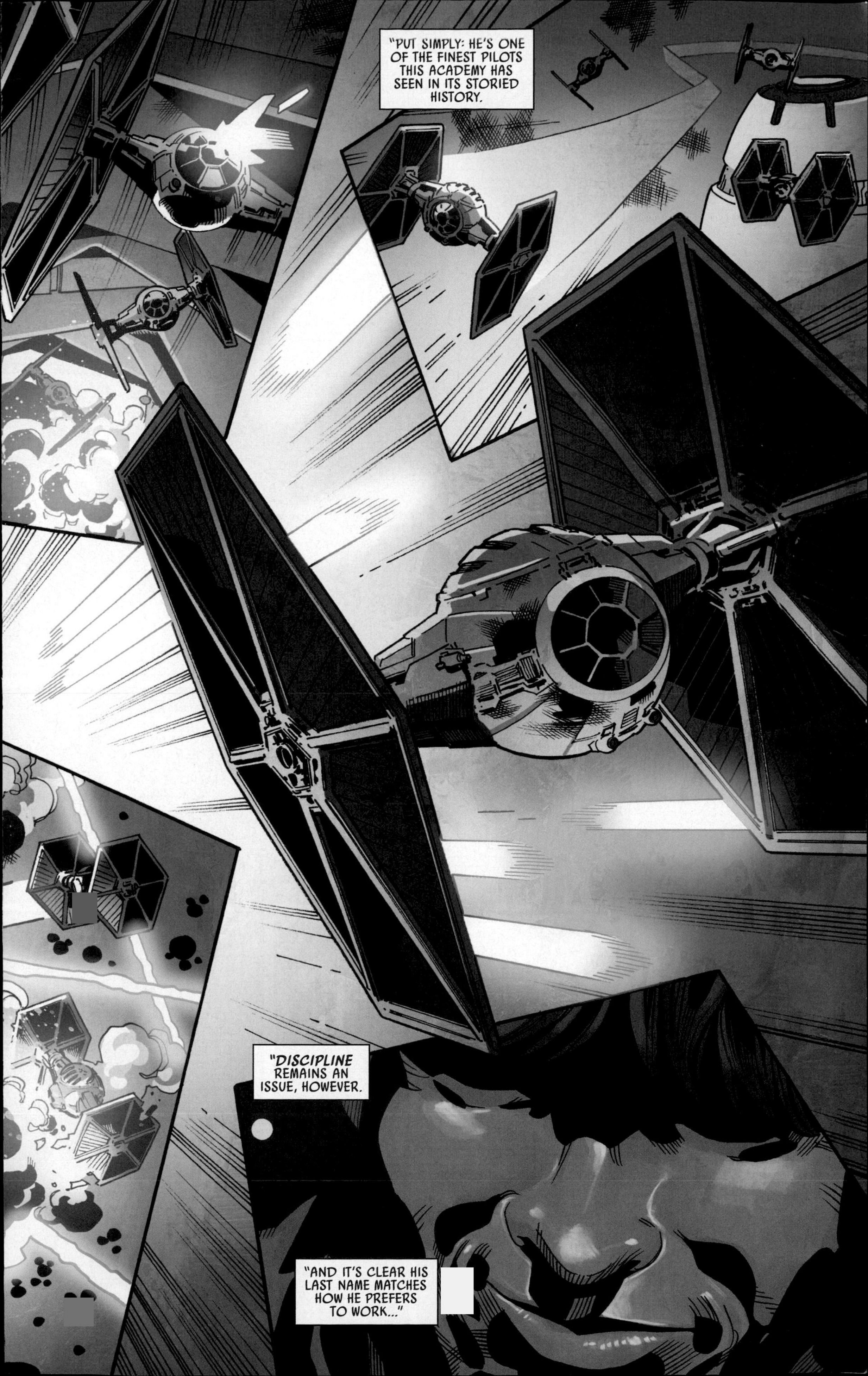
"PUT SIMPLY: HE'S ONE OF THE FINEST PILOTS THIS ACADEMY HAS SEEN IN ITS STORIED HISTORY.
"*DISCIPLINE* REMAINS AN ISSUE, HOWEVER.
"AND IT'S CLEAR HIS LAST NAME MATCHES HOW HE PREFERS TO WORK..."

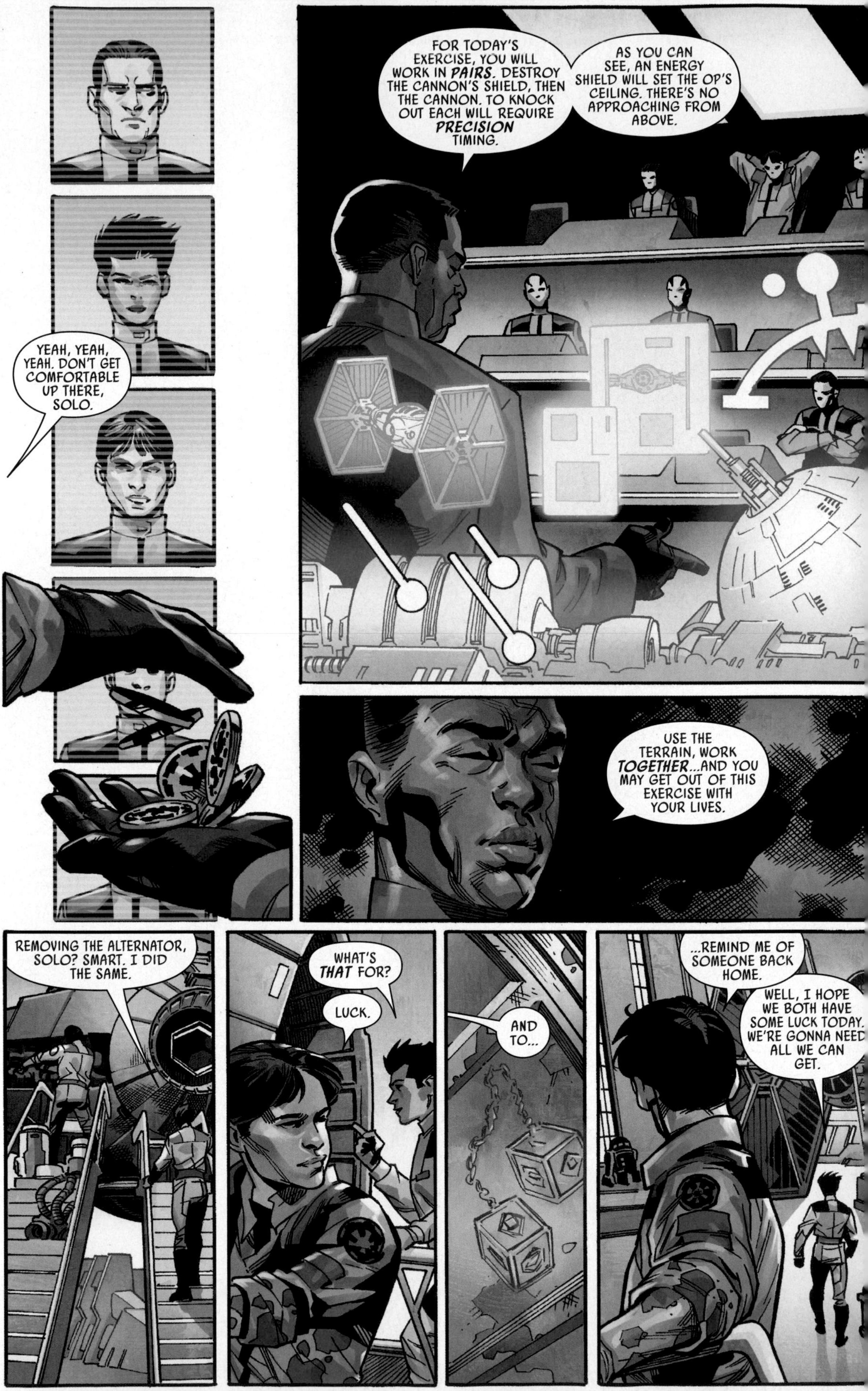
FOR TODAY'S EXERCISE, YOU WILL WORK IN PAIRS. DESTROY THE CANNON'S SHIELD, THEN THE CANNON. TO KNOCK OUT EACH WILL REQUIRE PRECISION TIMING.
AS YOU CAN SEE, AN ENERGY SHIELD WILL SET THE OP'S CEILING. THERE'S NO APPROACHING FROM ABOVE.
YEAH, YEAH, YEAH. DON'T GET COMFORTABLE UP THERE, SOLO.
USE THE TERRAIN, WORK TOGETHER...AND YOU MAY GET OUT OF THIS EXERCISE WITH YOUR LIVES.
REMOVING THE ALTERNATOR, SOLO? SMART. I DID THE SAME.
WHAT'S THAT FOR?
LUCK.
AND TO...
...REMIND ME OF SOMEONE BACK HOME.
WELL, I HOPE WE BOTH HAVE SOME LUCK TODAY. WE'RE GONNA NEED ALL WE CAN GET.

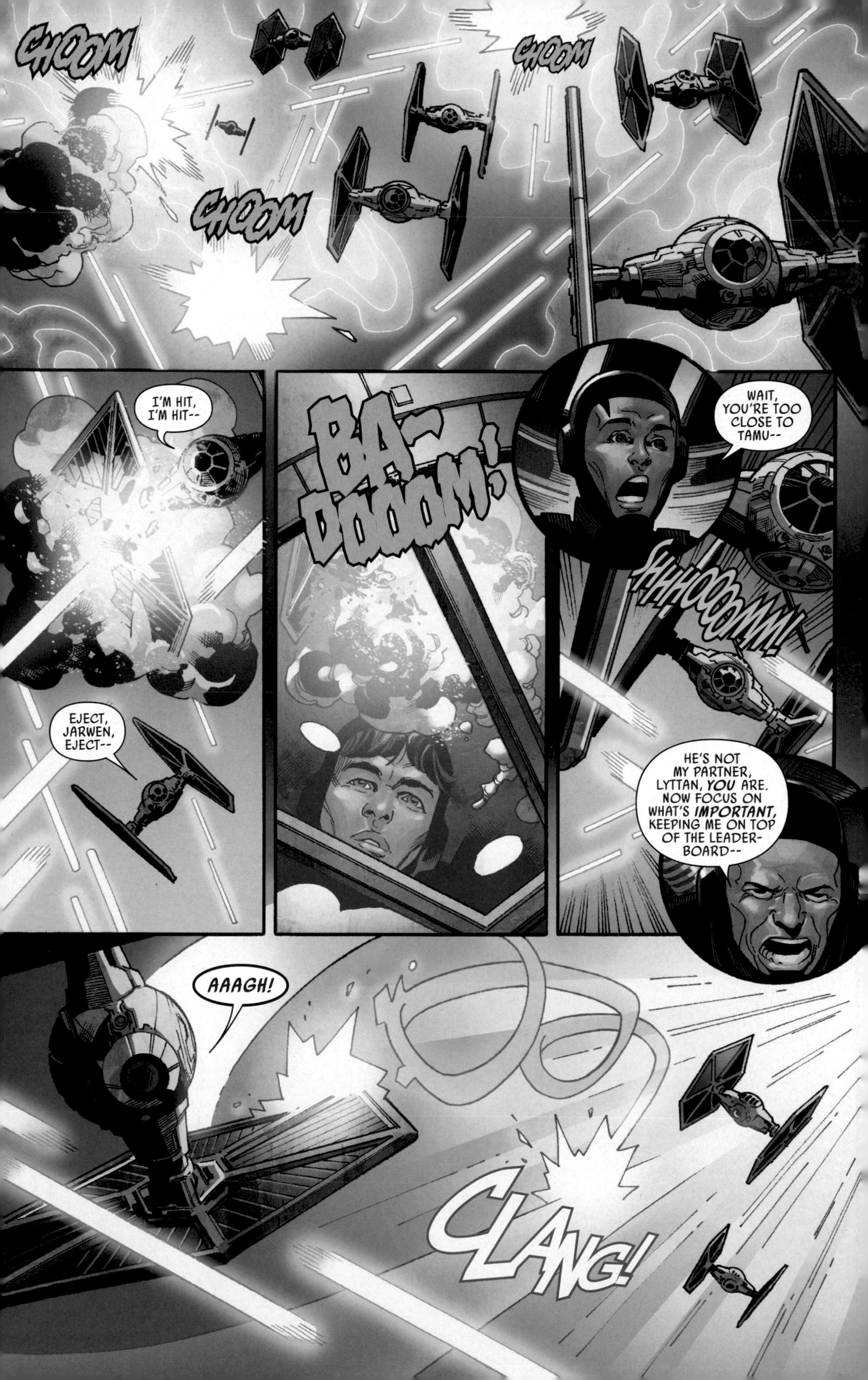
CHOOM
CHOOM
CHOOM
I'M HIT, I'M HIT--
EJECT, JARWEN, EJECT--
BA-DOOOM!
WAIT, YOU'RE TOO CLOSE TO TAMU--
SHHOOOMM!
HE'S NOT MY PARTNER, LYTTAN, YOU ARE. NOW FOCUS ON WHAT'S IMPORTANT, KEEPING ME ON TOP OF THE LEADER-BOARD--
AAAGH!
CLANG!

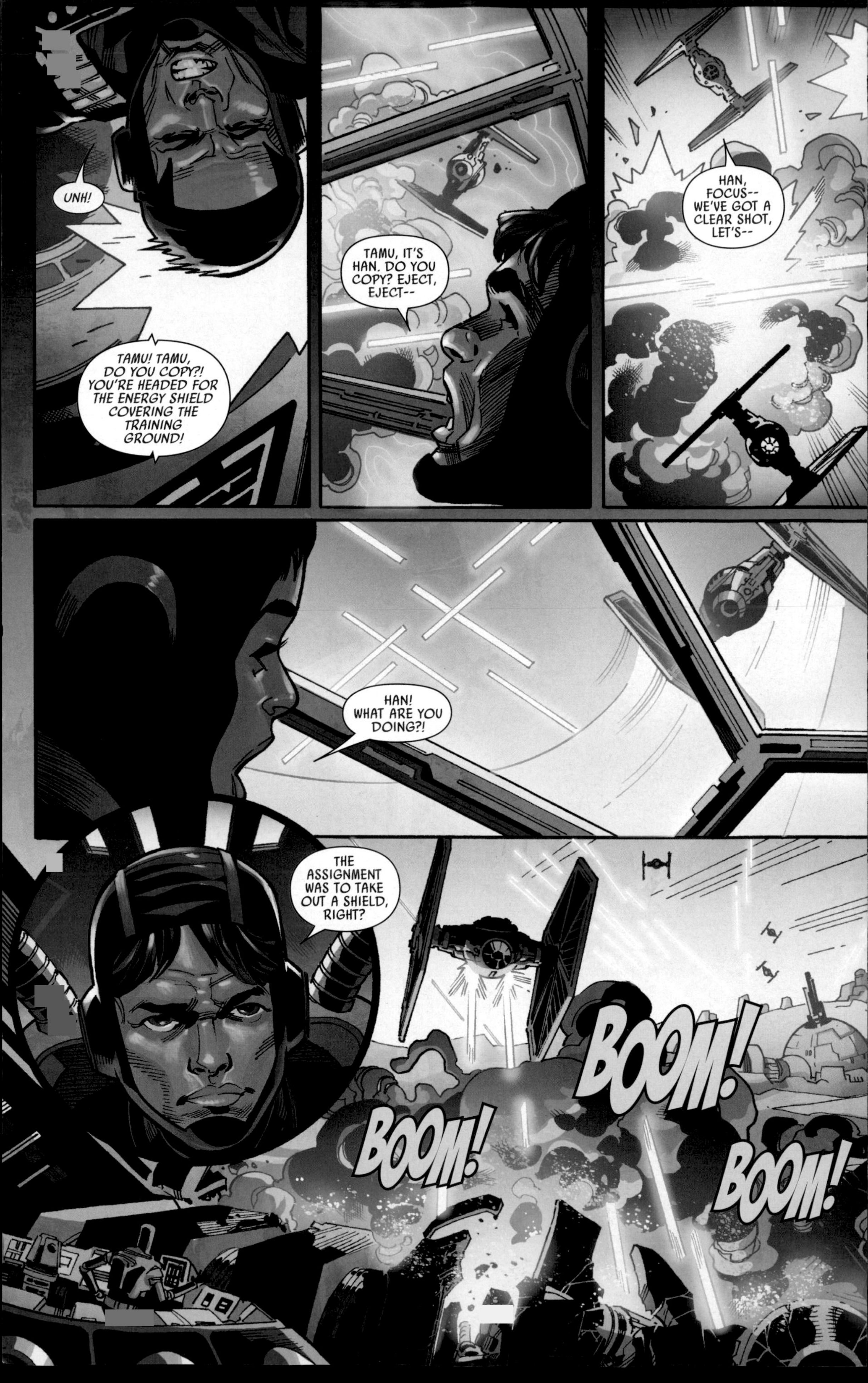
UNH!
TAMU! TAMU, DO YOU COPY?! YOU'RE HEADED FOR THE ENERGY SHIELD COVERING THE TRAINING GROUND!
TAMU, IT'S HAN. DO YOU COPY? EJECT, EJECT--
HAN, FOCUS-- WE'VE GOT A CLEAR SHOT, LET'S--
HAN! WHAT ARE YOU DOING?!
THE ASSIGNMENT WAS TO TAKE OUT A SHIELD, RIGHT?
BOOM!
BOOM!
BOOM!

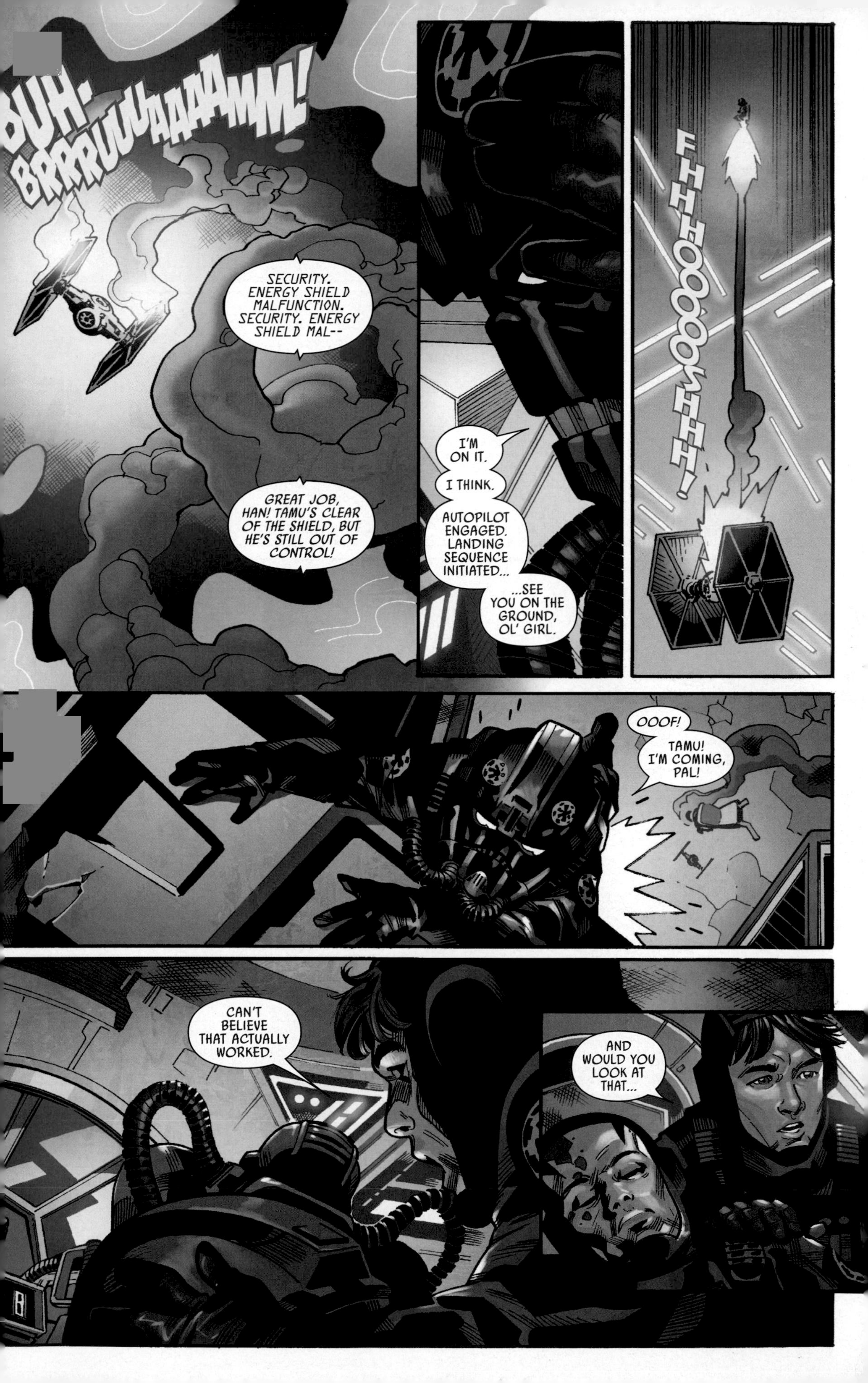
BUH-BRRRUUUAAAAMM!
SECURITY. ENERGY SHIELD MALFUNCTION. SECURITY. ENERGY SHIELD MAL--
GREAT JOB, HAN! TAMU'S CLEAR OF THE SHIELD, BUT HE'S STILL OUT OF CONTROL!
I'M ON IT.
I THINK.
AUTOPILOT ENGAGED. LANDING SEQUENCE INITIATED...
...SEE YOU ON THE GROUND, OL' GIRL.
FHHHOOOOOSHHH!
OOOF!
TAMU! I'M COMING, PAL!
CAN'T BELIEVE THAT ACTUALLY WORKED.
AND WOULD YOU LOOK AT THAT...

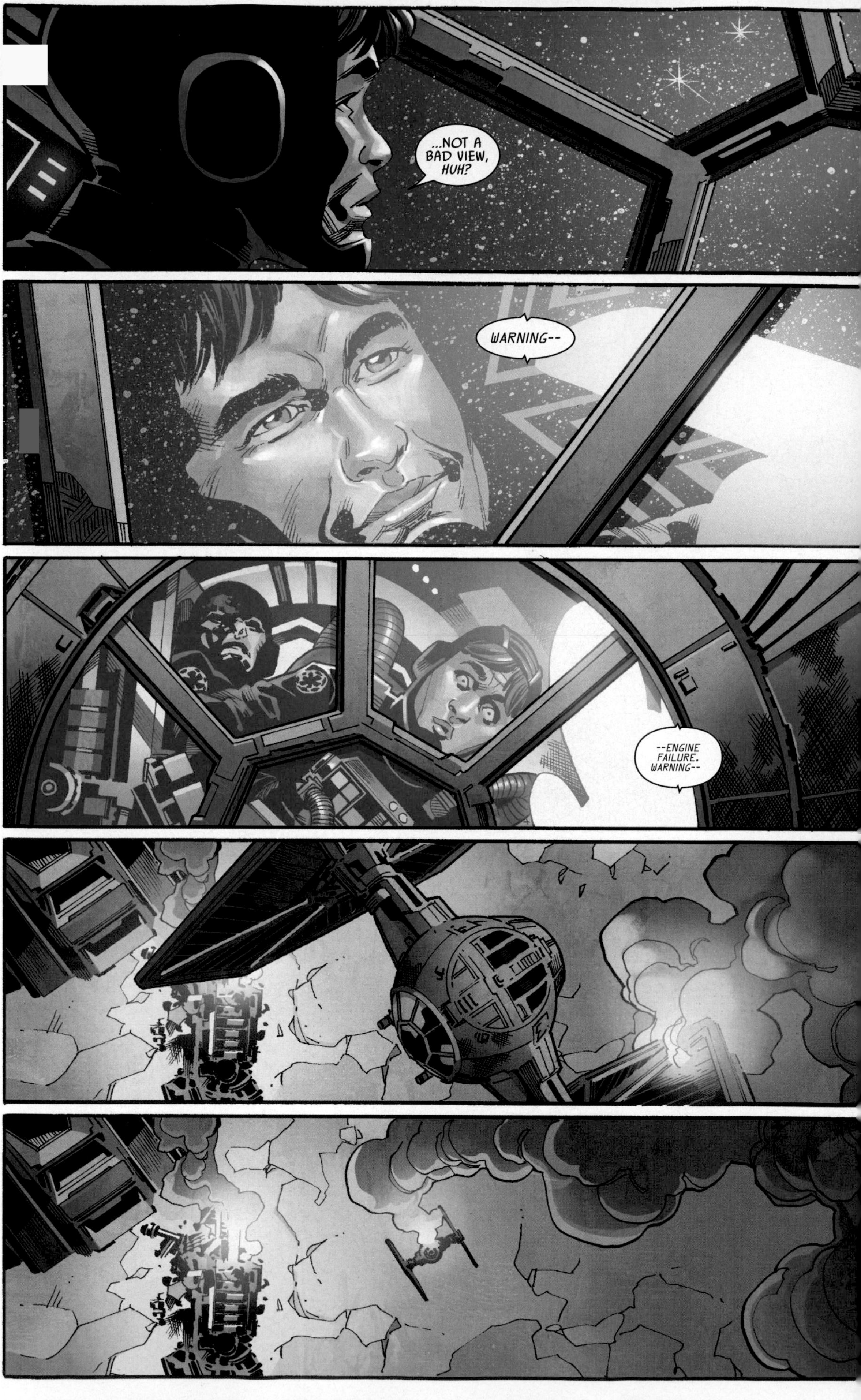
...NOT A BAD VIEW, HUH?
WARNING--
--ENGINE FAILURE. WARNING--

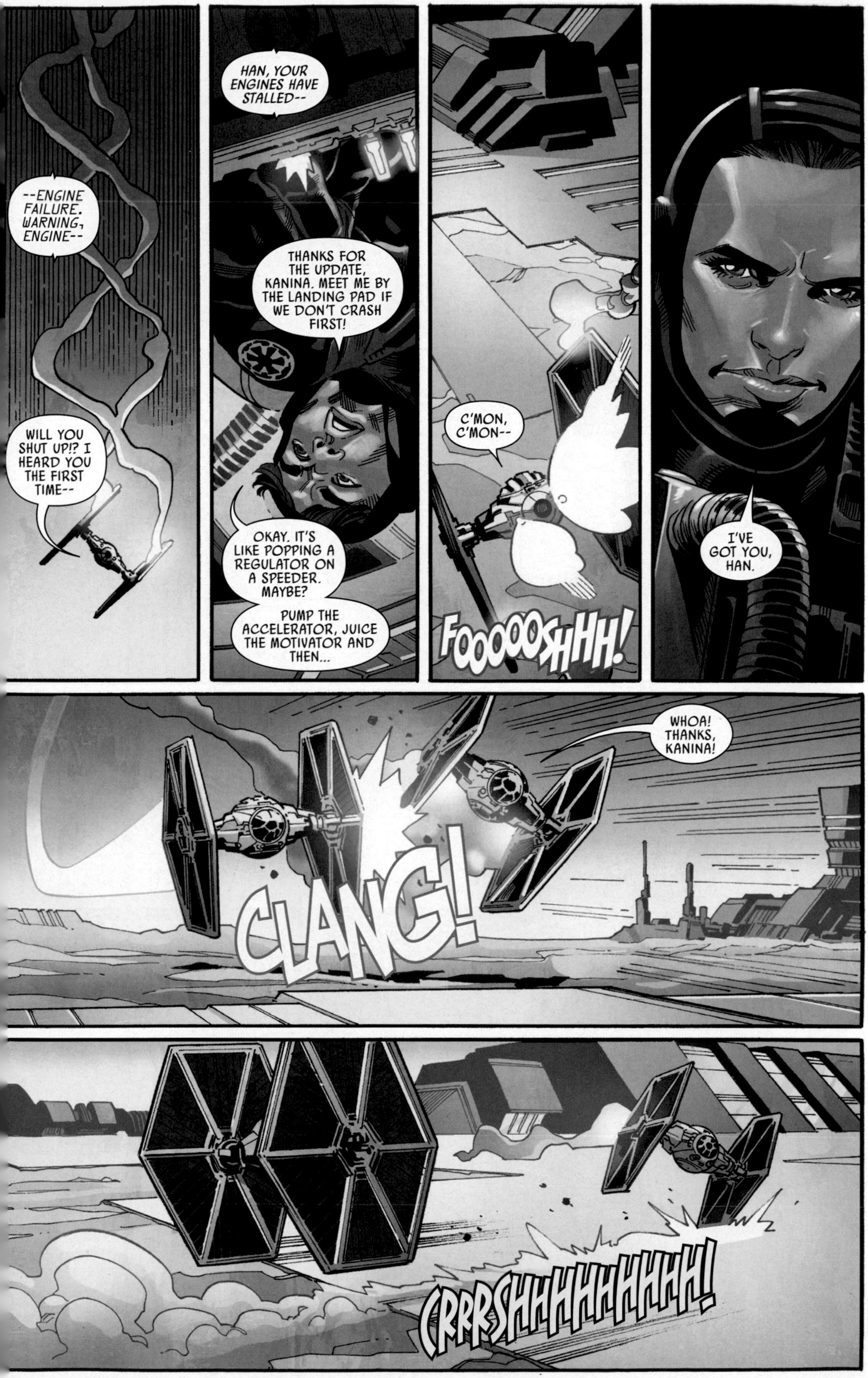
--ENGINE FAILURE. WARNING, ENGINE--
WILL YOU SHUT UP!? I HEARD YOU THE FIRST TIME--
HAN, YOUR ENGINES HAVE STALLED--
THANKS FOR THE UPDATE, KANINA. MEET ME BY THE LANDING PAD IF WE DON'T CRASH FIRST!
OKAY. IT'S LIKE POPPING A REGULATOR ON A SPEEDER. MAYBE?
PUMP THE ACCELERATOR, JUICE THE MOTIVATOR AND THEN...
C'MON, C'MON--
FOOOOOSHHH!
I'VE GOT YOU, HAN.
WHOA! THANKS, KANINA!
CLANG!
CRRRSHHHHHHHHH!

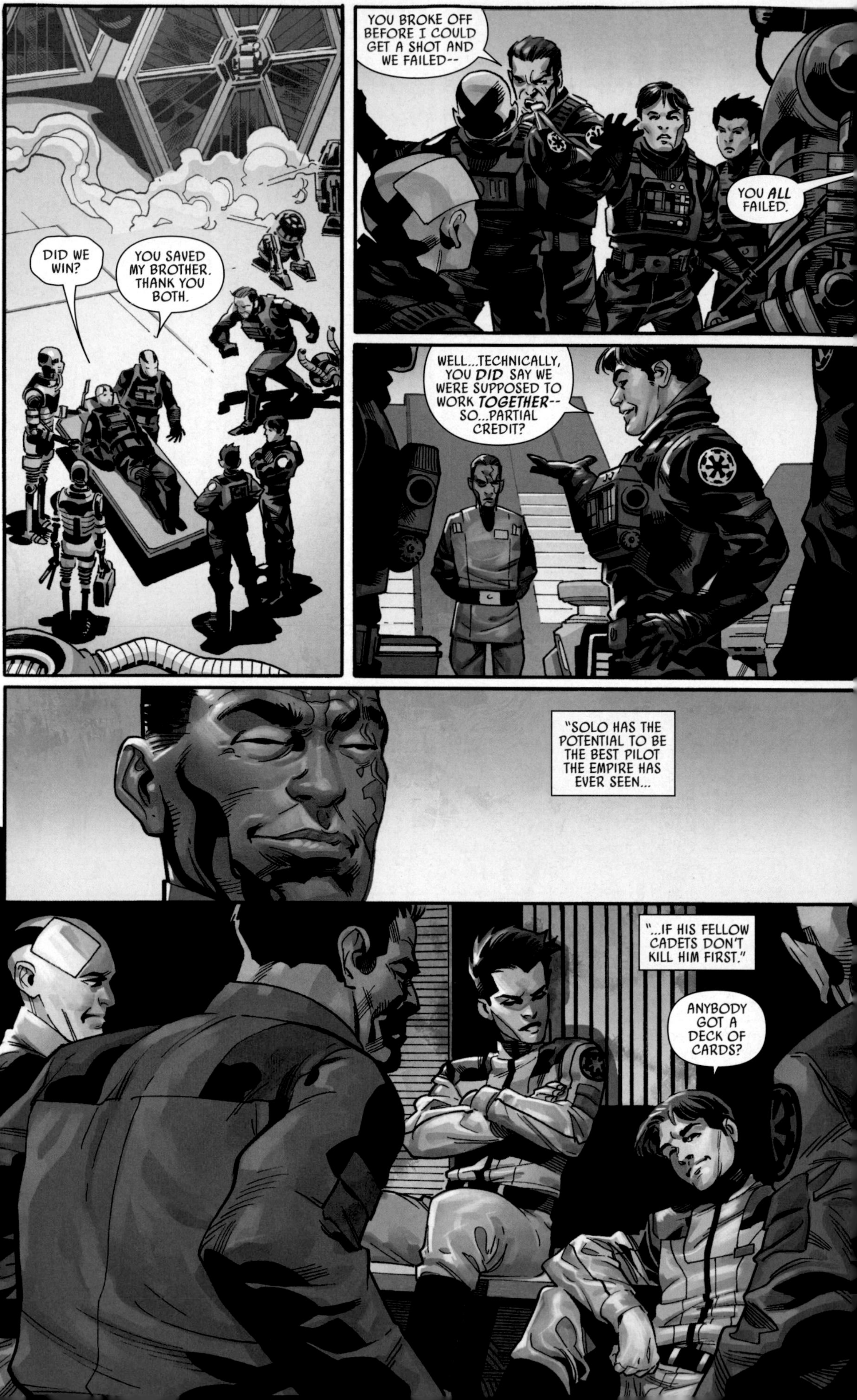
DID WE WIN?
YOU SAVED MY BROTHER. THANK YOU BOTH.
YOU BROKE OFF BEFORE I COULD GET A SHOT AND WE FAILED--
YOU ALL FAILED.
WELL...TECHNICALLY, YOU DID SAY WE WERE SUPPOSED TO WORK TOGETHER-- SO...PARTIAL CREDIT?
"SOLO HAS THE POTENTIAL TO BE THE BEST PILOT THE EMPIRE HAS EVER SEEN...
"...IF HIS FELLOW CADETS DON'T KILL HIM FIRST."
ANYBODY GOT A DECK OF CARDS?

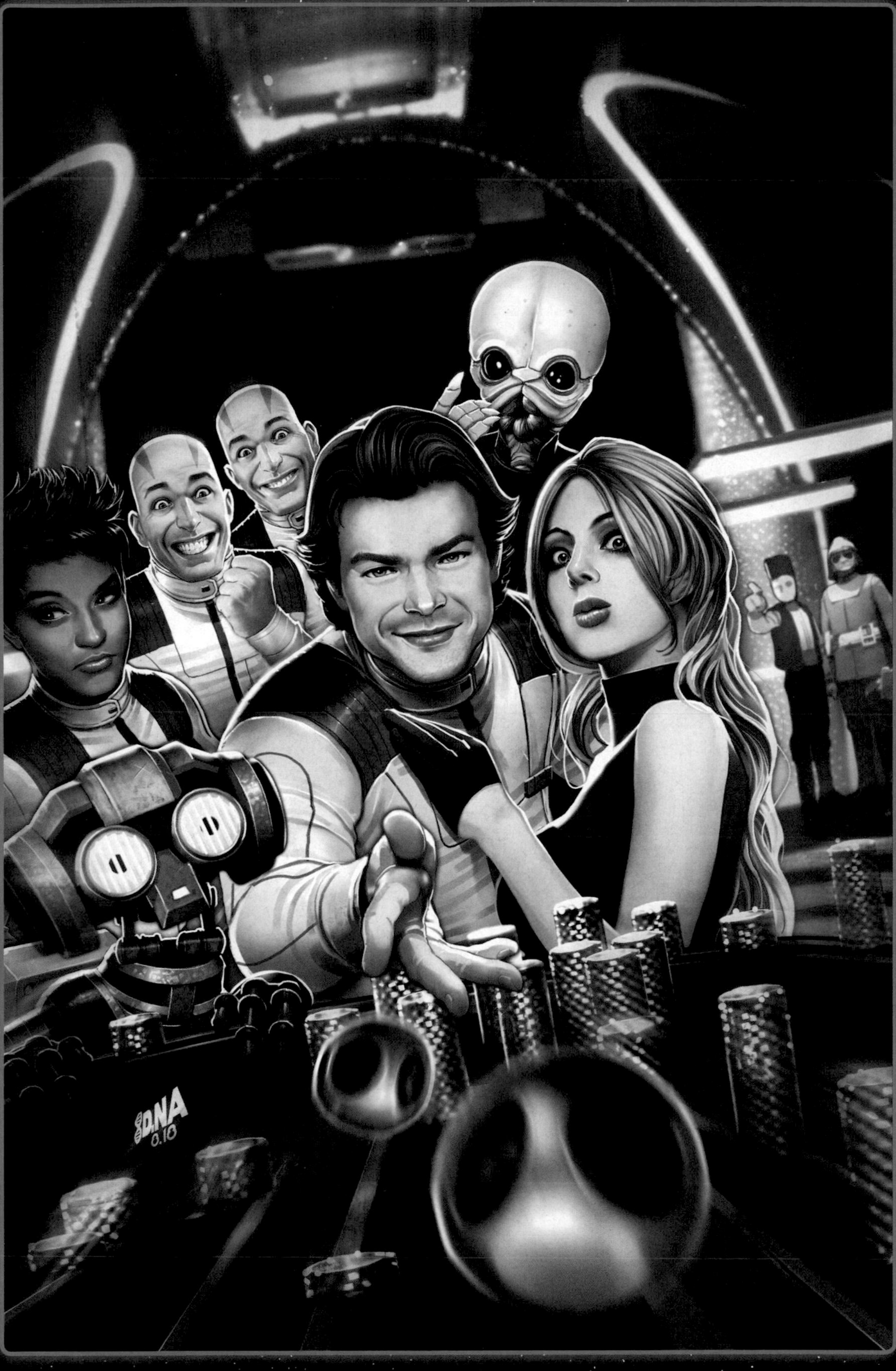
D.NA
8.18

3

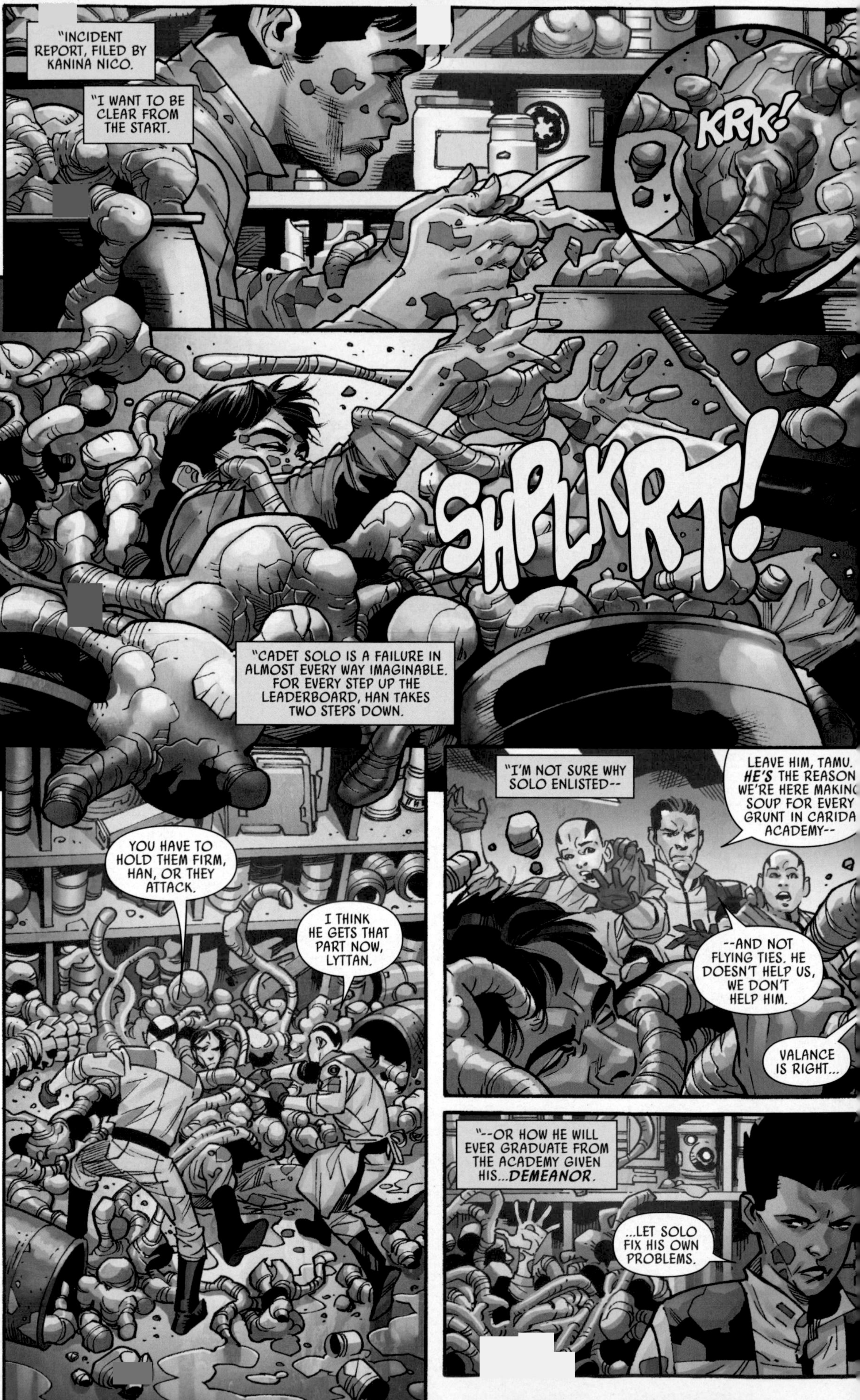
"INCIDENT REPORT, FILED BY KANINA NICO.
"I WANT TO BE CLEAR FROM THE START.
KRK!
SHPLKRT!
"CADET SOLO IS A FAILURE IN ALMOST EVERY WAY IMAGINABLE. FOR EVERY STEP UP THE LEADERBOARD, HAN TAKES TWO STEPS DOWN.
YOU HAVE TO HOLD THEM FIRM, HAN, OR THEY ATTACK.
I THINK HE GETS THAT PART NOW, LYTTAN.
"I'M NOT SURE WHY SOLO ENLISTED--
LEAVE HIM, TAMU. HE'S THE REASON WE'RE HERE MAKING SOUP FOR EVERY GRUNT IN CARIDA ACADEMY--
--AND NOT FLYING TIES. HE DOESN'T HELP US, WE DON'T HELP HIM.
VALANCE IS RIGHT...
"--OR HOW HE WILL EVER GRADUATE FROM THE ACADEMY GIVEN HIS...DEMEANOR.
...LET SOLO FIX HIS OWN PROBLEMS.

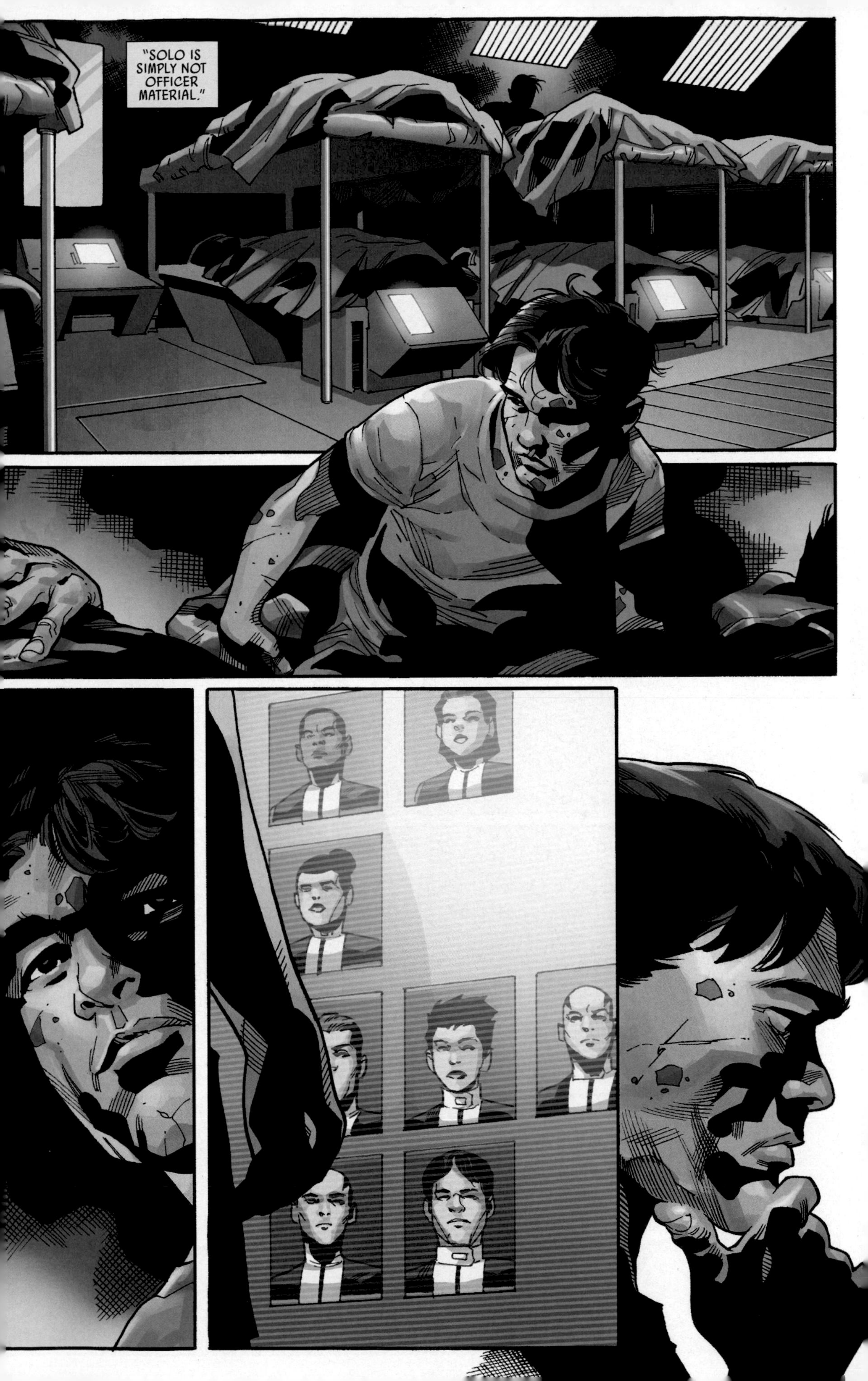
"SOLO IS SIMPLY NOT OFFICER MATERIAL."

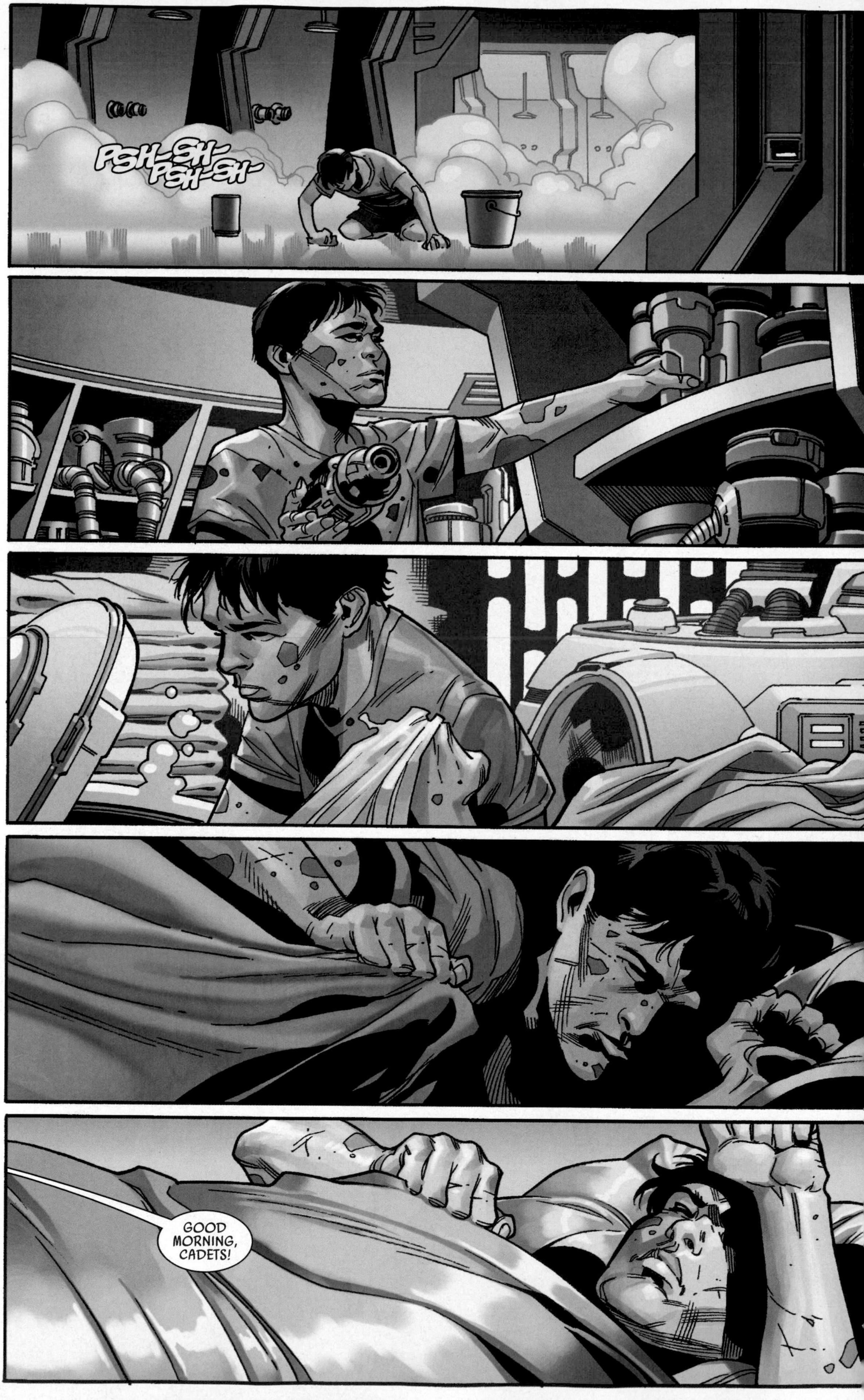
PSH-SH-
PSH-SH-
GOOD MORNING, CADETS!

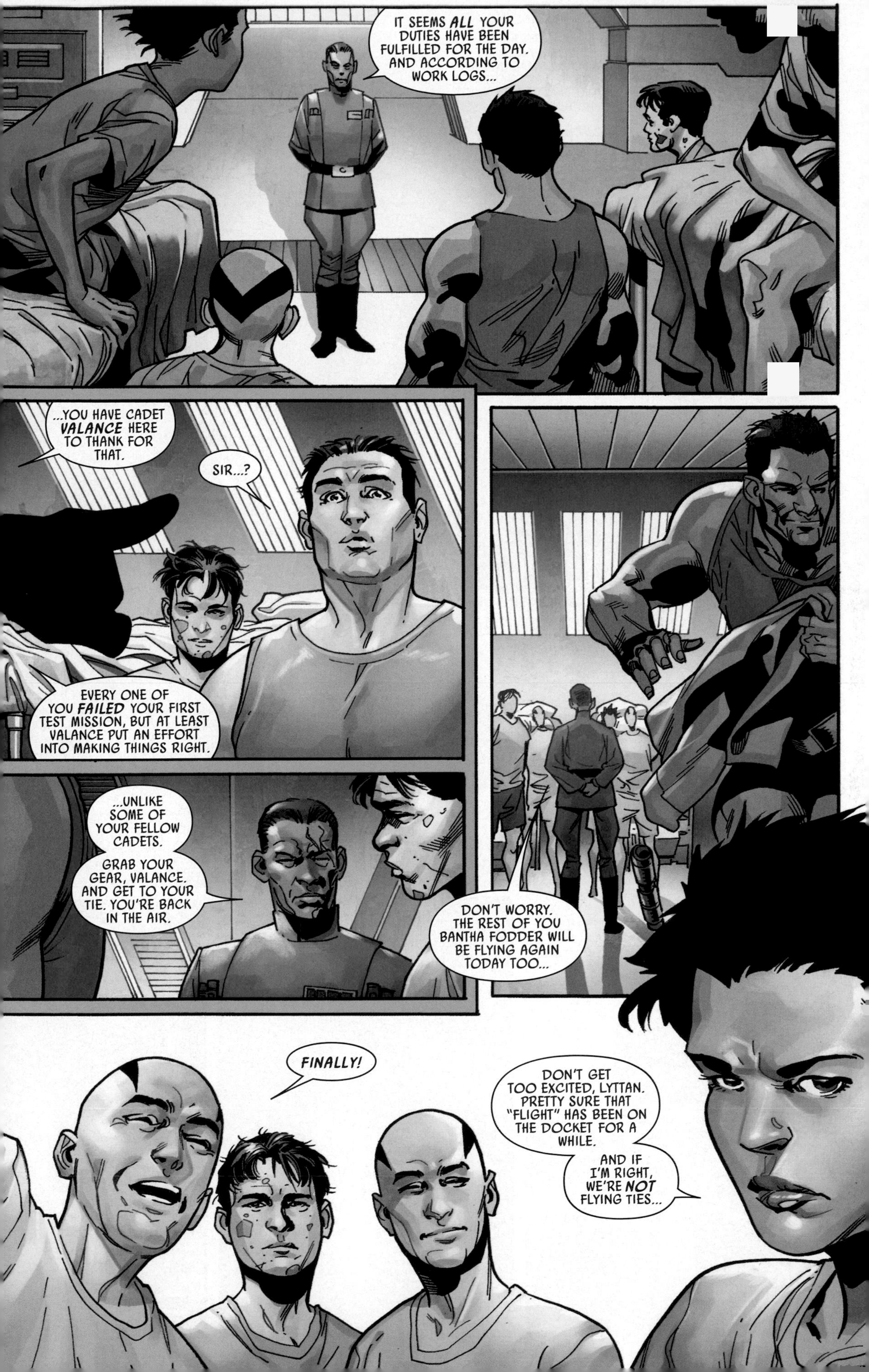
IT SEEMS ALL YOUR DUTIES HAVE BEEN FULFILLED FOR THE DAY. AND ACCORDING TO WORK LOGS...
...YOU HAVE CADET VALANCE HERE TO THANK FOR THAT.
SIR...?
EVERY ONE OF YOU FAILED YOUR FIRST TEST MISSION, BUT AT LEAST VALANCE PUT AN EFFORT INTO MAKING THINGS RIGHT.
...UNLIKE SOME OF YOUR FELLOW CADETS.
GRAB YOUR GEAR, VALANCE, AND GET TO YOUR TIE. YOU'RE BACK IN THE AIR.
DON'T WORRY. THE REST OF YOU BANTHA FODDER WILL BE FLYING AGAIN TODAY TOO...
FINALLY!
DON'T GET TOO EXCITED, LYTTAN. PRETTY SURE THAT "FLIGHT" HAS BEEN ON THE DOCKET FOR A WHILE.
AND IF I'M RIGHT, WE'RE NOT FLYING TIES...

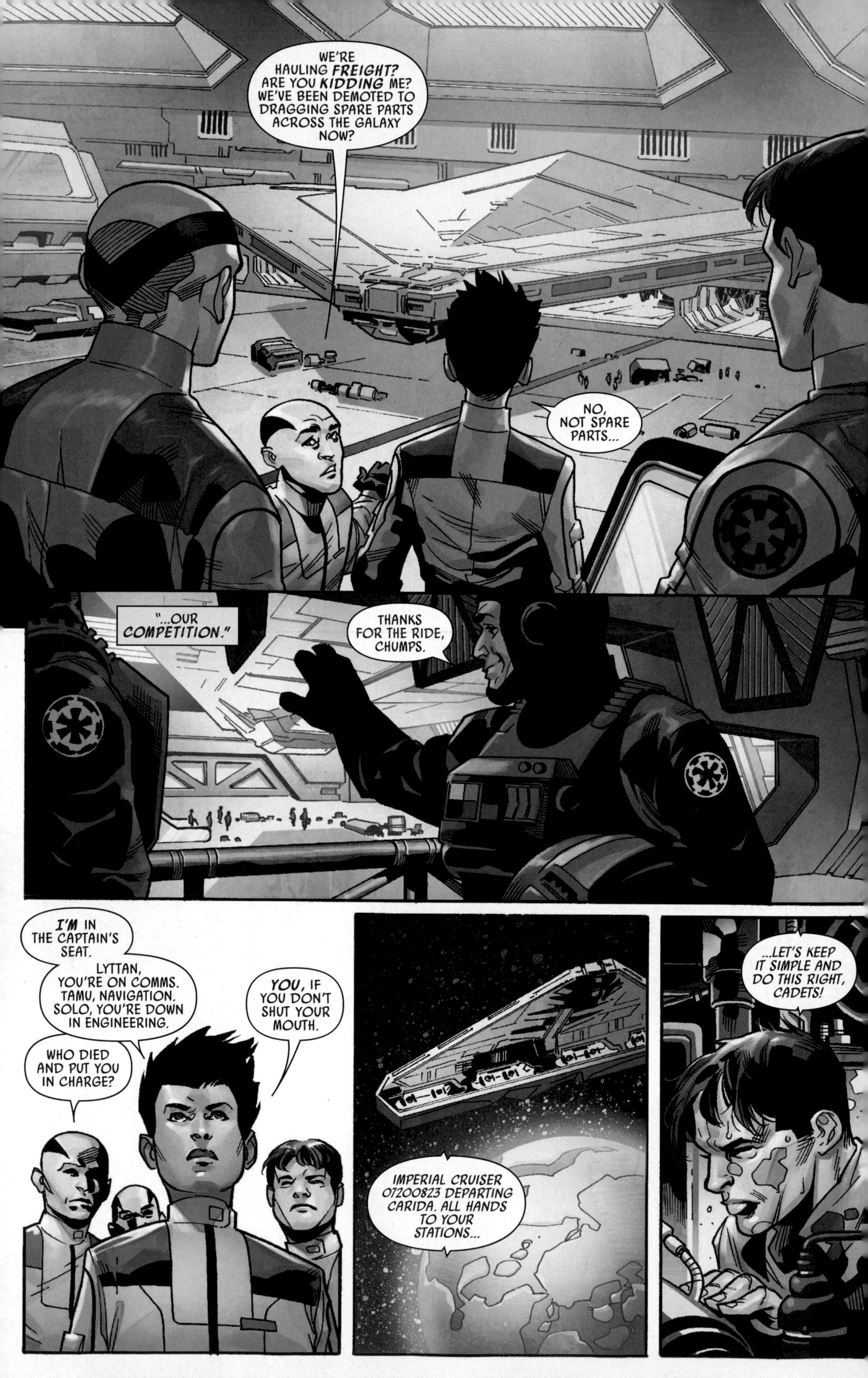
WE'RE HAULING FREIGHT? ARE YOU KIDDING ME? WE'VE BEEN DEMOTED TO DRAGGING SPARE PARTS ACROSS THE GALAXY NOW?
NO, NOT SPARE PARTS...
"...OUR COMPETITION."
THANKS FOR THE RIDE, CHUMPS.
I'M IN THE CAPTAIN'S SEAT.
LYTTAN, YOU'RE ON COMMS. TAMU, NAVIGATION. SOLO, YOU'RE DOWN IN ENGINEERING.
WHO DIED AND PUT YOU IN CHARGE?
YOU, IF YOU DON'T SHUT YOUR MOUTH.
IMPERIAL CRUISER 07200823 DEPARTING CARIDA. ALL HANDS TO YOUR STATIONS...
...LET'S KEEP IT SIMPLE AND DO THIS RIGHT, CADETS!

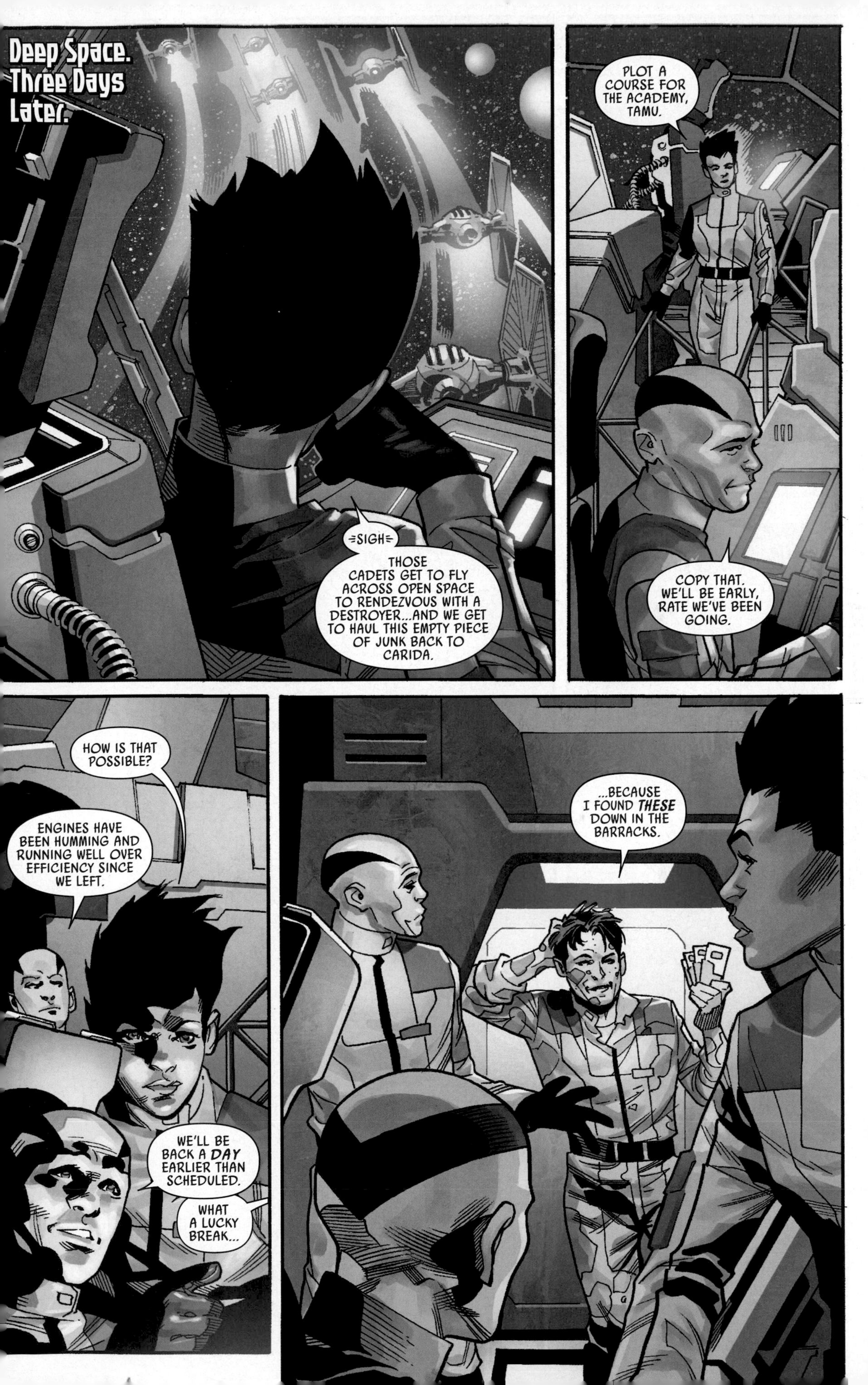
Deep Space. Three Days Later.
=SIGH=
THOSE CADETS GET TO FLY ACROSS OPEN SPACE TO RENDEZVOUS WITH A DESTROYER...AND WE GET TO HAUL THIS EMPTY PIECE OF JUNK BACK TO CARIDA.
PLOT A COURSE FOR THE ACADEMY, TAMU.
COPY THAT. WE'LL BE EARLY, RATE WE'VE BEEN GOING.
HOW IS THAT POSSIBLE?
ENGINES HAVE BEEN HUMMING AND RUNNING WELL OVER EFFICIENCY SINCE WE LEFT.
WE'LL BE BACK A DAY EARLIER THAN SCHEDULED.
WHAT A LUCKY BREAK...
...BECAUSE I FOUND THESE DOWN IN THE BARRACKS.

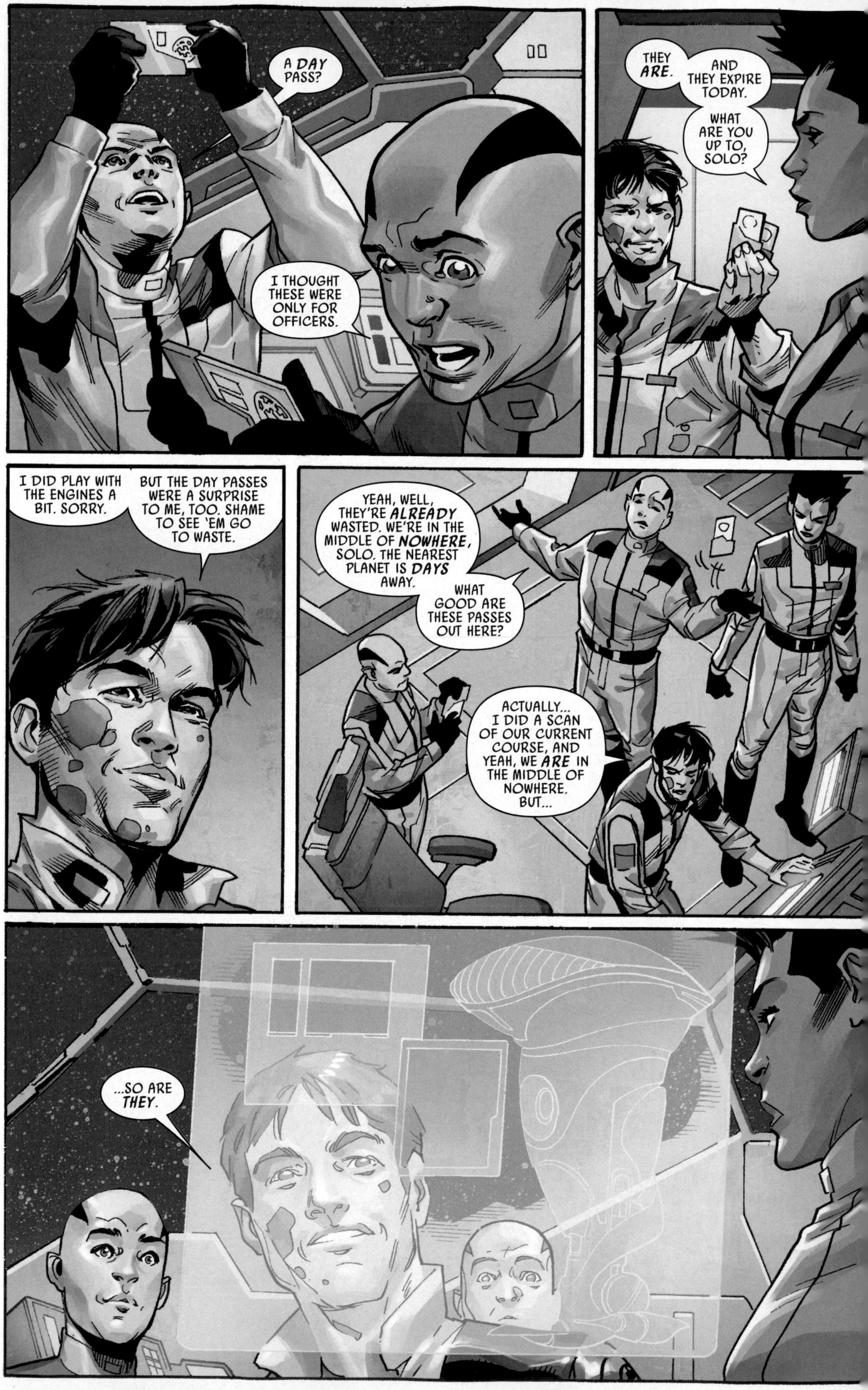
A DAY PASS?
I THOUGHT THESE WERE ONLY FOR OFFICERS.
THEY ARE.
AND THEY EXPIRE TODAY.
WHAT ARE YOU UP TO, SOLO?
I DID PLAY WITH THE ENGINES A BIT. SORRY.
BUT THE DAY PASSES WERE A SURPRISE TO ME, TOO. SHAME TO SEE 'EM GO TO WASTE.
YEAH, WELL, THEY'RE ALREADY WASTED. WE'RE IN THE MIDDLE OF NOWHERE, SOLO. THE NEAREST PLANET IS DAYS AWAY.
WHAT GOOD ARE THESE PASSES OUT HERE?
ACTUALLY... I DID A SCAN OF OUR CURRENT COURSE, AND YEAH, WE ARE IN THE MIDDLE OF NOWHERE. BUT...
...SO ARE THEY.

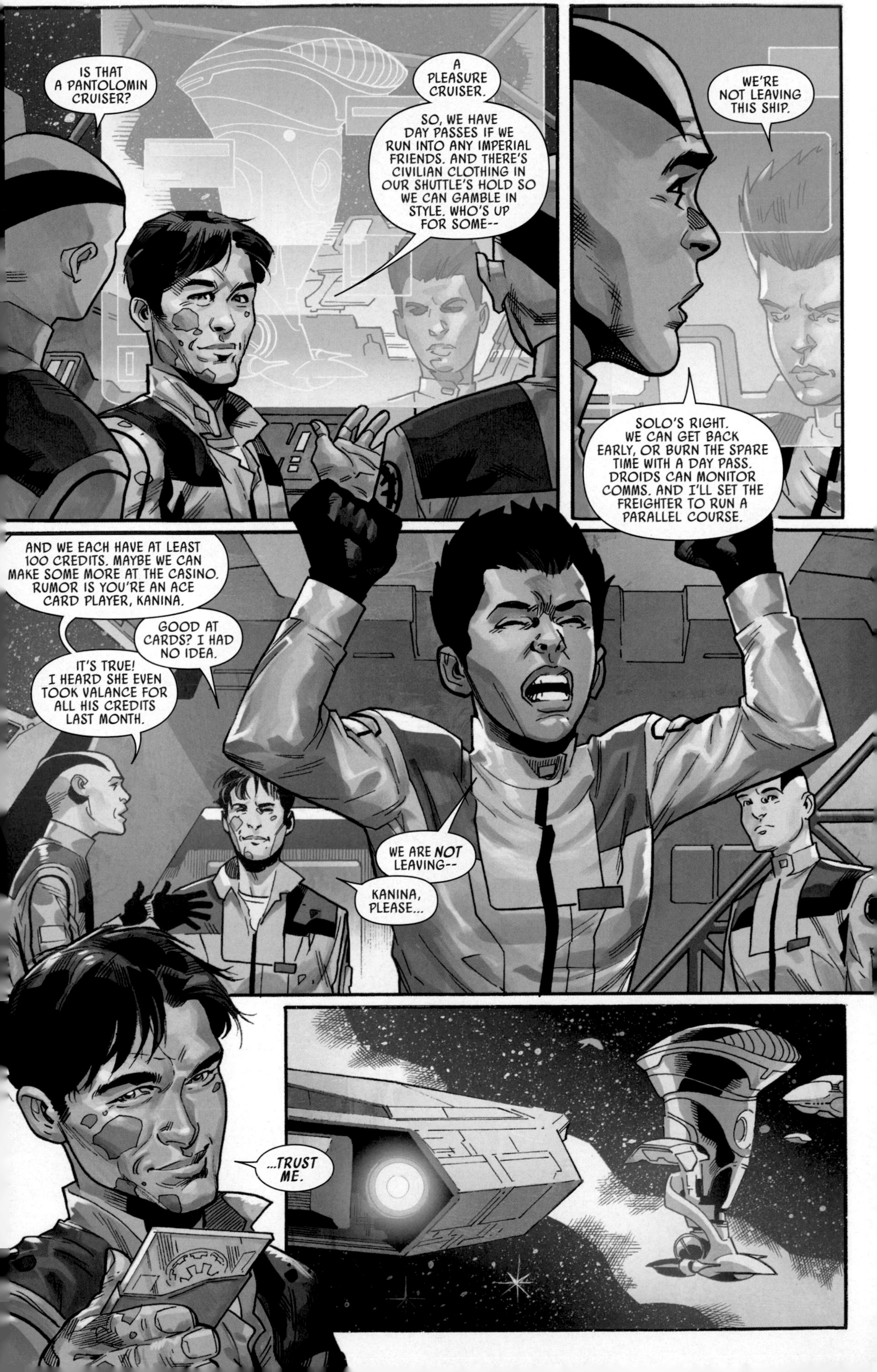
IS THAT A PANTOLOMIN CRUISER?
A PLEASURE CRUISER.
SO, WE HAVE DAY PASSES IF WE RUN INTO ANY IMPERIAL FRIENDS. AND THERE'S CIVILIAN CLOTHING IN OUR SHUTTLE'S HOLD SO WE CAN GAMBLE IN STYLE. WHO'S UP FOR SOME--
WE'RE NOT LEAVING THIS SHIP.
SOLO'S RIGHT. WE CAN GET BACK EARLY, OR BURN THE SPARE TIME WITH A DAY PASS. DROIDS CAN MONITOR COMMS. AND I'LL SET THE FREIGHTER TO RUN A PARALLEL COURSE.
AND WE EACH HAVE AT LEAST 100 CREDITS. MAYBE WE CAN MAKE SOME MORE AT THE CASINO. RUMOR IS YOU'RE AN ACE CARD PLAYER, KANINA.
GOOD AT CARDS? I HAD NO IDEA.
IT'S TRUE! I HEARD SHE EVEN TOOK VALANCE FOR ALL HIS CREDITS LAST MONTH.
WE ARE NOT LEAVING--
KANINA, PLEASE...
...TRUST ME.

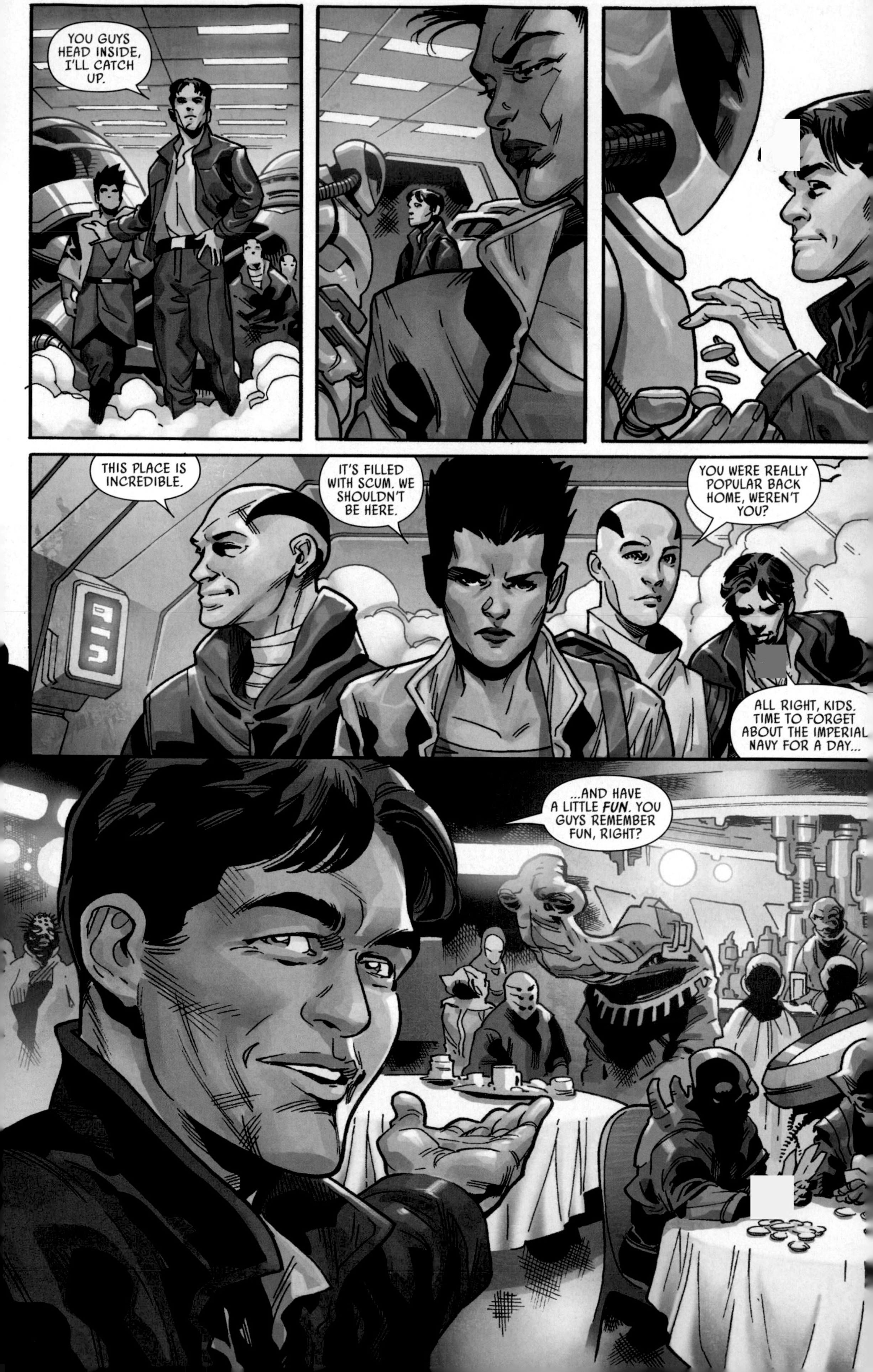
YOU GUYS HEAD INSIDE, I'LL CATCH UP.
THIS PLACE IS INCREDIBLE.
IT'S FILLED WITH SCUM. WE SHOULDN'T BE HERE.
YOU WERE REALLY POPULAR BACK HOME, WEREN'T YOU?
ALL RIGHT, KIDS. TIME TO FORGET ABOUT THE IMPERIAL NAVY FOR A DAY...
...AND HAVE A LITTLE FUN. YOU GUYS REMEMBER FUN, RIGHT?

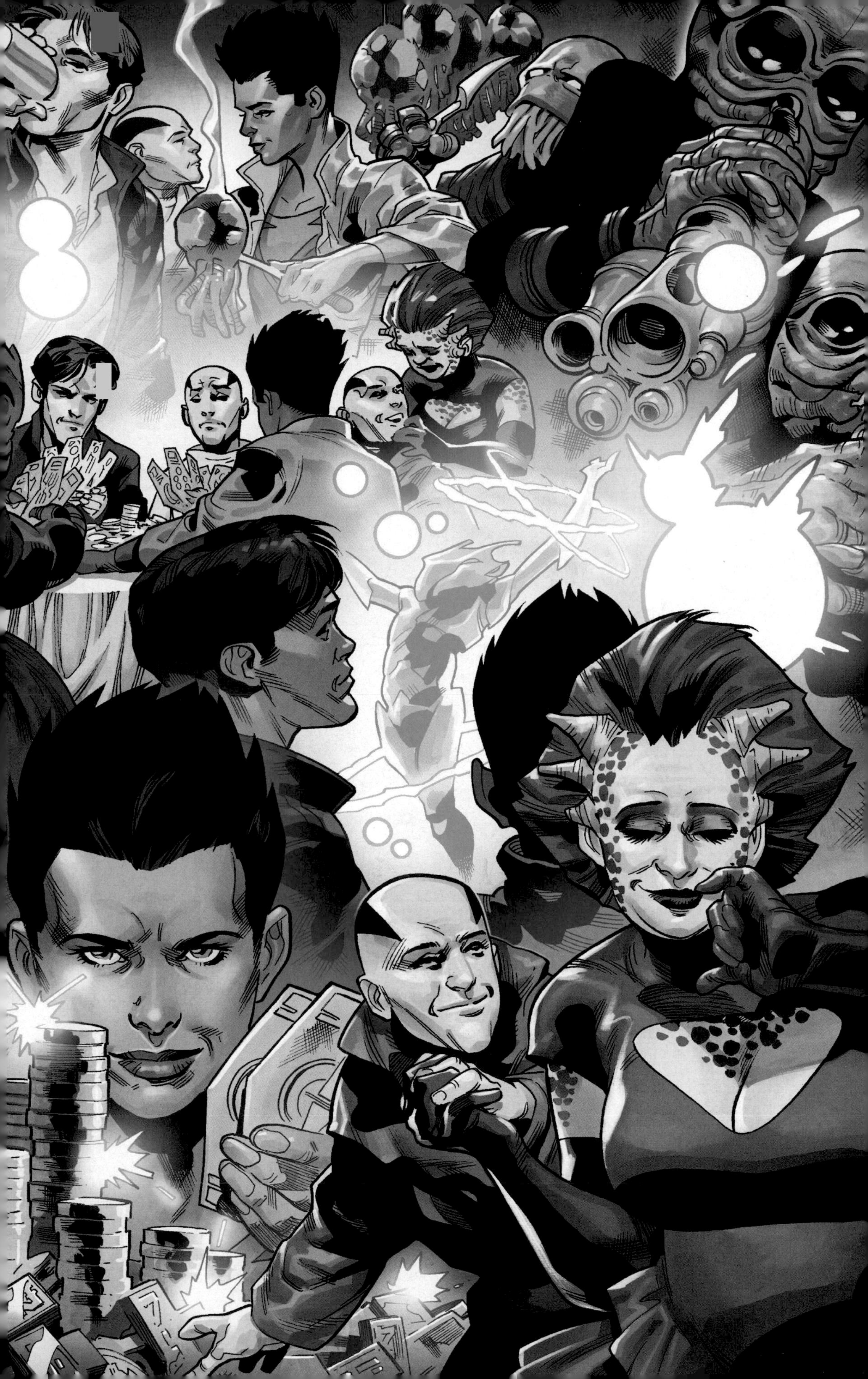

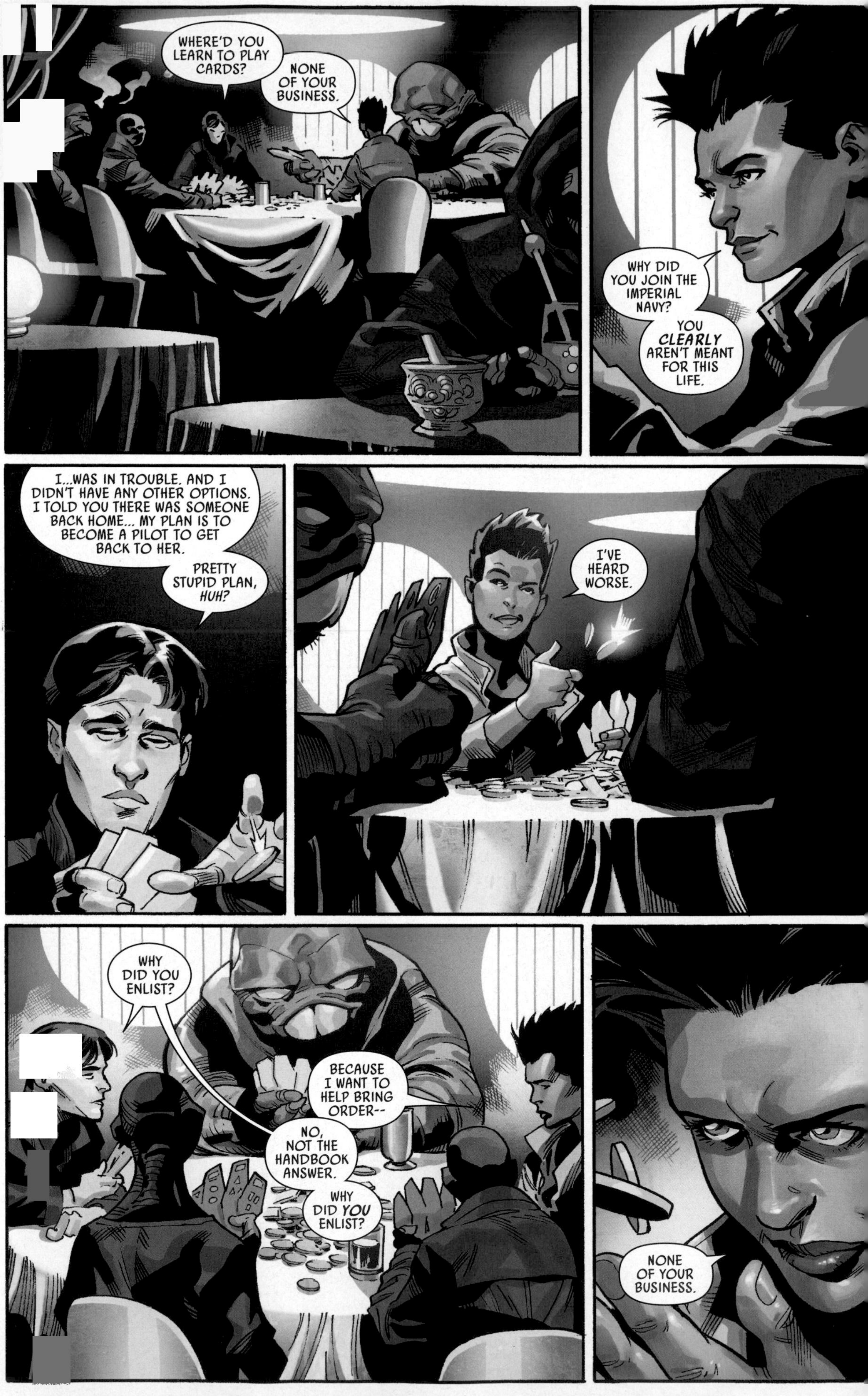
WHERE'D YOU LEARN TO PLAY CARDS?
NONE OF YOUR BUSINESS.
WHY DID YOU JOIN THE IMPERIAL NAVY?
YOU CLEARLY AREN'T MEANT FOR THIS LIFE.
I...WAS IN TROUBLE. AND I DIDN'T HAVE ANY OTHER OPTIONS. I TOLD YOU THERE WAS SOMEONE BACK HOME... MY PLAN IS TO BECOME A PILOT TO GET BACK TO HER.
PRETTY STUPID PLAN, HUH?
I'VE HEARD WORSE.
WHY DID YOU ENLIST?
BECAUSE I WANT TO HELP BRING ORDER--
NO, NOT THE HANDBOOK ANSWER.
WHY DID YOU ENLIST?
NONE OF YOUR BUSINESS.

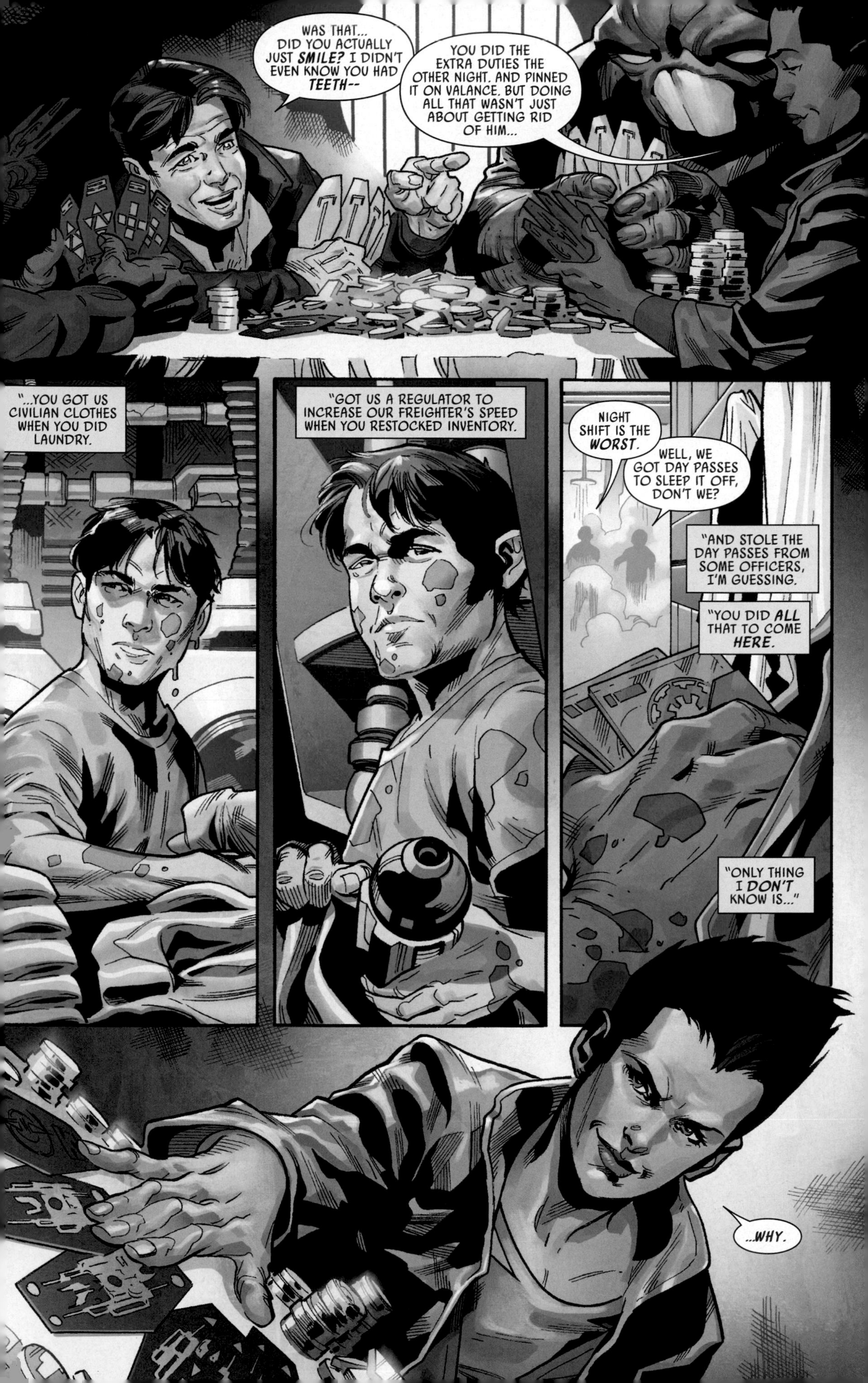
WAS THAT... DID YOU ACTUALLY JUST SMILE? I DIDN'T EVEN KNOW YOU HAD TEETH--
YOU DID THE EXTRA DUTIES THE OTHER NIGHT. AND PINNED IT ON VALANCE. BUT DOING ALL THAT WASN'T JUST ABOUT GETTING RID OF HIM...
"...YOU GOT US CIVILIAN CLOTHES WHEN YOU DID LAUNDRY.
"GOT US A REGULATOR TO INCREASE OUR FREIGHTER'S SPEED WHEN YOU RESTOCKED INVENTORY.
NIGHT SHIFT IS THE WORST.
WELL, WE GOT DAY PASSES TO SLEEP IT OFF, DON'T WE?
"AND STOLE THE DAY PASSES FROM SOME OFFICERS, I'M GUESSING.
"YOU DID ALL THAT TO COME HERE.
"ONLY THING I DON'T KNOW IS..."
...WHY.

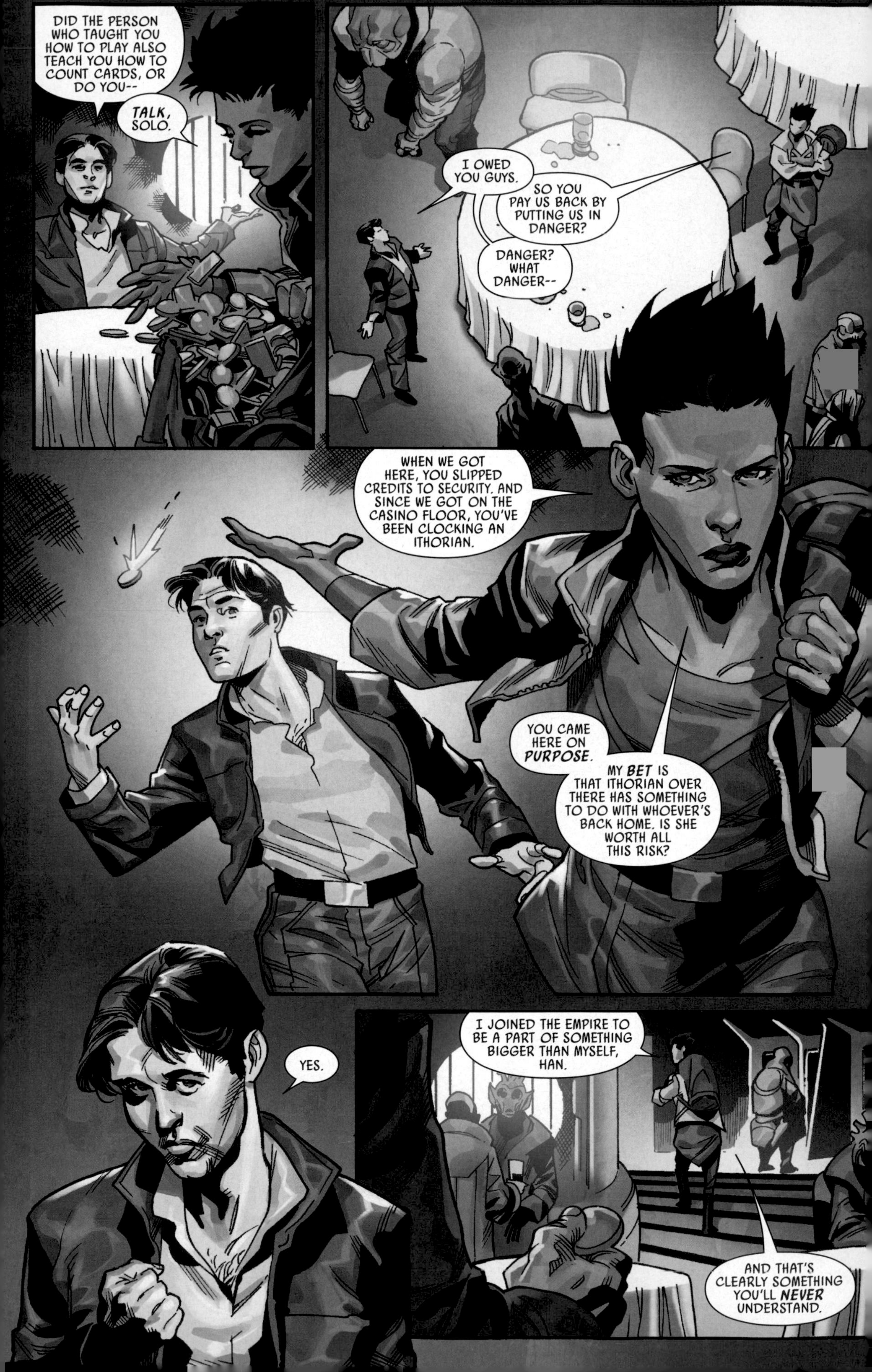
DID THE PERSON WHO TAUGHT YOU HOW TO PLAY ALSO TEACH YOU HOW TO COUNT CARDS, OR DO YOU--
TALK, SOLO.
I OWED YOU GUYS.
SO YOU PAY US BACK BY PUTTING US IN DANGER?
DANGER? WHAT DANGER--
WHEN WE GOT HERE, YOU SLIPPED CREDITS TO SECURITY. AND SINCE WE GOT ON THE CASINO FLOOR, YOU'VE BEEN CLOCKING AN ITHORIAN.
YOU CAME HERE ON PURPOSE.
MY BET IS THAT ITHORIAN OVER THERE HAS SOMETHING TO DO WITH WHOEVER'S BACK HOME. IS SHE WORTH ALL THIS RISK?
YES.
I JOINED THE EMPIRE TO BE A PART OF SOMETHING BIGGER THAN MYSELF, HAN.
AND THAT'S CLEARLY SOMETHING YOU'LL NEVER UNDERSTAND.

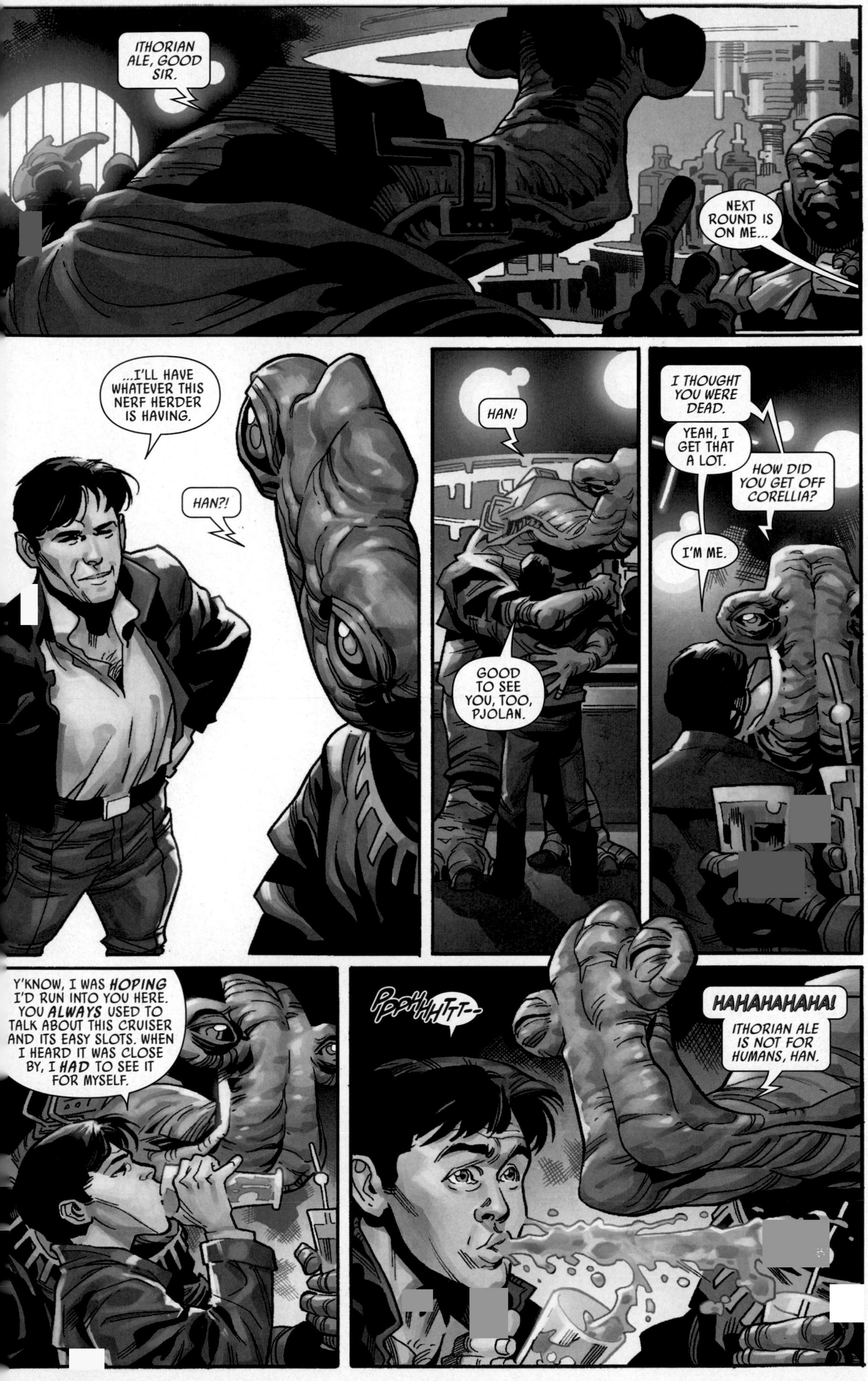
ITHORIAN ALE, GOOD SIR.
NEXT ROUND IS ON ME...
...I'LL HAVE WHATEVER THIS NERF HERDER IS HAVING.
HAN?!
HAN!
GOOD TO SEE YOU, TOO, PJOLAN.
I THOUGHT YOU WERE DEAD.
YEAH, I GET THAT A LOT.
HOW DID YOU GET OFF CORELLIA?
I'M ME.
Y'KNOW, I WAS HOPING I'D RUN INTO YOU HERE. YOU ALWAYS USED TO TALK ABOUT THIS CRUISER AND ITS EASY SLOTS. WHEN I HEARD IT WAS CLOSE BY, I HAD TO SEE IT FOR MYSELF.
PPPHHHTTT--
HAHAHAHAHA! ITHORIAN ALE IS NOT FOR HUMANS, HAN.

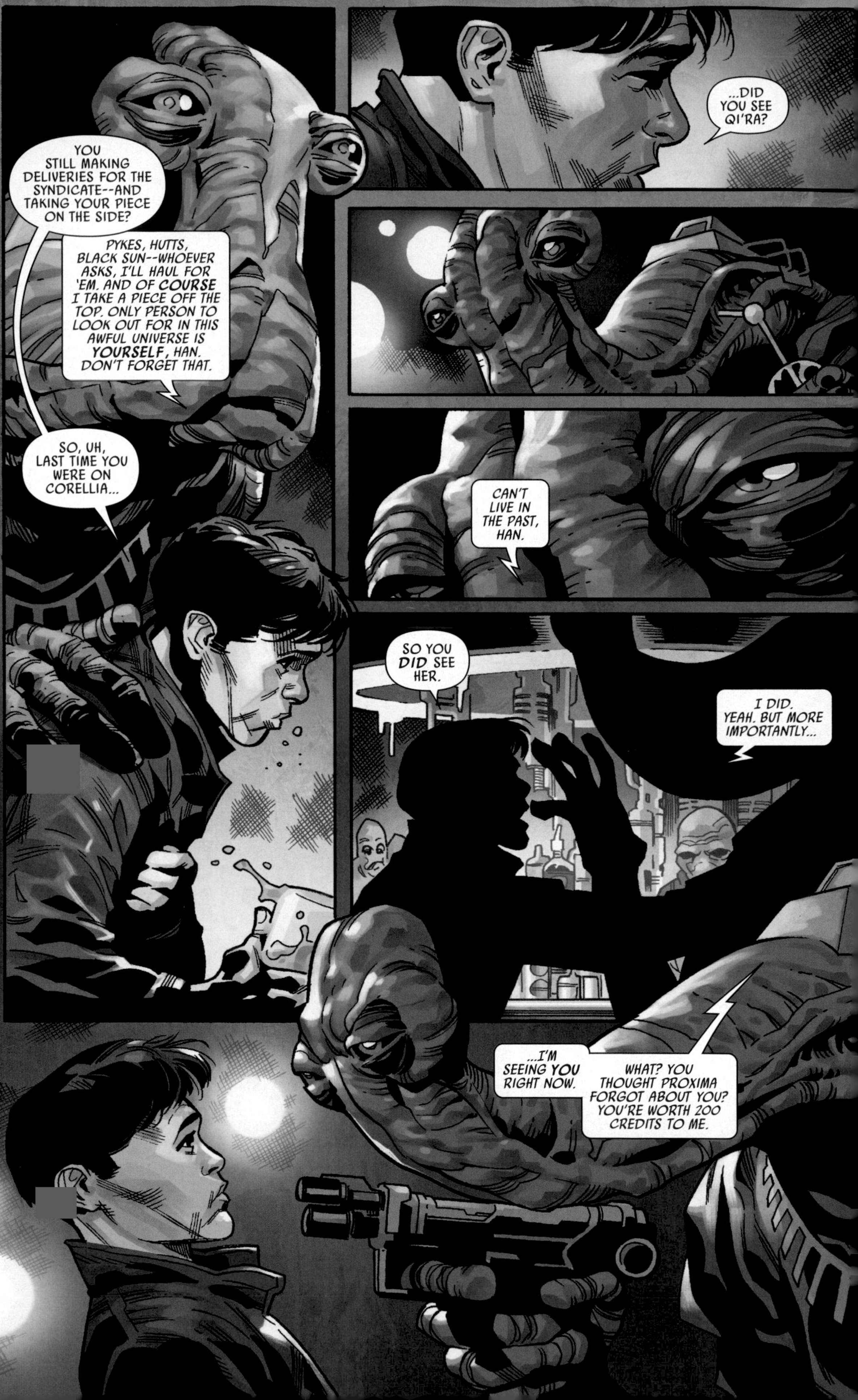
YOU STILL MAKING DELIVERIES FOR THE SYNDICATE--AND TAKING YOUR PIECE ON THE SIDE?
PYKES, HUTTS, BLACK SUN--WHOEVER ASKS, I'LL HAUL FOR 'EM. AND OF COURSE I TAKE A PIECE OFF THE TOP. ONLY PERSON TO LOOK OUT FOR IN THIS AWFUL UNIVERSE IS YOURSELF, HAN. DON'T FORGET THAT.
SO, UH, LAST TIME YOU WERE ON CORELLIA...
...DID YOU SEE QI'RA?
CAN'T LIVE IN THE PAST, HAN.
SO YOU DID SEE HER.
I DID. YEAH. BUT MORE IMPORTANTLY...
...I'M SEEING YOU RIGHT NOW.
WHAT? YOU THOUGHT PROXIMA FORGOT ABOUT YOU? YOU'RE WORTH 200 CREDITS TO ME.

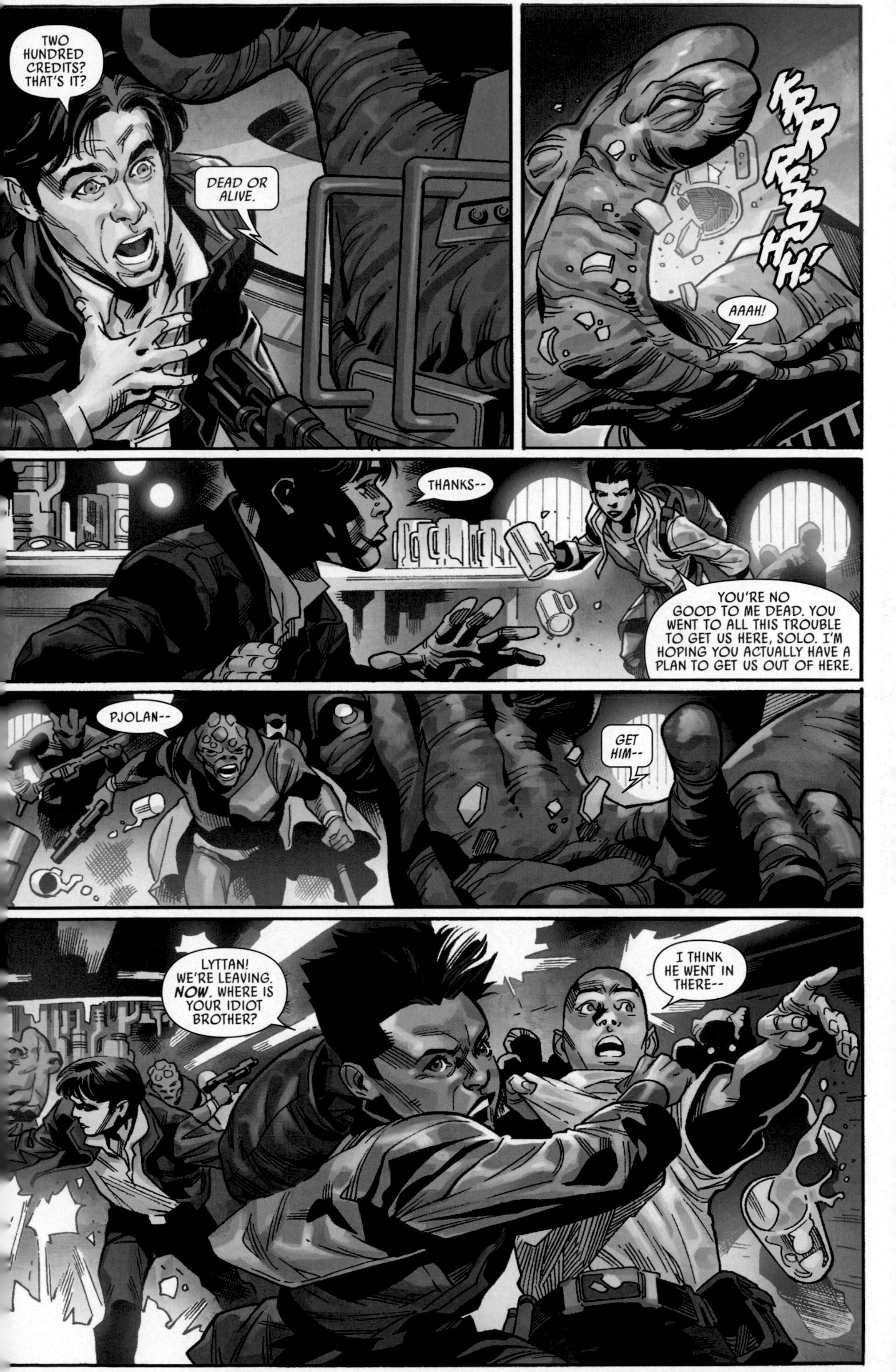

TWO HUNDRED CREDITS? THAT'S IT?
DEAD OR ALIVE.
KRRESHH!
AAAH!
THANKS--
YOU'RE NO GOOD TO ME DEAD. YOU WENT TO ALL THIS TROUBLE TO GET US HERE, SOLO. I'M HOPING YOU ACTUALLY HAVE A PLAN TO GET US OUT OF HERE.
PJOLAN--
GET HIM--
LYTTAN! WE'RE LEAVING. NOW. WHERE IS YOUR IDIOT BROTHER?
I THINK HE WENT IN THERE--

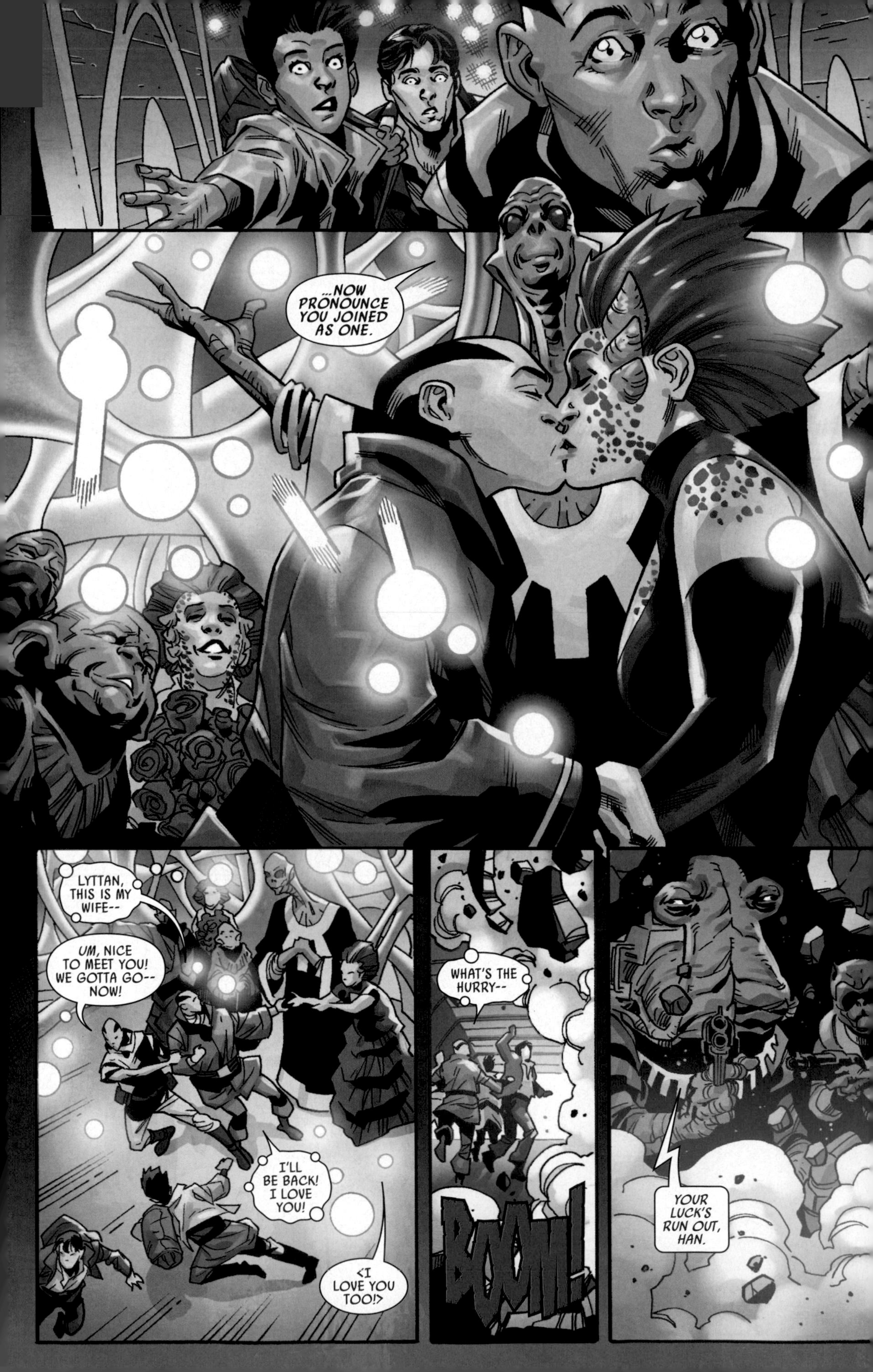
...NOW PRONOUNCE YOU JOINED AS ONE.
LYTTAN, THIS IS MY WIFE--
UM, NICE TO MEET YOU! WE GOTTA GO-- NOW!
I'LL BE BACK! I LOVE YOU!
<I LOVE YOU TOO!>
WHAT'S THE HURRY--
BOOM!
YOUR LUCK'S RUN OUT, HAN.

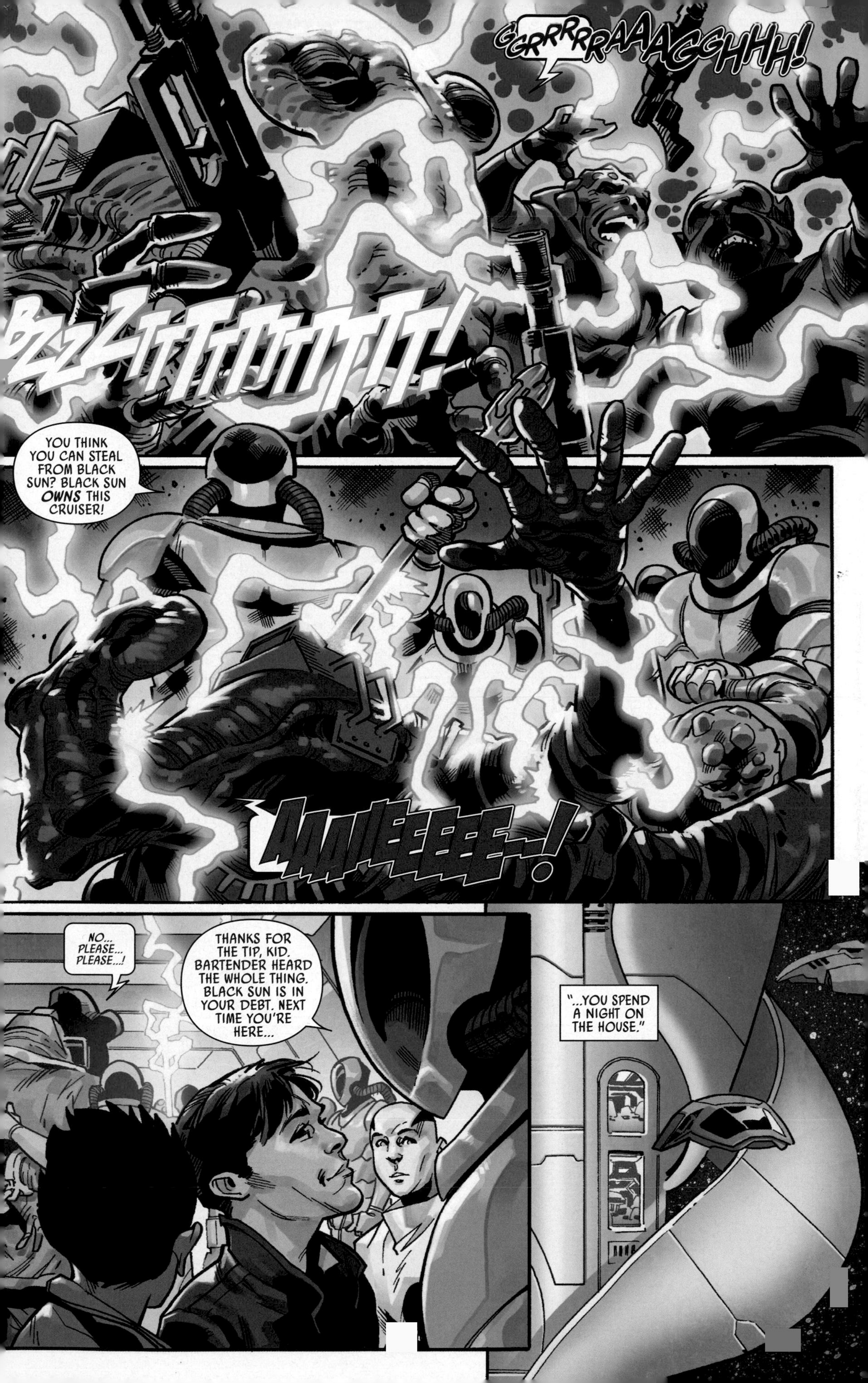
GGRRRRRAAAAGGHHH!
BZZZTTTTTTTTTT!
YOU THINK YOU CAN STEAL FROM BLACK SUN? BLACK SUN *OWNS* THIS CRUISER!
AAAIIEEEEE...!
NO... PLEASE... PLEASE...!
THANKS FOR THE TIP, KID. BARTENDER HEARD THE WHOLE THING. BLACK SUN IS IN YOUR DEBT. NEXT TIME YOU'RE HERE...
"...YOU SPEND A NIGHT ON THE HOUSE."

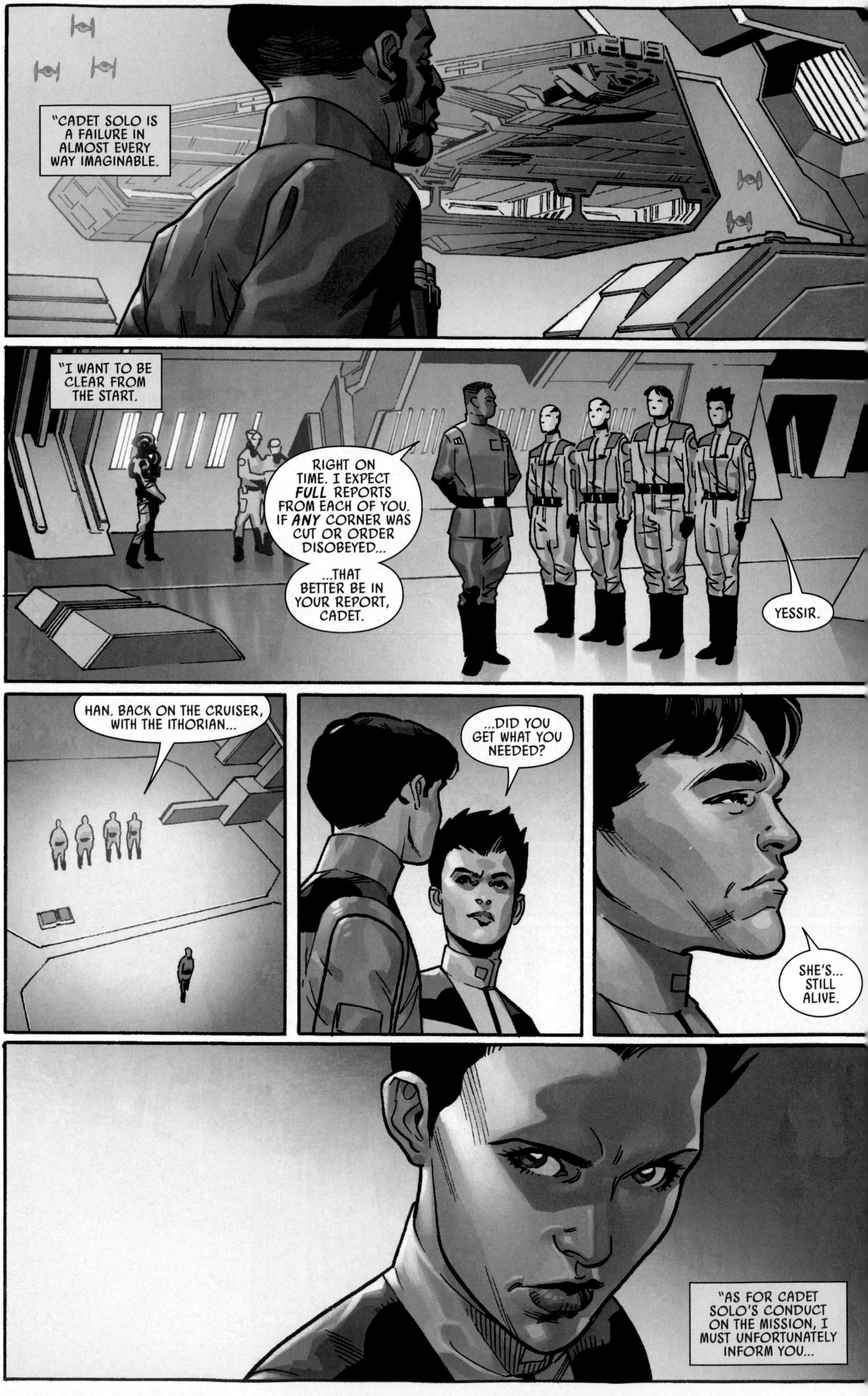
"CADET SOLO IS A FAILURE IN ALMOST EVERY WAY IMAGINABLE.
"I WANT TO BE CLEAR FROM THE START.
RIGHT ON TIME. I EXPECT FULL REPORTS FROM EACH OF YOU. IF ANY CORNER WAS CUT OR ORDER DISOBEYED...
...THAT BETTER BE IN YOUR REPORT, CADET.
YESSIR.
HAN. BACK ON THE CRUISER, WITH THE ITHORIAN...
...DID YOU GET WHAT YOU NEEDED?
SHE'S... STILL ALIVE.
"AS FOR CADET SOLO'S CONDUCT ON THE MISSION, I MUST UNFORTUNATELY INFORM YOU...

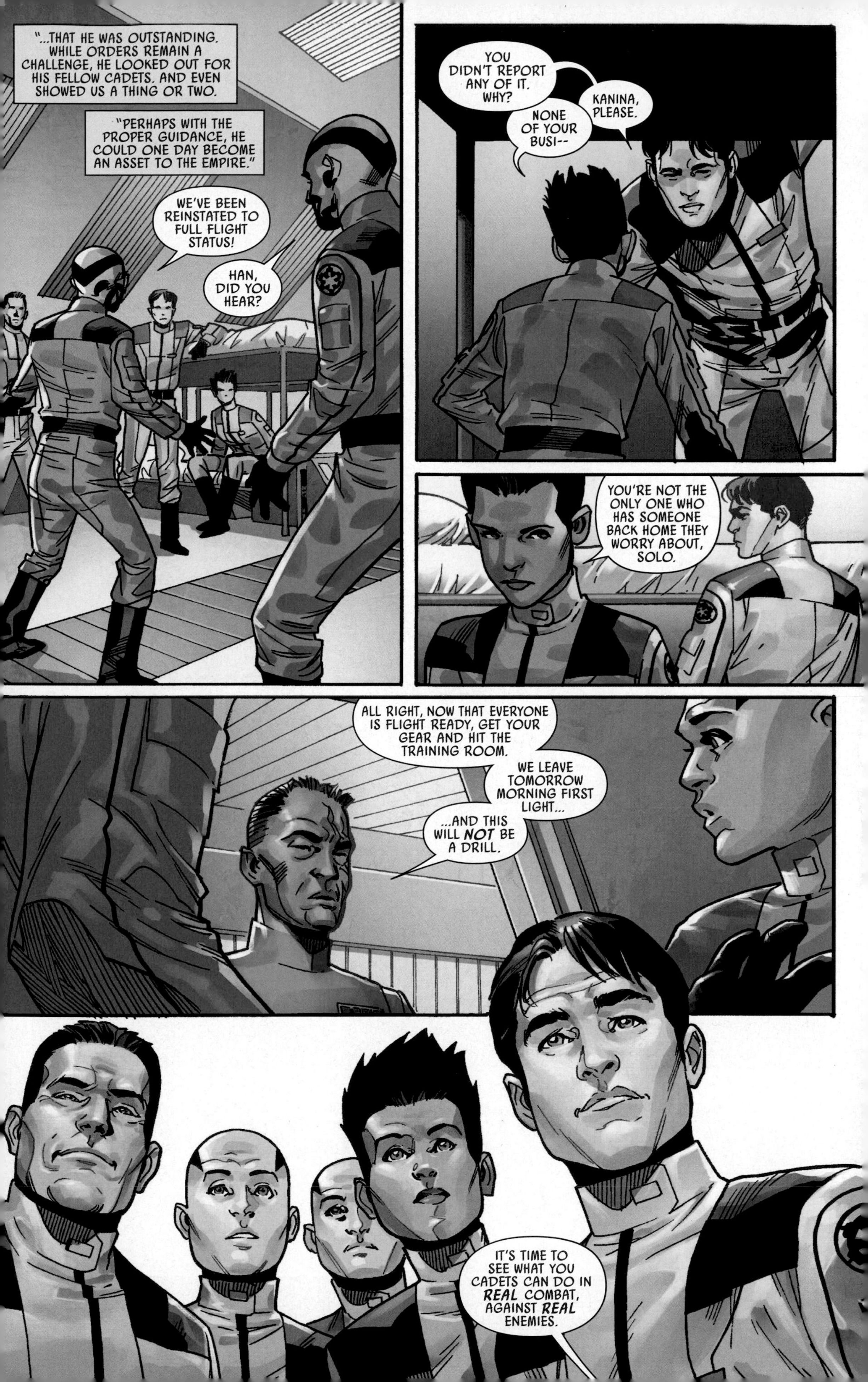
"...THAT HE WAS OUTSTANDING. WHILE ORDERS REMAIN A CHALLENGE, HE LOOKED OUT FOR HIS FELLOW CADETS. AND EVEN SHOWED US A THING OR TWO.
"PERHAPS WITH THE PROPER GUIDANCE, HE COULD ONE DAY BECOME AN ASSET TO THE EMPIRE."
WE'VE BEEN REINSTATED TO FULL FLIGHT STATUS!
HAN, DID YOU HEAR?
YOU DIDN'T REPORT ANY OF IT. WHY?
NONE OF YOUR BUSI--
KANINA, PLEASE.
YOU'RE NOT THE ONLY ONE WHO HAS SOMEONE BACK HOME THEY WORRY ABOUT, SOLO.
ALL RIGHT, NOW THAT EVERYONE IS FLIGHT READY, GET YOUR GEAR AND HIT THE TRAINING ROOM.
WE LEAVE TOMORROW MORNING FIRST LIGHT...
...AND THIS WILL NOT BE A DRILL.
IT'S TIME TO SEE WHAT YOU CADETS CAN DO IN REAL COMBAT, AGAINST REAL ENEMIES.

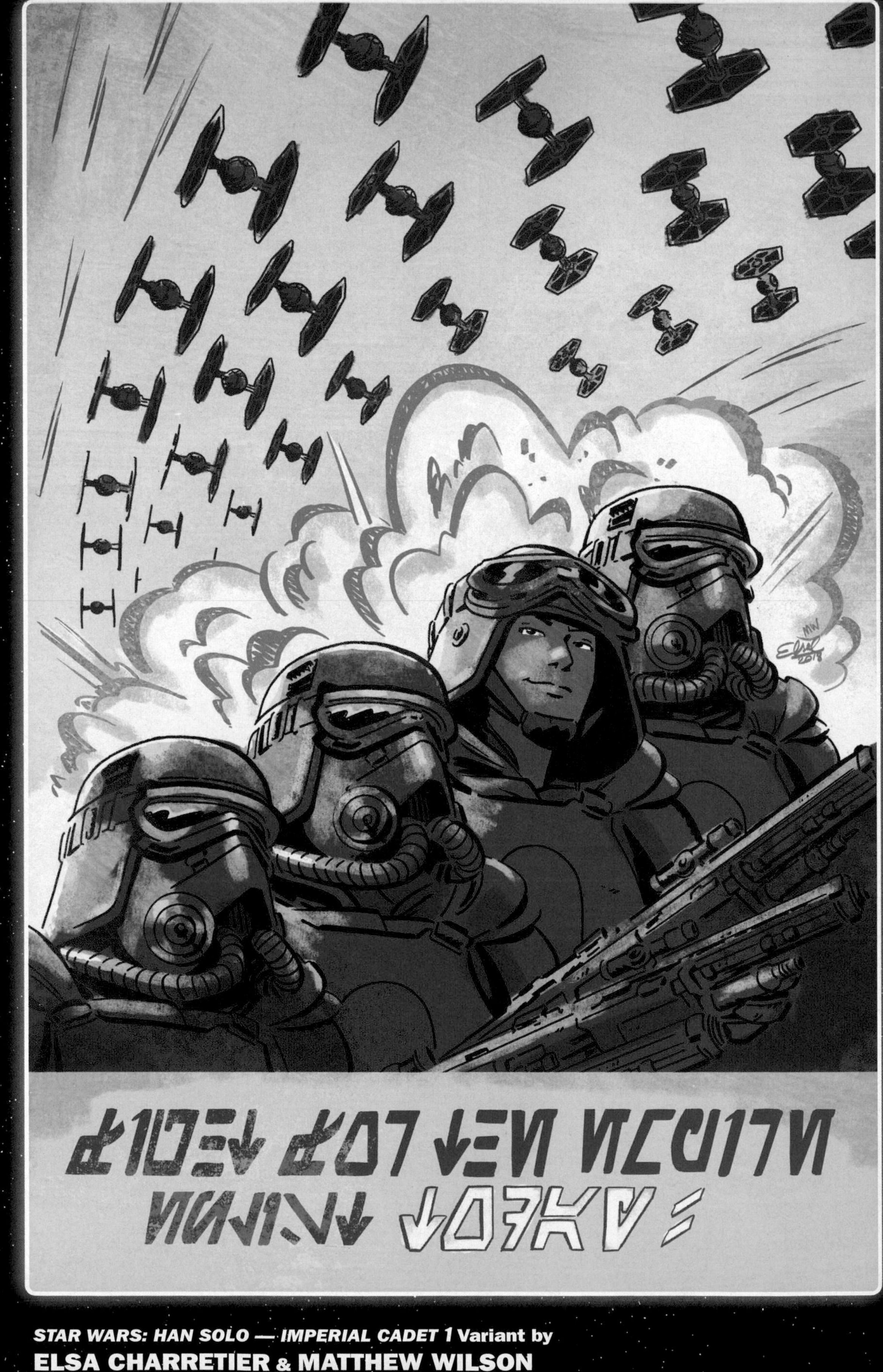

STAR WARS: HAN SOLO — IMPERIAL CADET 1 **Variant by**

ELSA CHARRETIER & MATTHEW WILSON

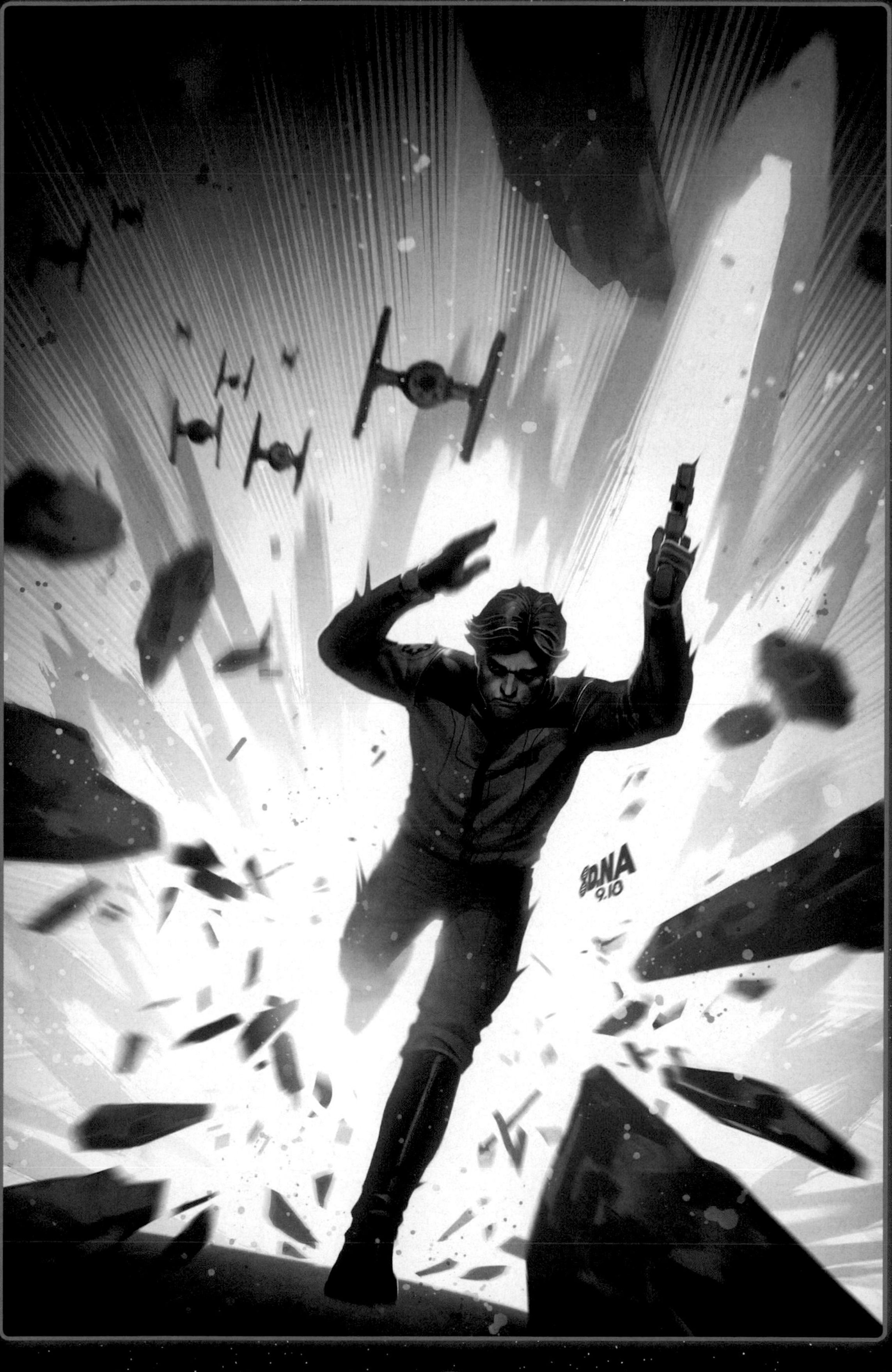

4

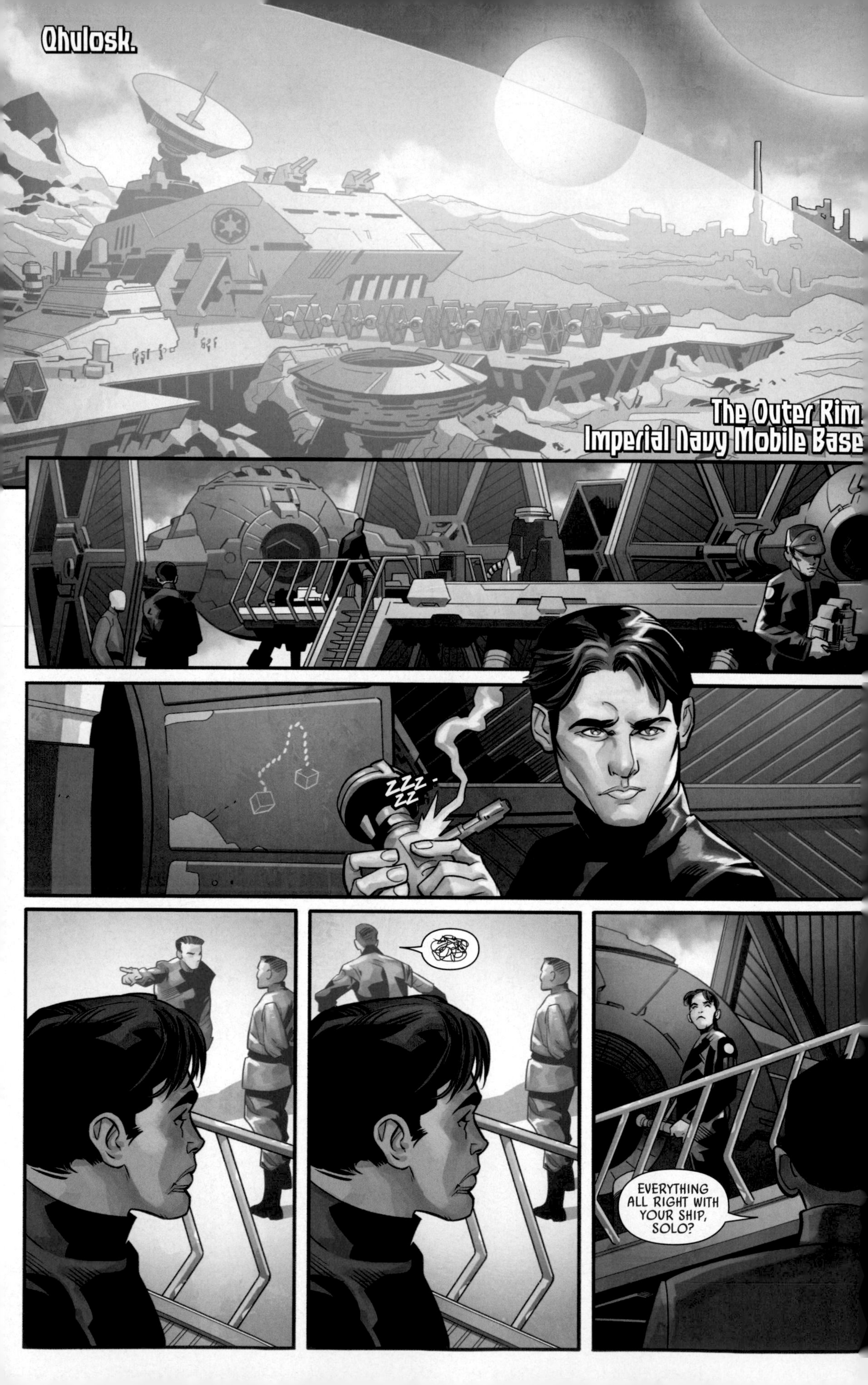
Qhulosk.
The Outer Rim
Imperial Navy Mobile Base
ZZZ-
ZZ
EVERYTHING ALL RIGHT WITH YOUR SHIP, SOLO?

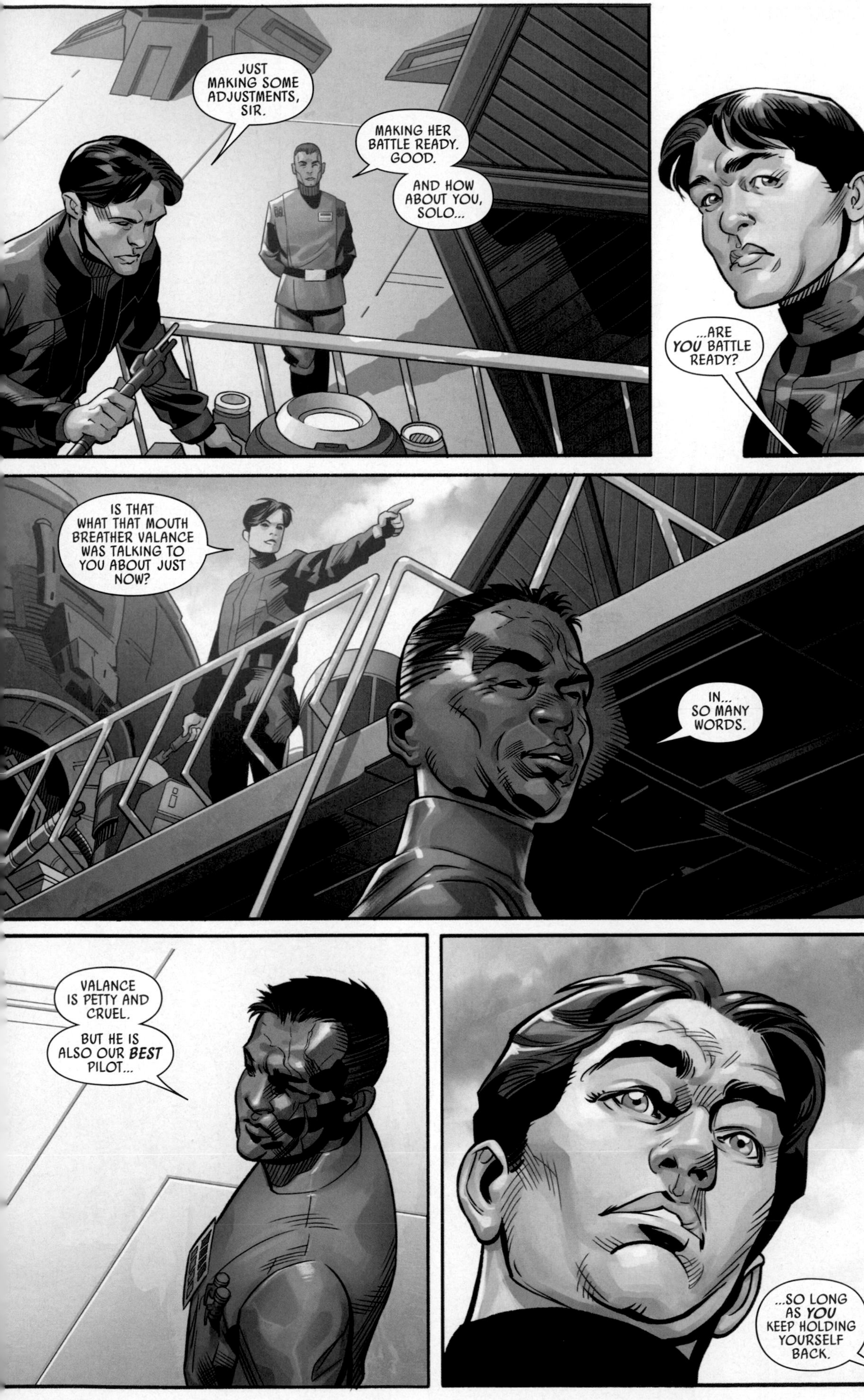
JUST MAKING SOME ADJUSTMENTS, SIR.
MAKING HER BATTLE READY. GOOD.
AND HOW ABOUT YOU, SOLO...
...ARE *YOU* BATTLE READY?
IS THAT WHAT THAT MOUTH BREATHER VALANCE WAS TALKING TO YOU ABOUT JUST NOW?
IN... SO MANY WORDS.
VALANCE IS PETTY AND CRUEL.
BUT HE IS ALSO OUR *BEST* PILOT...
...SO LONG AS *YOU* KEEP HOLDING YOURSELF BACK.

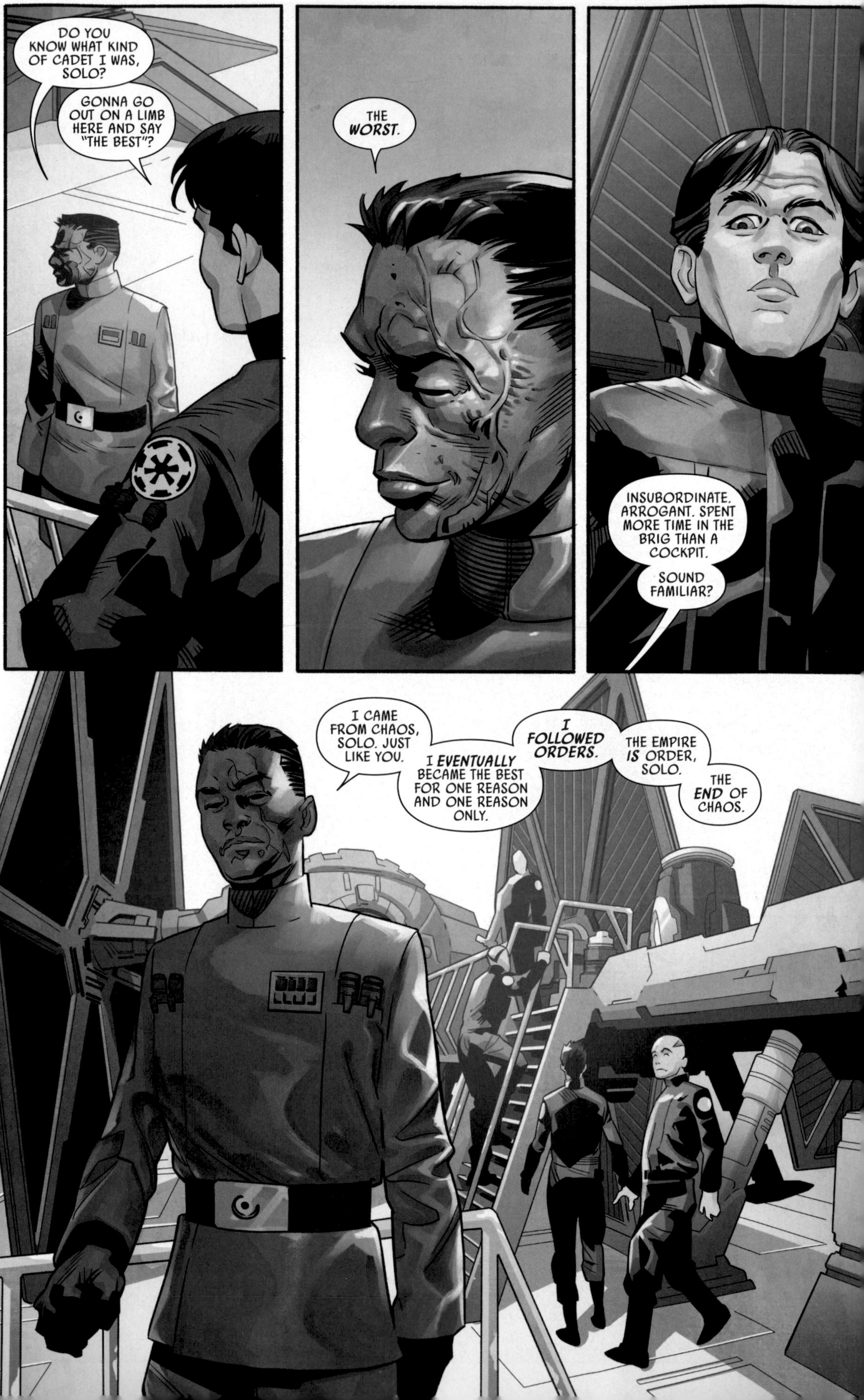
DO YOU KNOW WHAT KIND OF CADET I WAS, SOLO?
GONNA GO OUT ON A LIMB HERE AND SAY "THE BEST"?
THE WORST.
INSUBORDINATE. ARROGANT. SPENT MORE TIME IN THE BRIG THAN A COCKPIT.
SOUND FAMILIAR?
I CAME FROM CHAOS, SOLO. JUST LIKE YOU.
I EVENTUALLY BECAME THE BEST FOR ONE REASON AND ONE REASON ONLY.
I FOLLOWED ORDERS.
THE EMPIRE IS ORDER, SOLO.
THE END OF CHAOS.

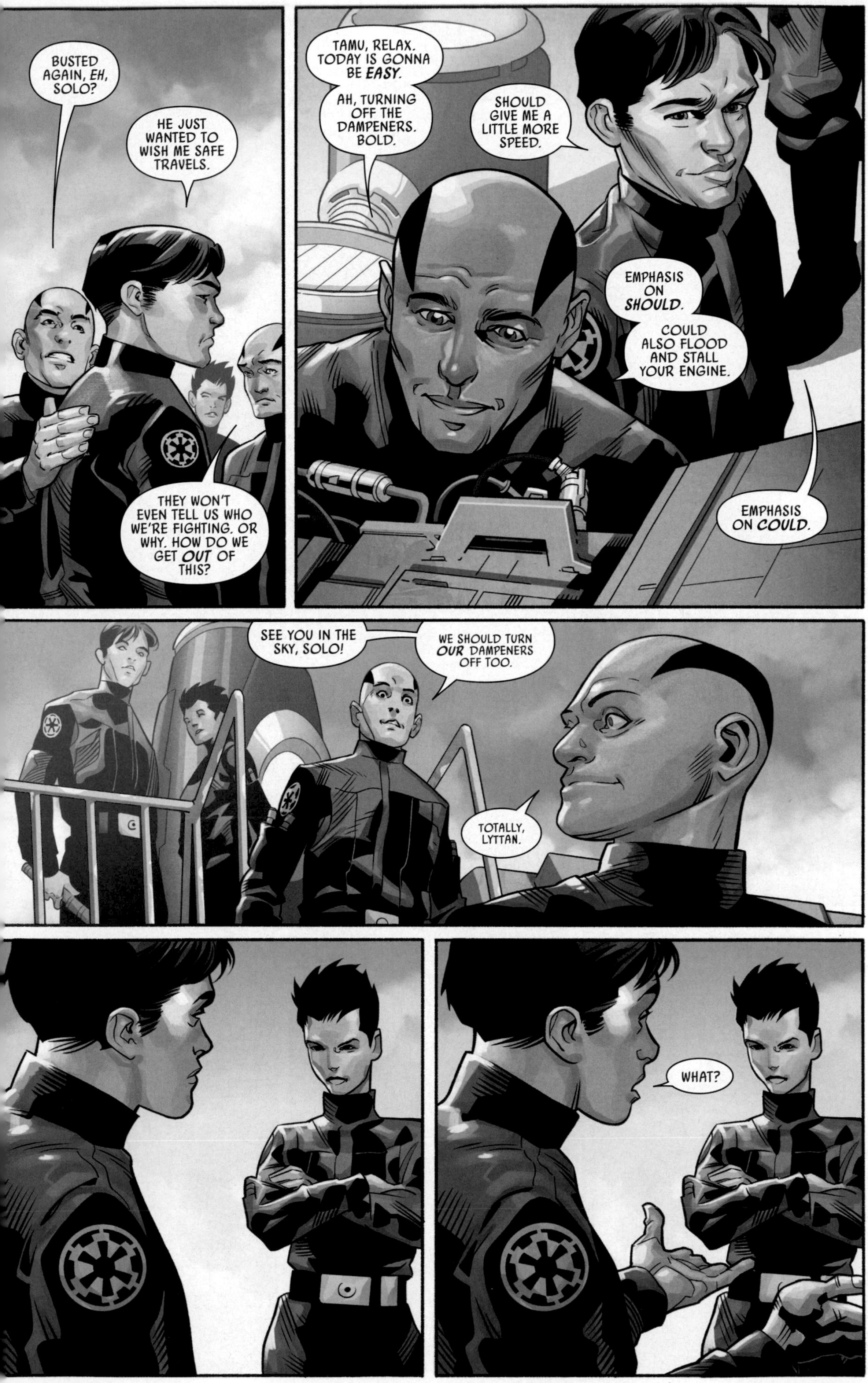
BUSTED AGAIN, EH, SOLO?
HE JUST WANTED TO WISH ME SAFE TRAVELS.
THEY WON'T EVEN TELL US WHO WE'RE FIGHTING. OR WHY. HOW DO WE GET OUT OF THIS?
TAMU, RELAX. TODAY IS GONNA BE EASY.
AH, TURNING OFF THE DAMPENERS. BOLD.
SHOULD GIVE ME A LITTLE MORE SPEED.
EMPHASIS ON SHOULD.
COULD ALSO FLOOD AND STALL YOUR ENGINE.
EMPHASIS ON COULD.
SEE YOU IN THE SKY, SOLO!
WE SHOULD TURN OUR DAMPENERS OFF TOO.
TOTALLY, LYTTAN.
WHAT?

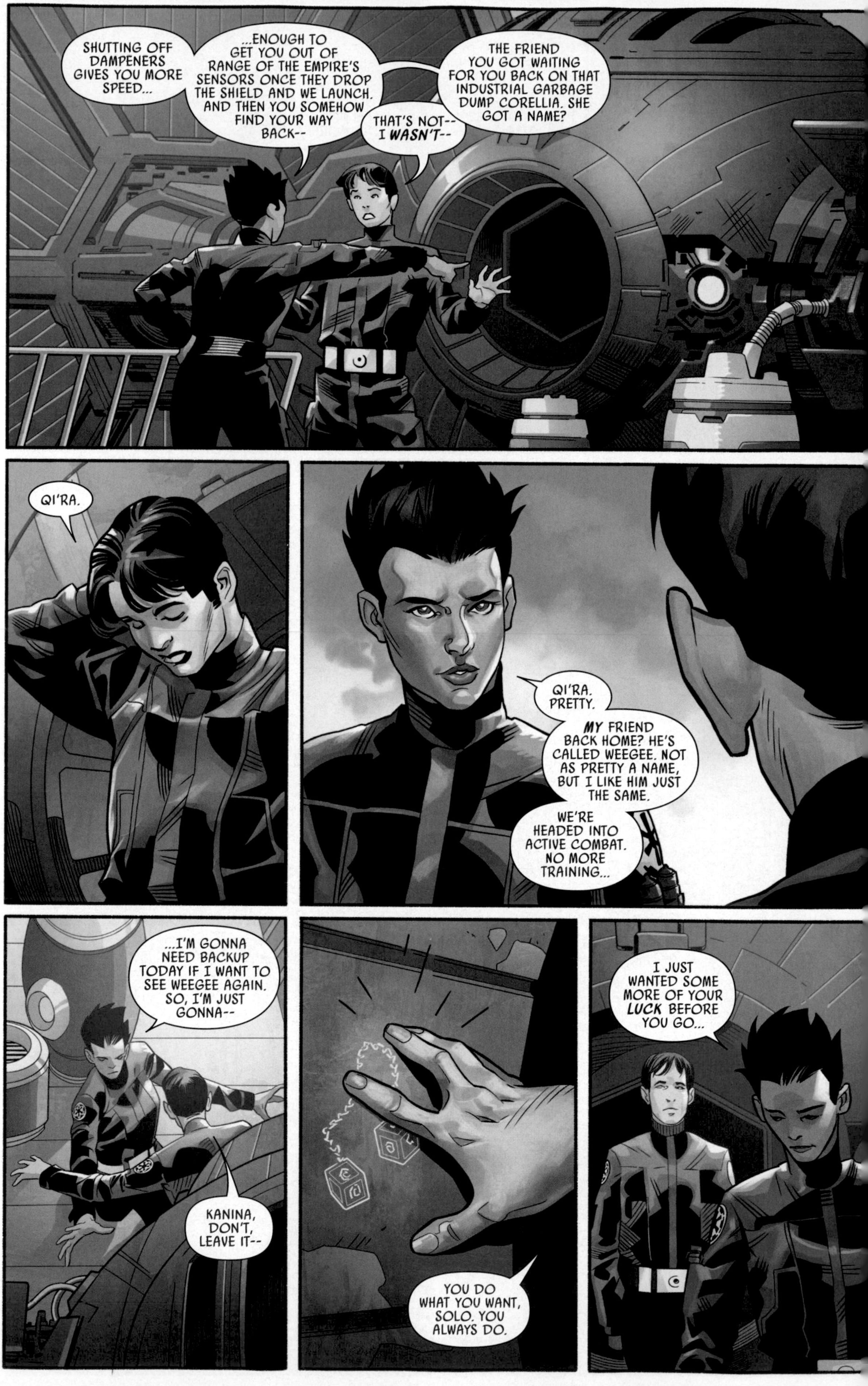
SHUTTING OFF DAMPENERS GIVES YOU MORE SPEED...
...ENOUGH TO GET YOU OUT OF RANGE OF THE EMPIRE'S SENSORS ONCE THEY DROP THE SHIELD AND WE LAUNCH. AND THEN YOU SOMEHOW FIND YOUR WAY BACK--
THAT'S NOT-- I WASN'T--
THE FRIEND YOU GOT WAITING FOR YOU BACK ON THAT INDUSTRIAL GARBAGE DUMP CORELLIA. SHE GOT A NAME?
QI'RA.
QI'RA. PRETTY.
MY FRIEND BACK HOME? HE'S CALLED WEEGEE. NOT AS PRETTY A NAME, BUT I LIKE HIM JUST THE SAME.
WE'RE HEADED INTO ACTIVE COMBAT. NO MORE TRAINING...
...I'M GONNA NEED BACKUP TODAY IF I WANT TO SEE WEEGEE AGAIN. SO, I'M JUST GONNA--
KANINA, DON'T, LEAVE IT--
YOU DO WHAT YOU WANT, SOLO. YOU ALWAYS DO.
I JUST WANTED SOME MORE OF YOUR LUCK BEFORE YOU GO...

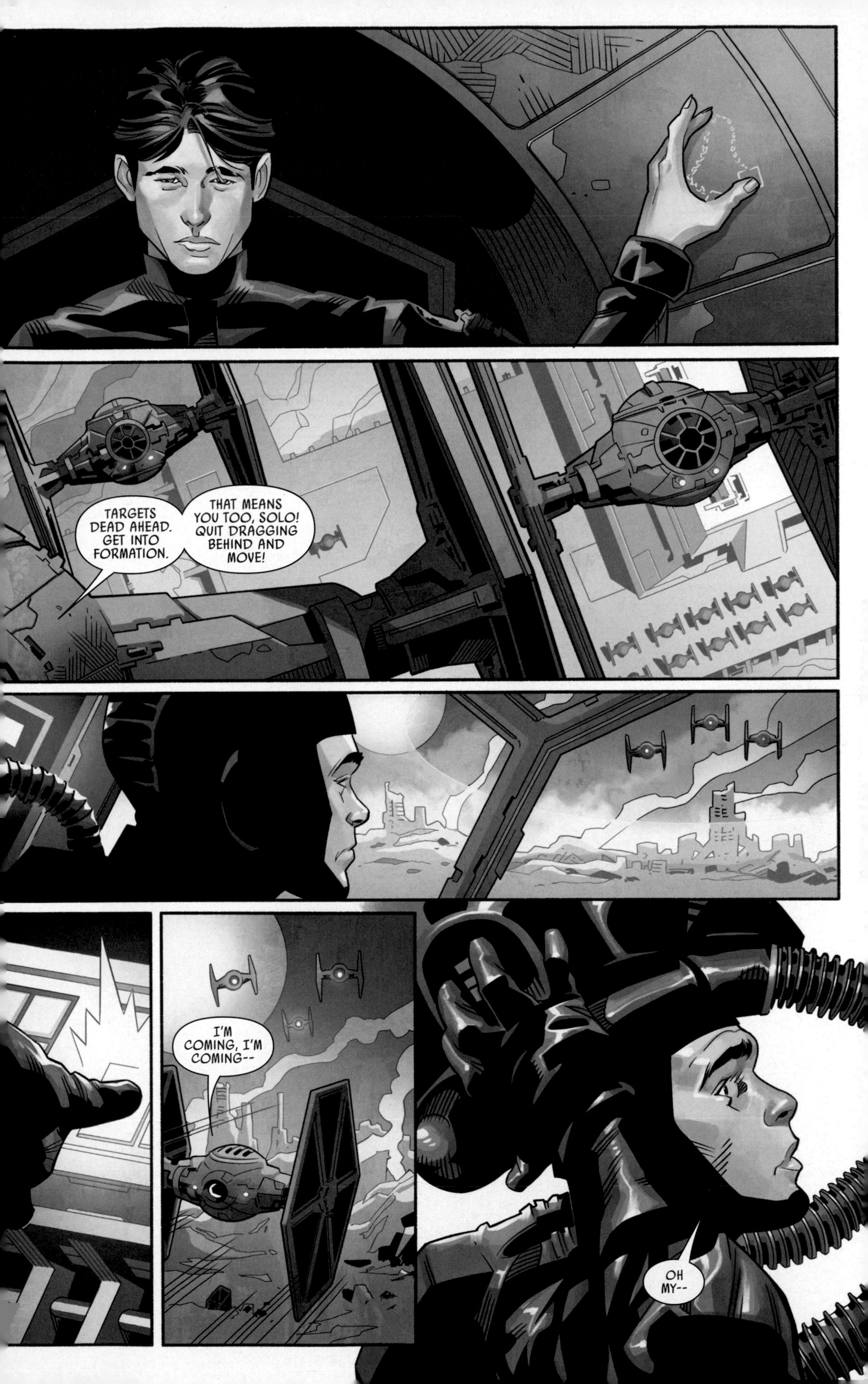
TARGETS DEAD AHEAD. GET INTO FORMATION.
THAT MEANS YOU TOO, SOLO! QUIT DRAGGING BEHIND AND MOVE!
I'M COMING, I'M COMING--
OH MY--

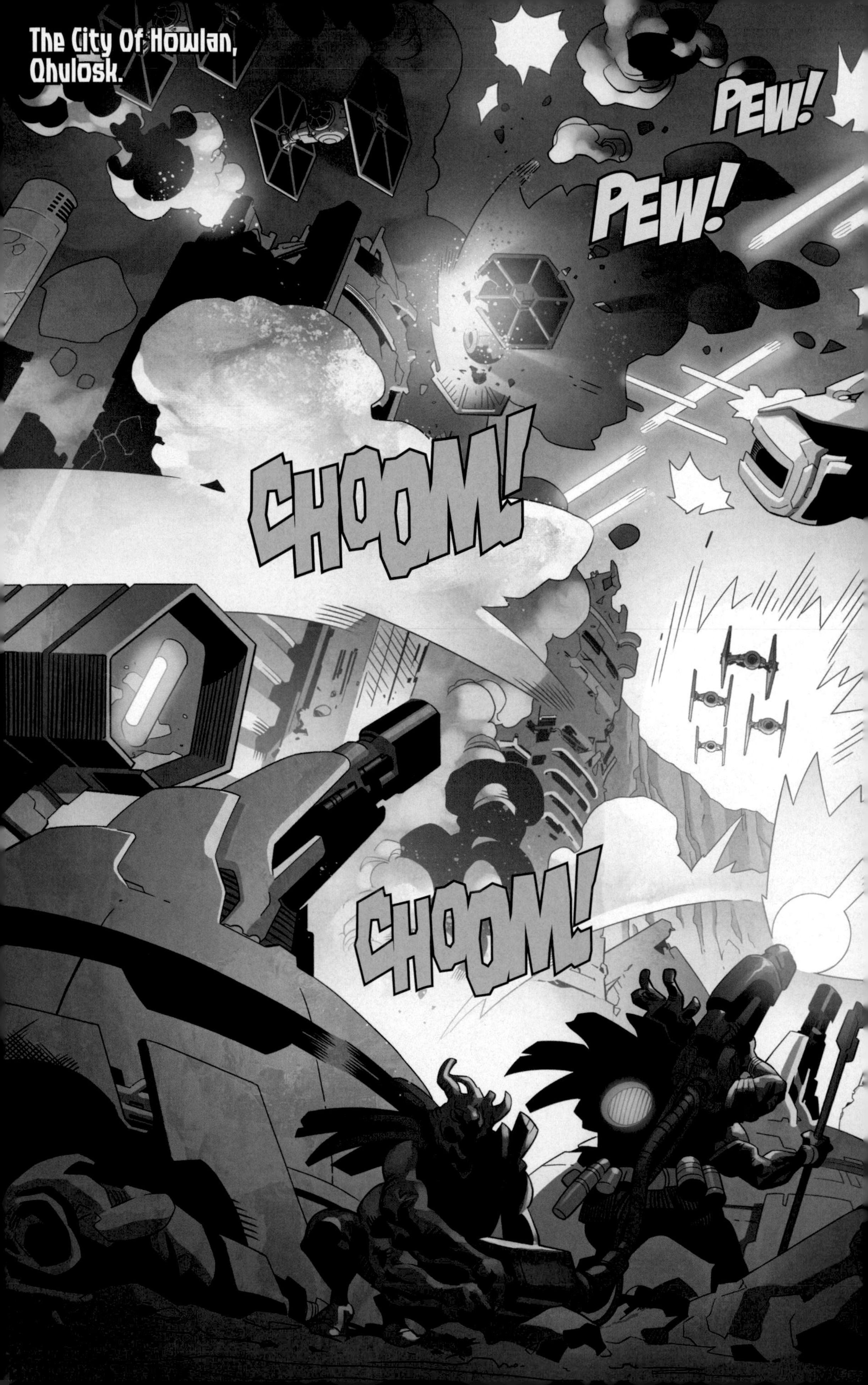
The City Of Howlan,
Qhulosk.
PEW!
PEW!
CHOOM!
CHOOM!

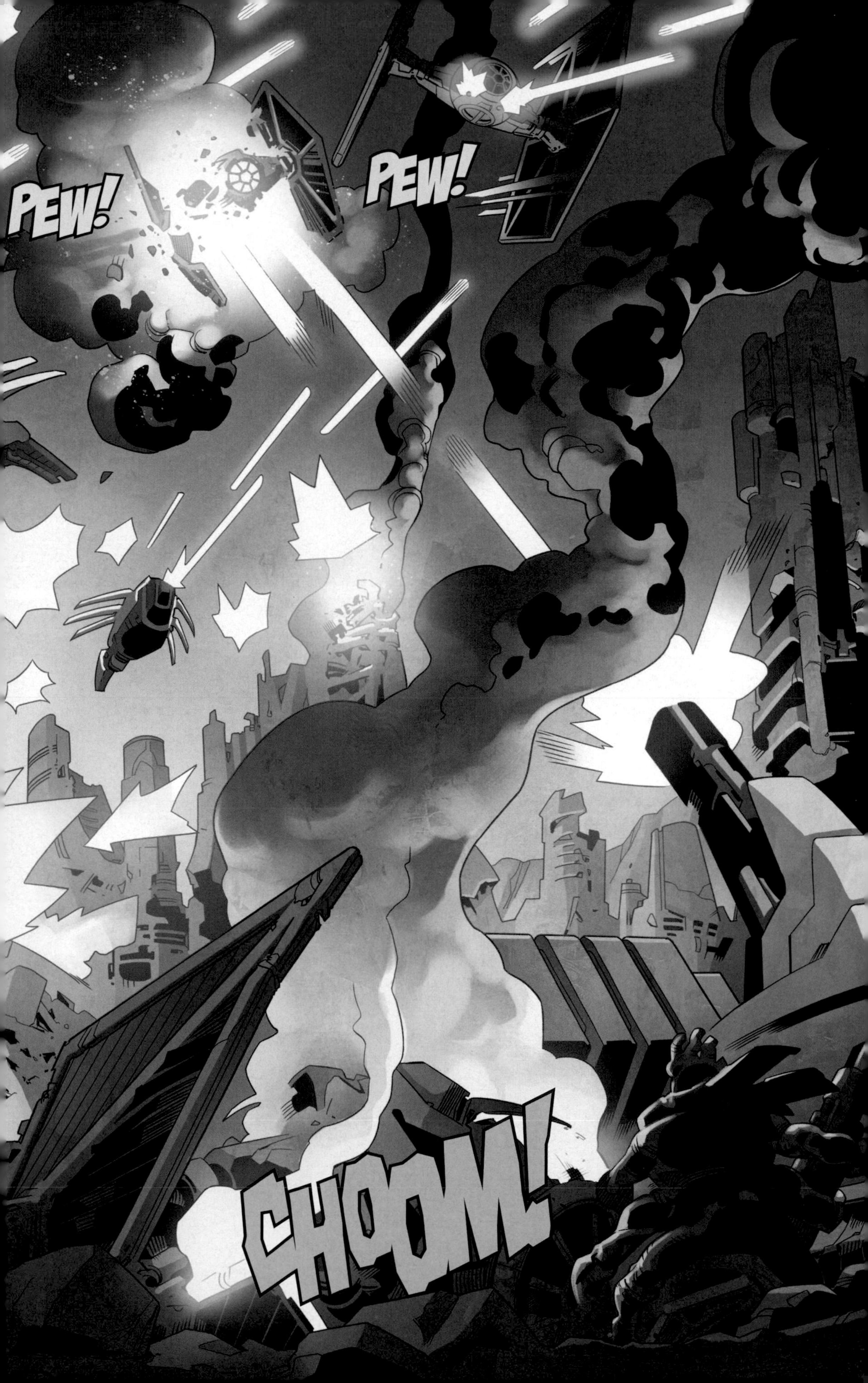
PEW!
PEW!
CHOOM!

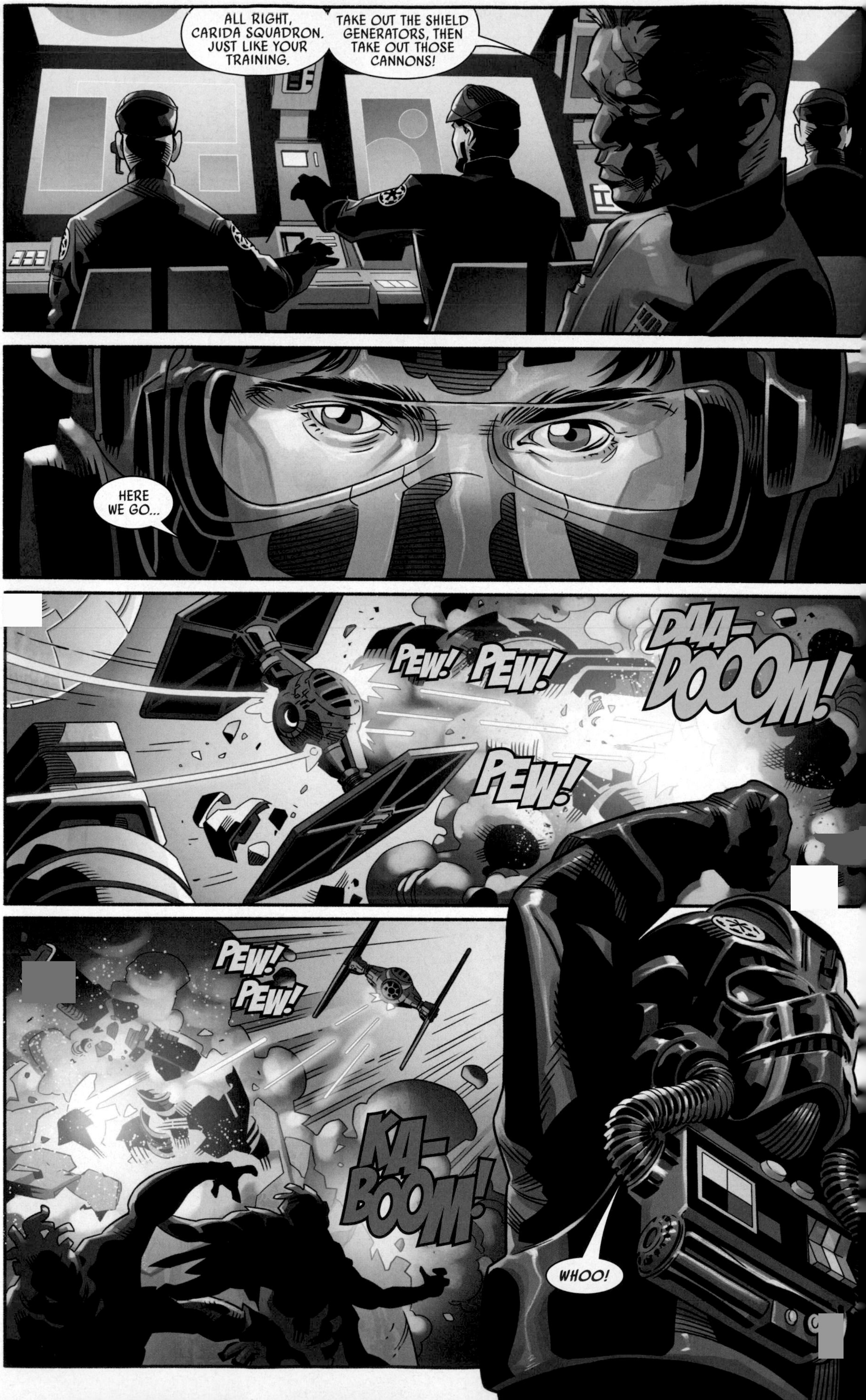
ALL RIGHT, CARIDA SQUADRON. JUST LIKE YOUR TRAINING.
TAKE OUT THE SHIELD GENERATORS, THEN TAKE OUT THOSE CANNONS!
HERE WE GO...
PEW! PEW!
DAA-DOOOOM!
PEW!
PEW! PEW!
KA-BOOM!
WHOO!

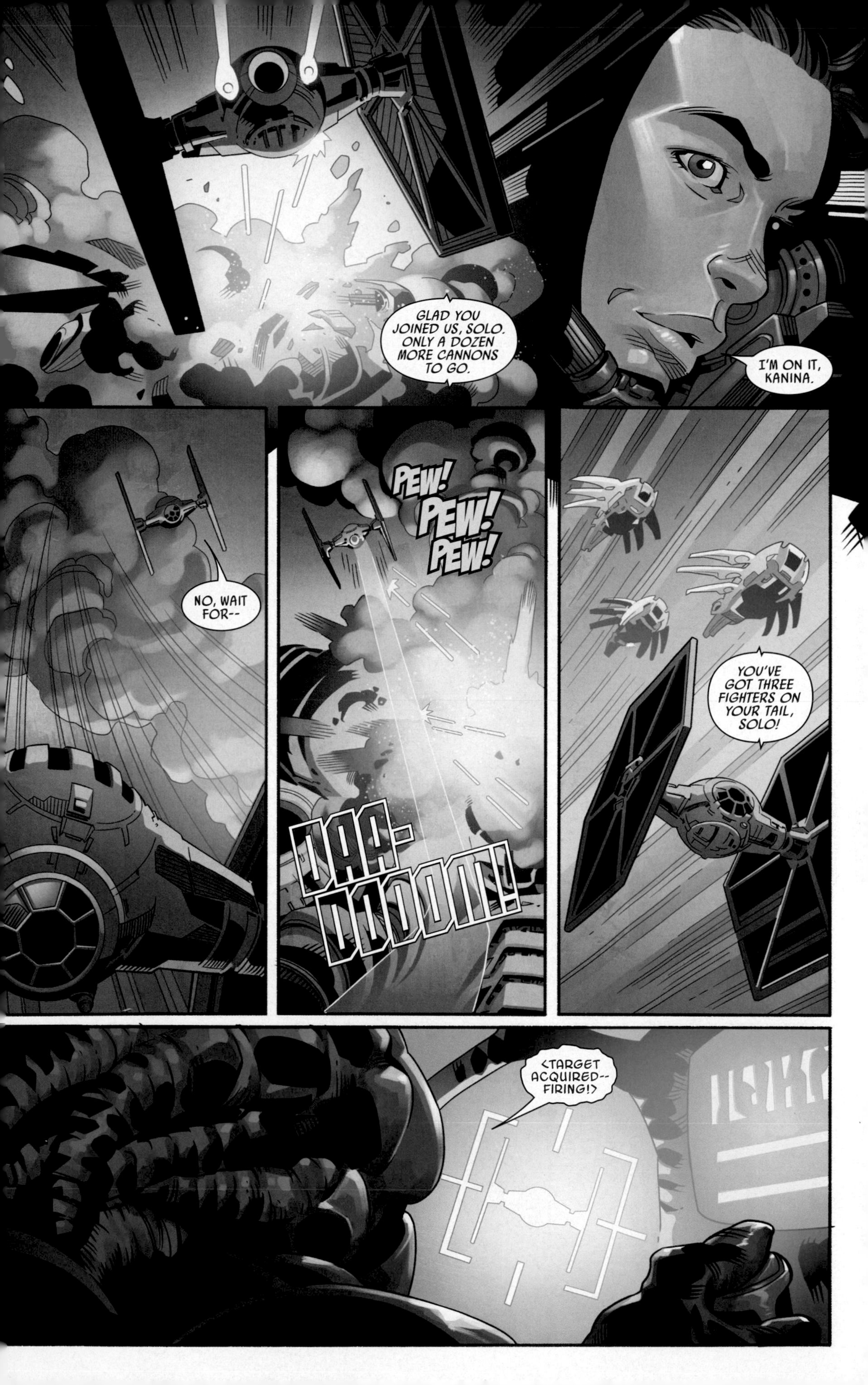

GLAD YOU JOINED US, SOLO. ONLY A DOZEN MORE CANNONS TO GO.
I'M ON IT, KANINA.
NO, WAIT FOR--
PEW! PEW! PEW!
VAA-DOOOM!
YOU'VE GOT THREE FIGHTERS ON YOUR TAIL, SOLO!
<TARGET ACQUIRED-- FIRING!>

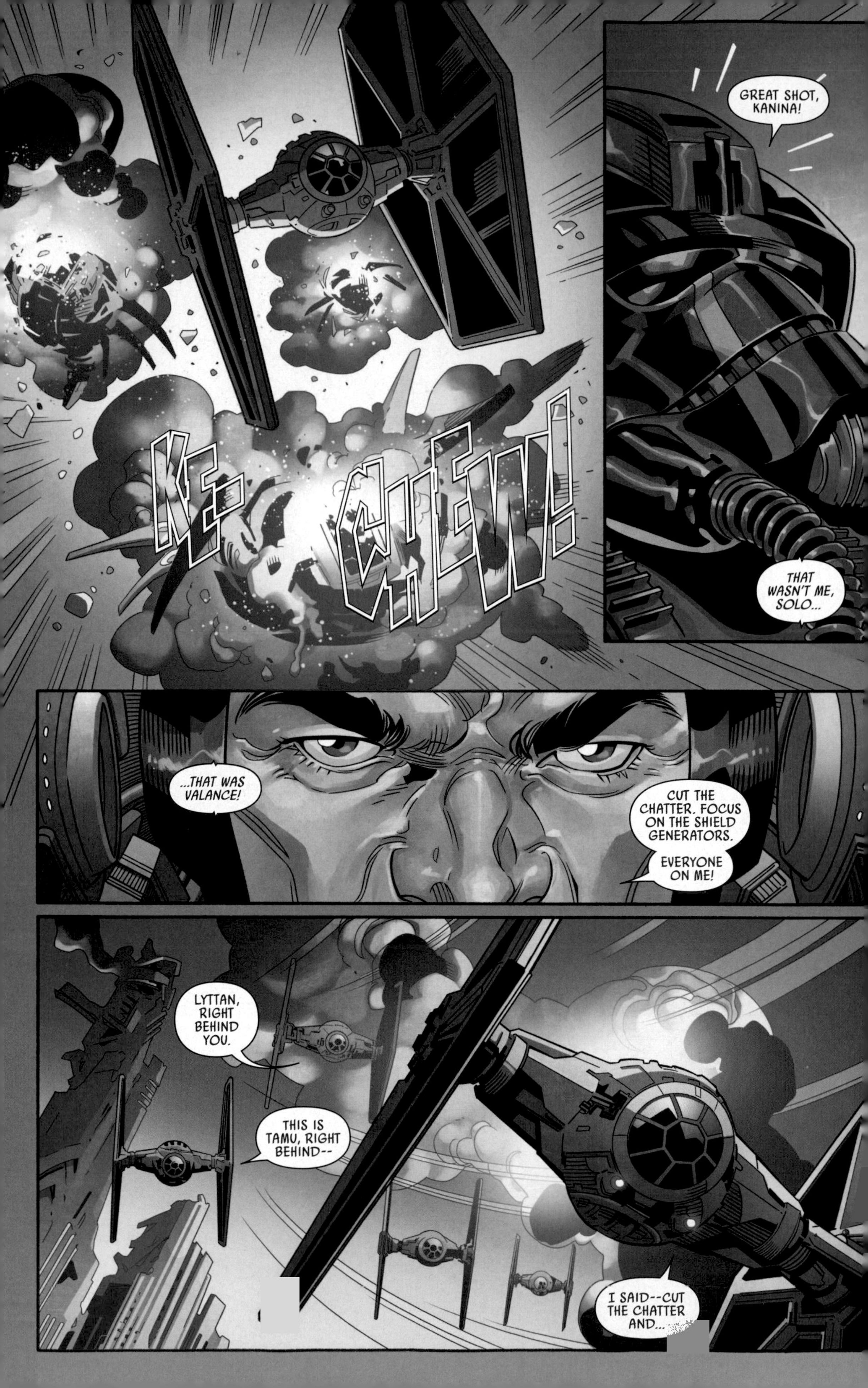
KE-CHEW!
GREAT SHOT, KANINA!
THAT WASN'T ME, SOLO...
...THAT WAS VALANCE!
CUT THE CHATTER. FOCUS ON THE SHIELD GENERATORS.
EVERYONE ON ME!
LYTTAN, RIGHT BEHIND YOU.
THIS IS TAMU, RIGHT BEHIND--
I SAID--CUT THE CHATTER AND...

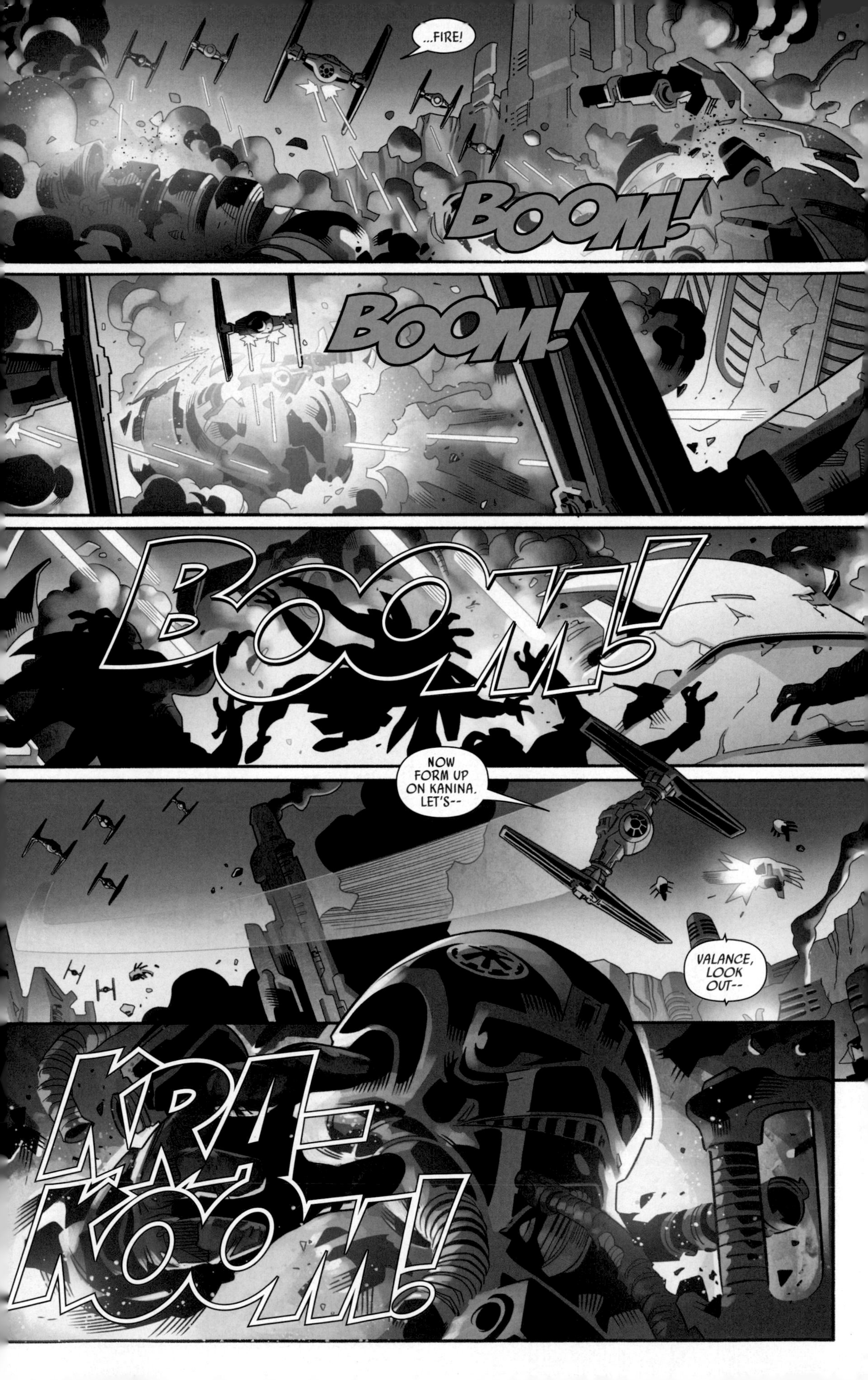
...FIRE!
BOOM!
BOOM!
BOOM!
NOW FORM UP ON KANINA. LET'S--
VALANCE, LOOK OUT--
KRA-KOOM!

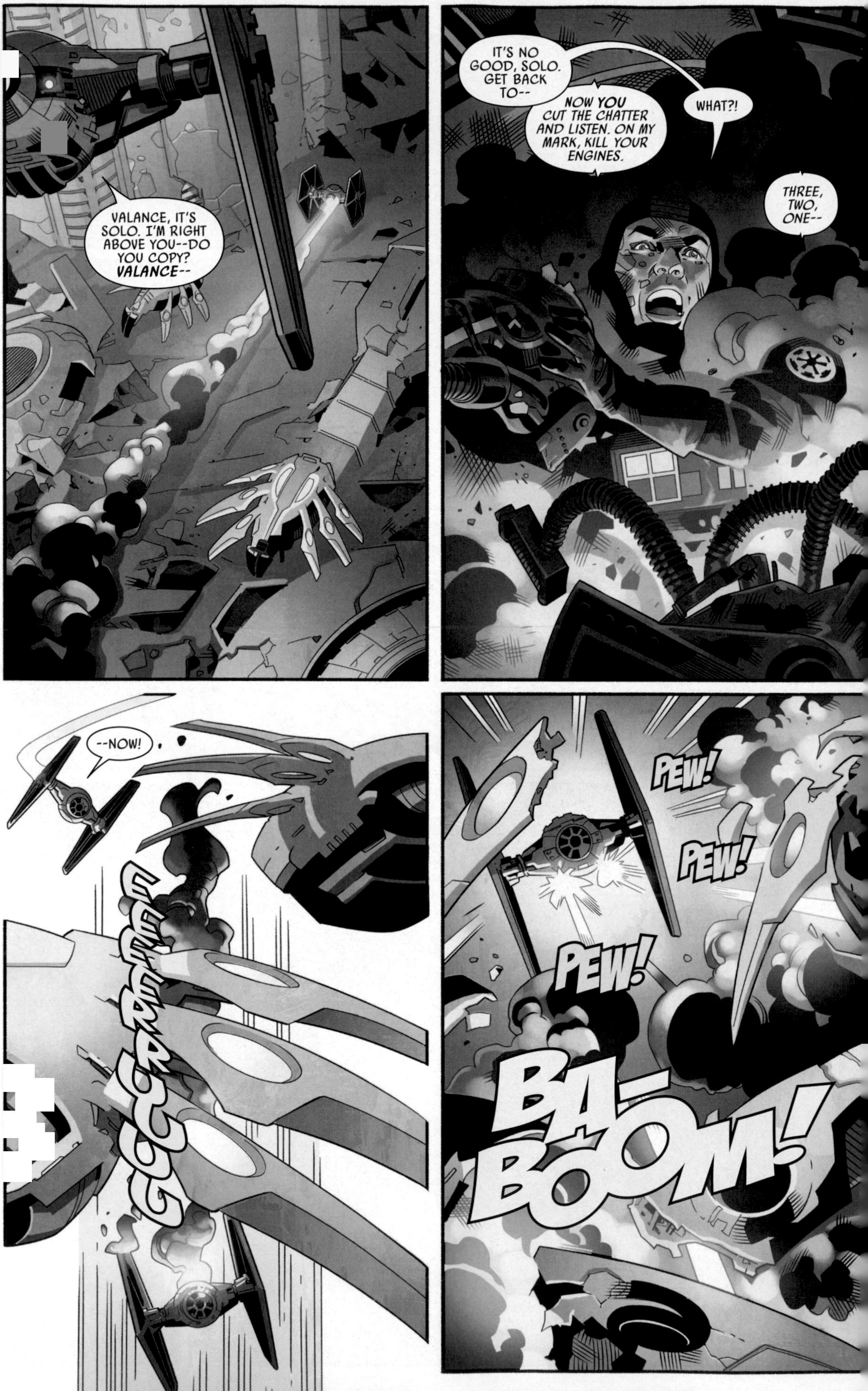
VALANCE, IT'S SOLO. I'M RIGHT ABOVE YOU--DO YOU COPY? VALANCE--
IT'S NO GOOD, SOLO. GET BACK TO--
NOW YOU CUT THE CHATTER AND LISTEN. ON MY MARK, KILL YOUR ENGINES.
WHAT?!
THREE, TWO, ONE--
--NOW!
PEW!
PEW!
PEW!
BA-BOOM!

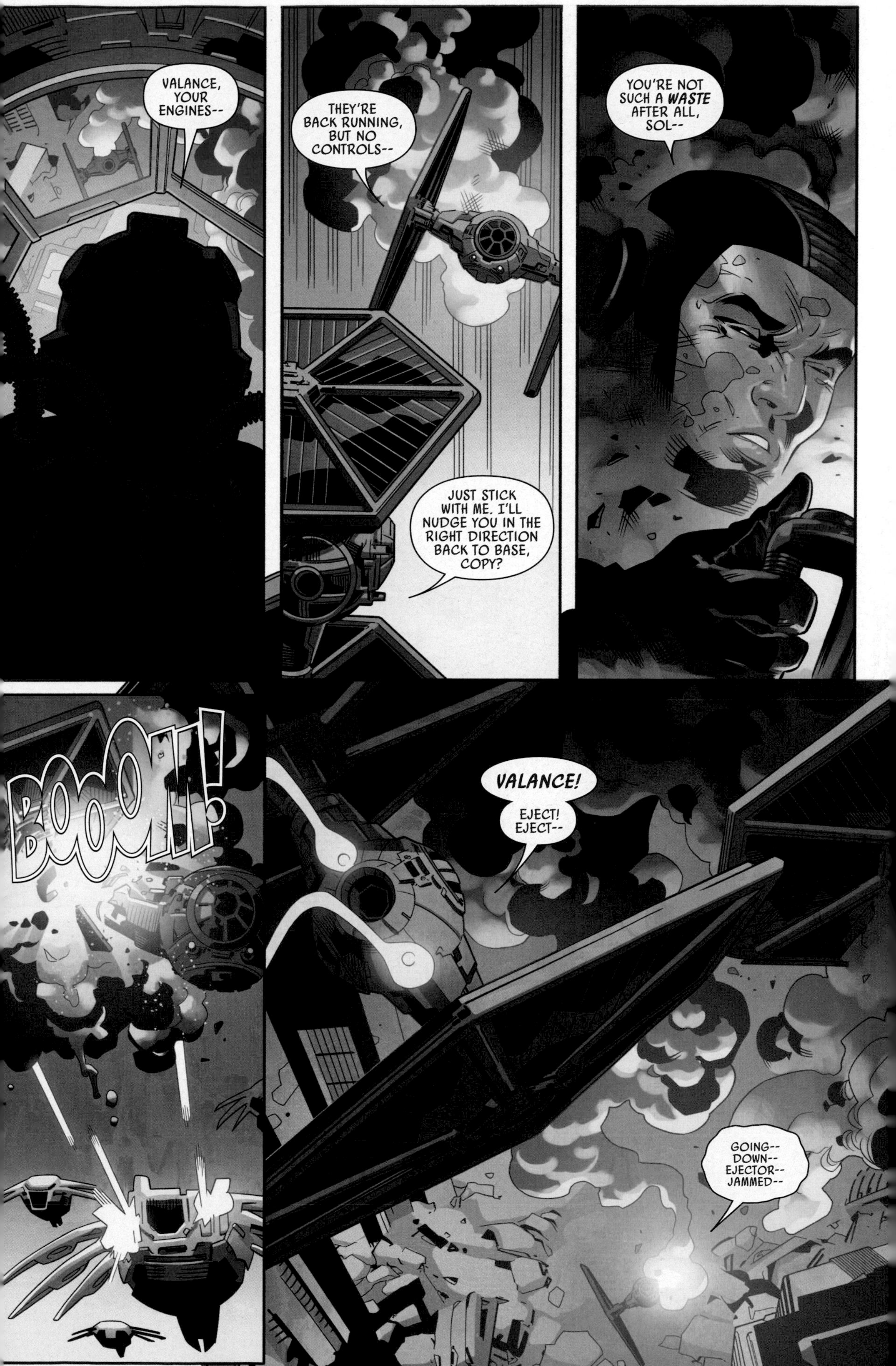
VALANCE, YOUR ENGINES--
THEY'RE BACK RUNNING, BUT NO CONTROLS--
JUST STICK WITH ME. I'LL NUDGE YOU IN THE RIGHT DIRECTION BACK TO BASE, COPY?
YOU'RE NOT SUCH A WASTE AFTER ALL, SOL--
BOOOM!
VALANCE!
EJECT! EJECT--
GOING-- DOWN-- EJECTOR-- JAMMED--

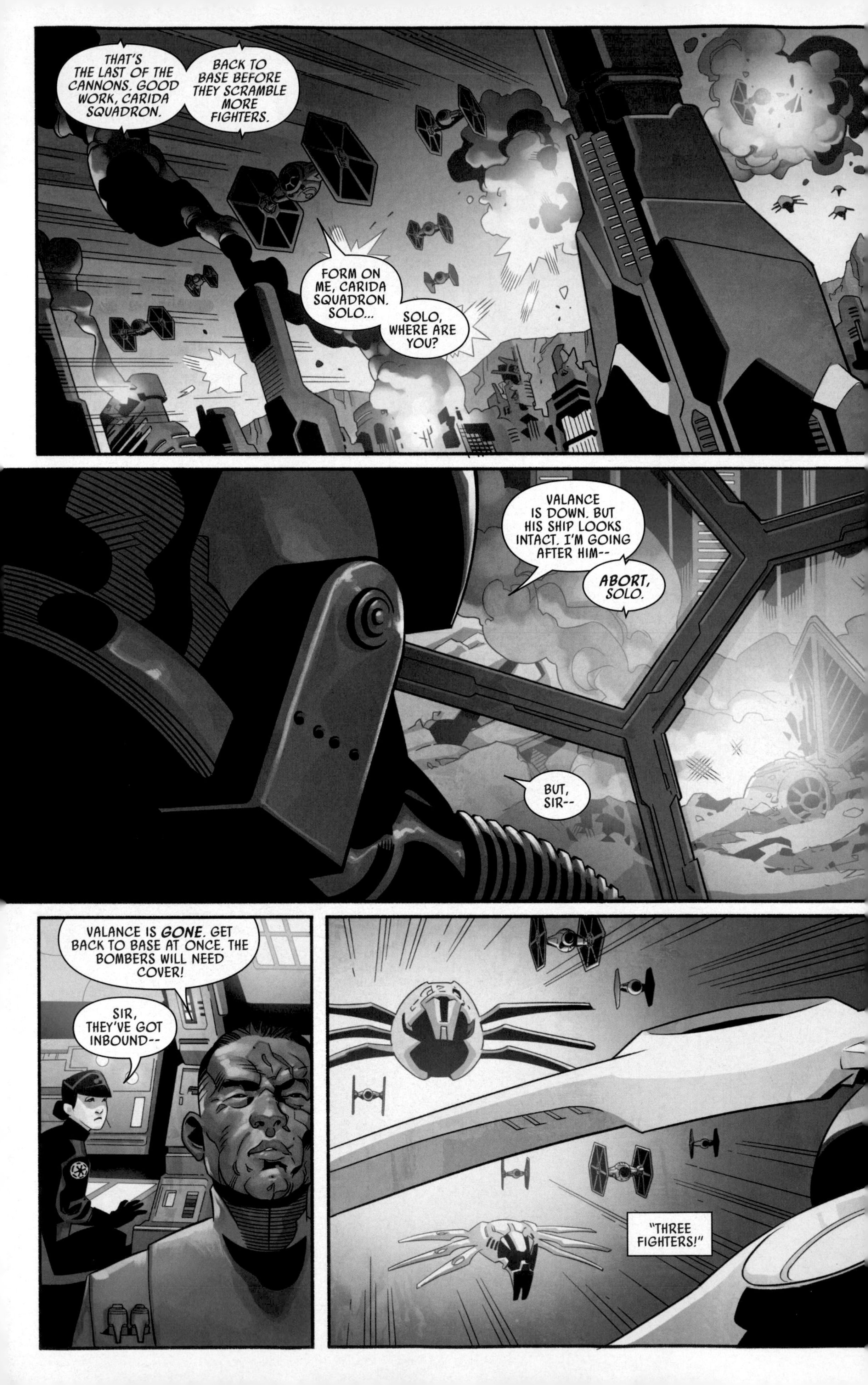
THAT'S THE LAST OF THE CANNONS. GOOD WORK, CARIDA SQUADRON.
BACK TO BASE BEFORE THEY SCRAMBLE MORE FIGHTERS.
FORM ON ME, CARIDA SQUADRON. SOLO...
SOLO, WHERE ARE YOU?
VALANCE IS DOWN. BUT HIS SHIP LOOKS INTACT. I'M GOING AFTER HIM--
ABORT, SOLO.
BUT, SIR--
VALANCE IS GONE. GET BACK TO BASE AT ONCE. THE BOMBERS WILL NEED COVER!
SIR, THEY'VE GOT INBOUND--
"THREE FIGHTERS!"

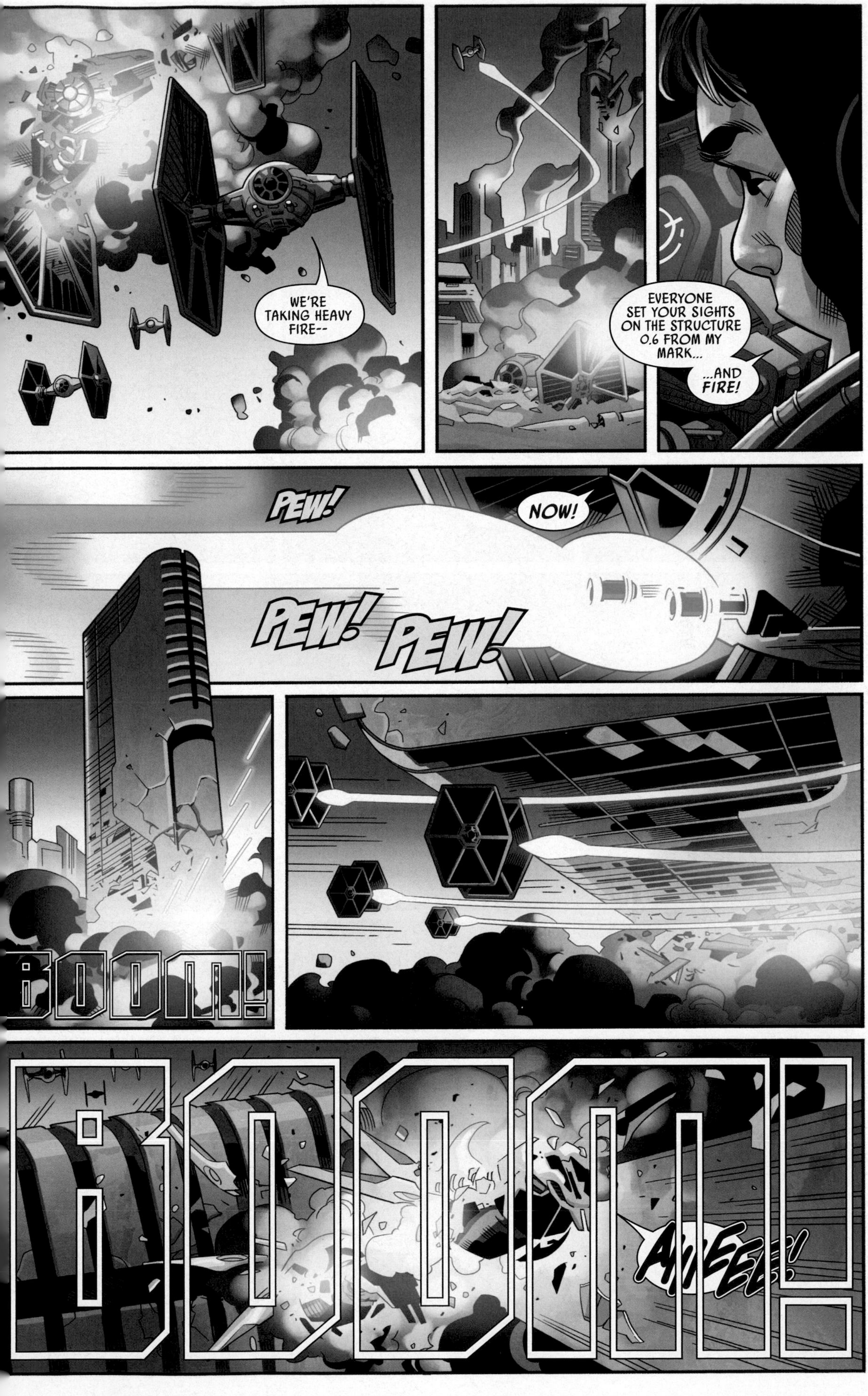
WE'RE TAKING HEAVY FIRE--
EVERYONE SET YOUR SIGHTS ON THE STRUCTURE 0.6 FROM MY MARK...
...AND FIRE!
PEW!
NOW!
PEW! PEW!
BOOM!
BOOM!
AAIEEE!

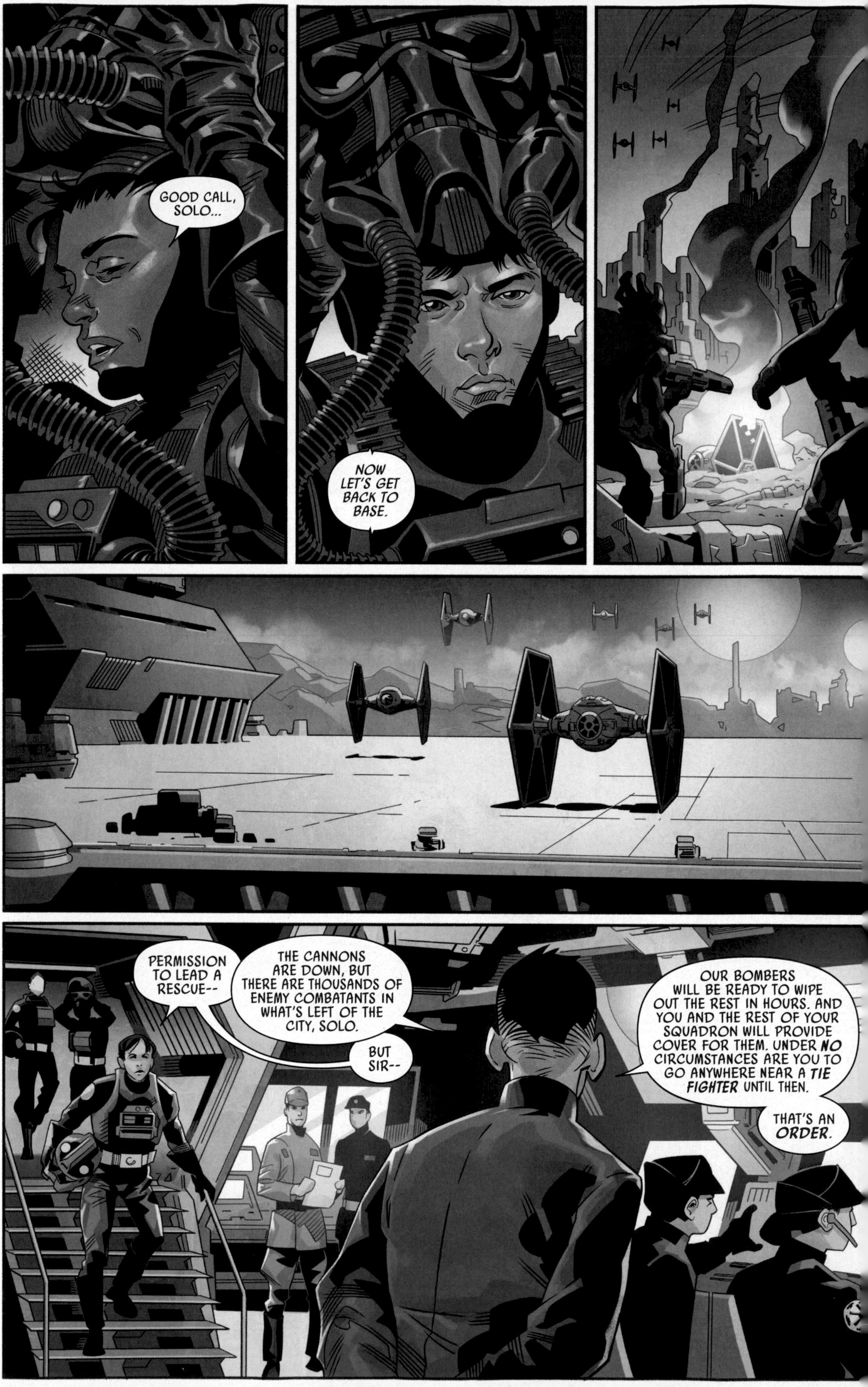
GOOD CALL, SOLO...
NOW LET'S GET BACK TO BASE.
PERMISSION TO LEAD A RESCUE--
THE CANNONS ARE DOWN, BUT THERE ARE THOUSANDS OF ENEMY COMBATANTS IN WHAT'S LEFT OF THE CITY, SOLO.
BUT SIR--
OUR BOMBERS WILL BE READY TO WIPE OUT THE REST IN HOURS. AND YOU AND THE REST OF YOUR SQUADRON WILL PROVIDE COVER FOR THEM. UNDER NO CIRCUMSTANCES ARE YOU TO GO ANYWHERE NEAR A TIE FIGHTER UNTIL THEN.
THAT'S AN ORDER.

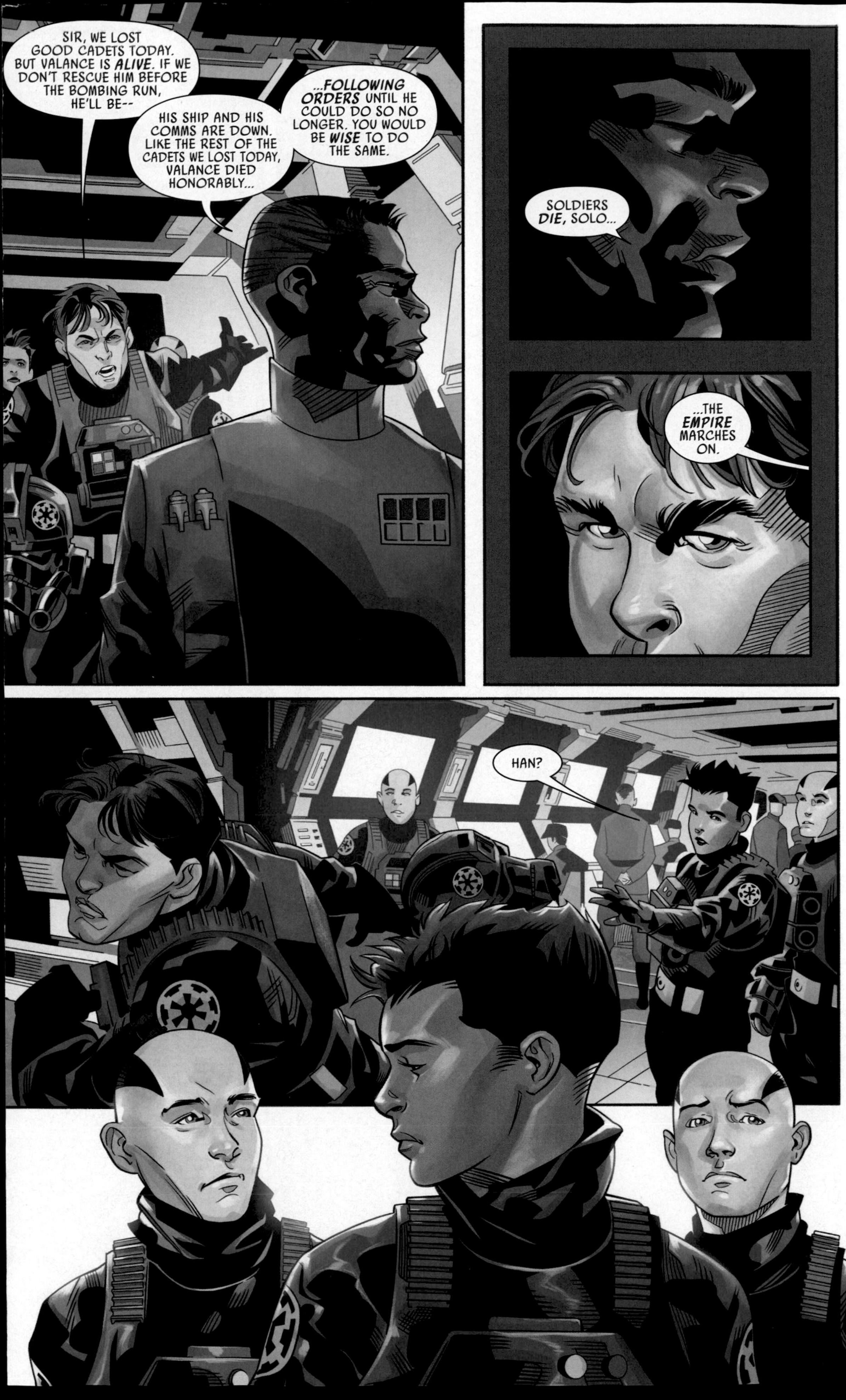
SIR, WE LOST GOOD CADETS TODAY. BUT VALANCE IS ALIVE. IF WE DON'T RESCUE HIM BEFORE THE BOMBING RUN, HE'LL BE--
HIS SHIP AND HIS COMMS ARE DOWN. LIKE THE REST OF THE CADETS WE LOST TODAY, VALANCE DIED HONORABLY...
...FOLLOWING ORDERS UNTIL HE COULD DO SO NO LONGER. YOU WOULD BE WISE TO DO THE SAME.
SOLDIERS DIE, SOLO...
...THE EMPIRE MARCHES ON.
HAN?

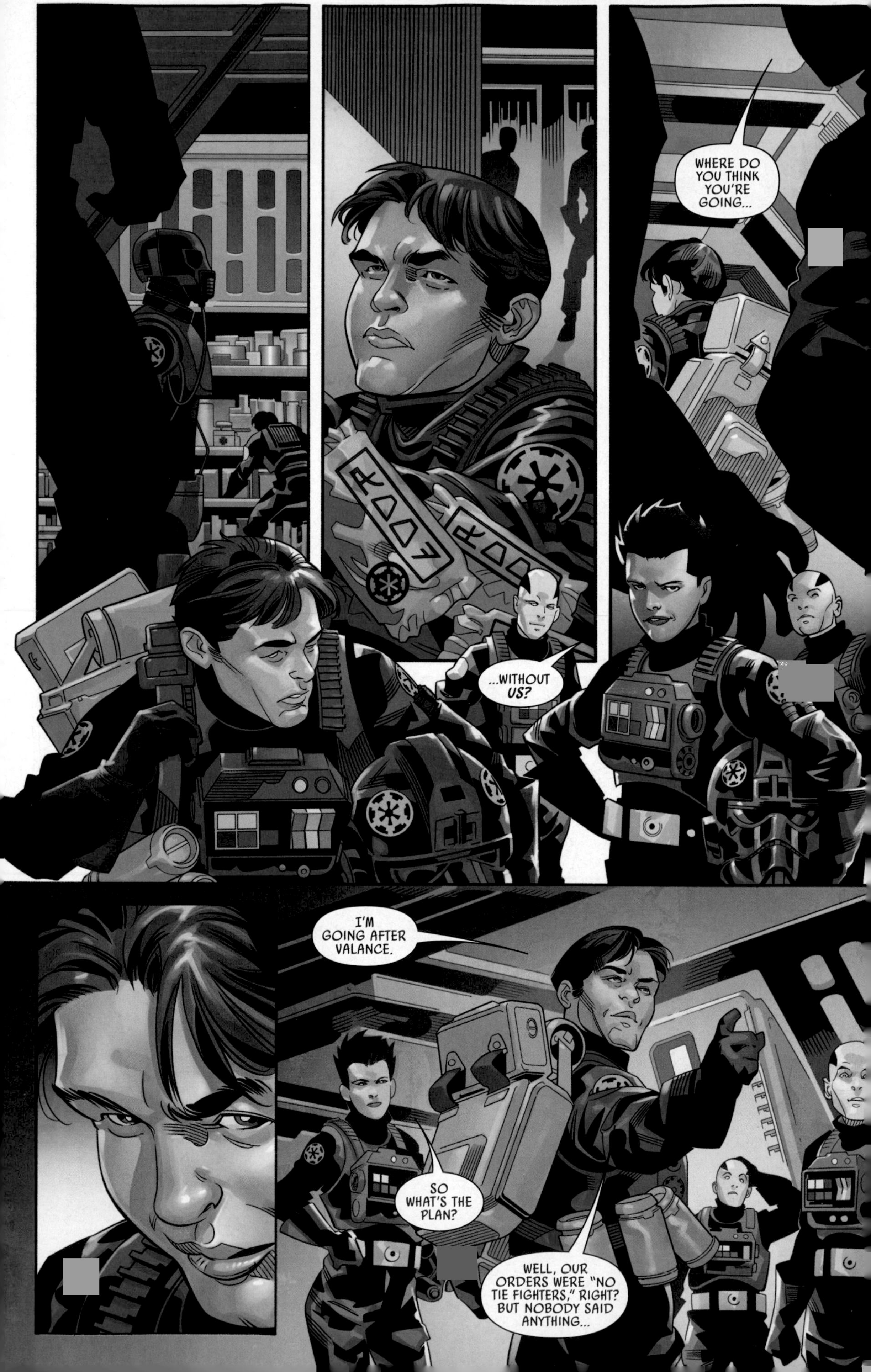
WHERE DO YOU THINK YOU'RE GOING...
...WITHOUT US?
I'M GOING AFTER VALANCE.
SO WHAT'S THE PLAN?
WELL, OUR ORDERS WERE "NO TIE FIGHTERS," RIGHT? BUT NOBODY SAID ANYTHING...

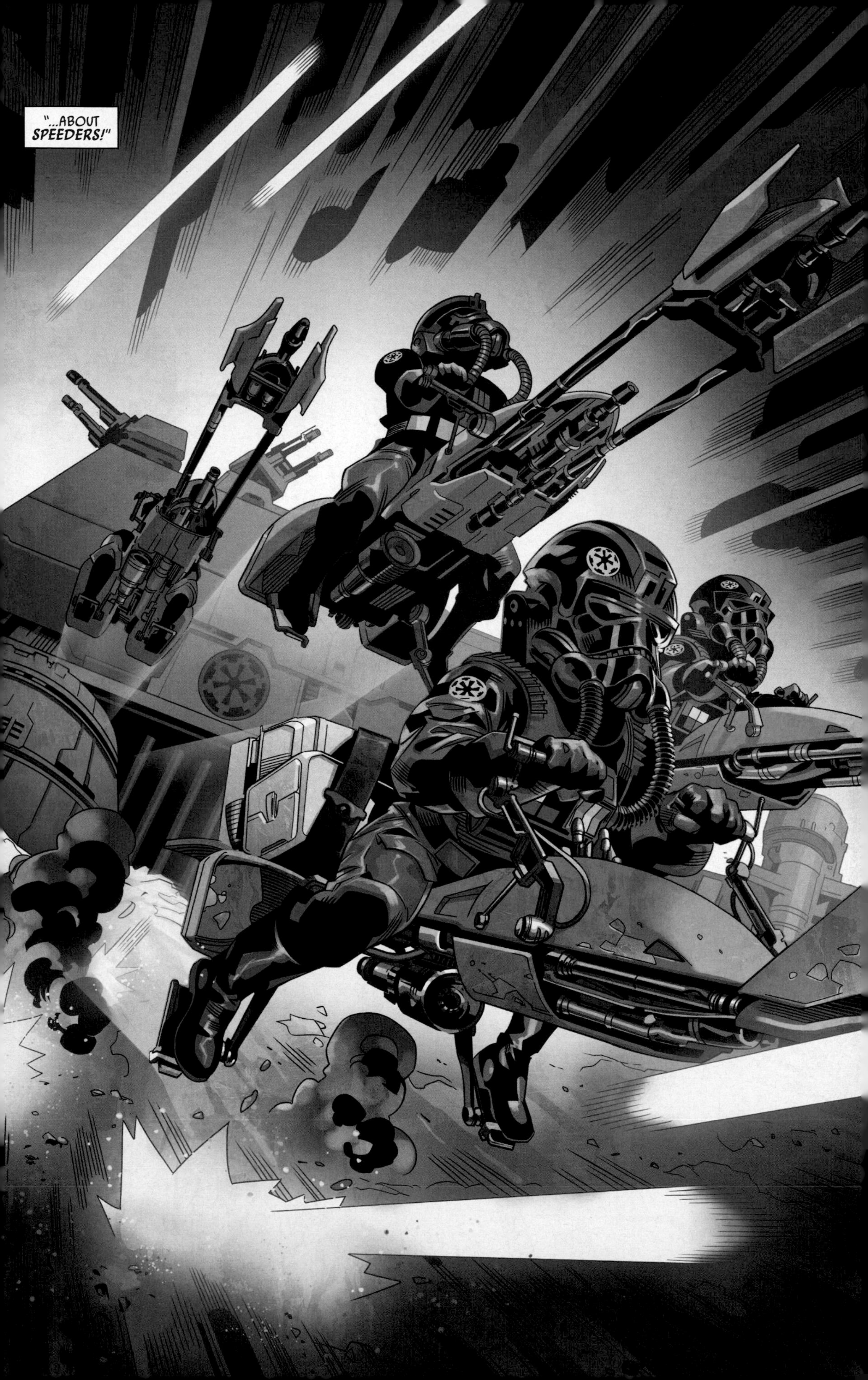
"...ABOUT SPEEDERS!"

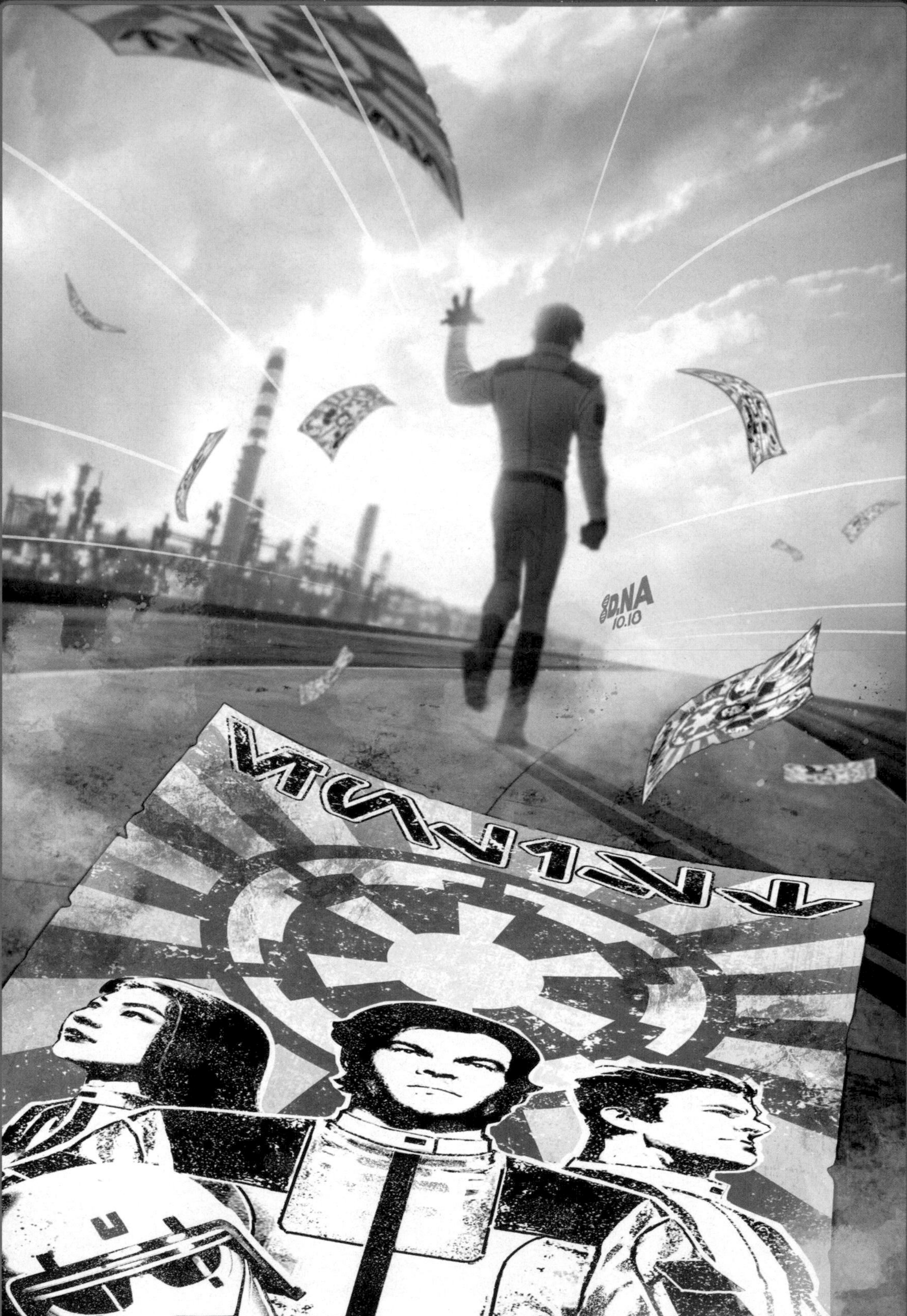
D.NA
10.18

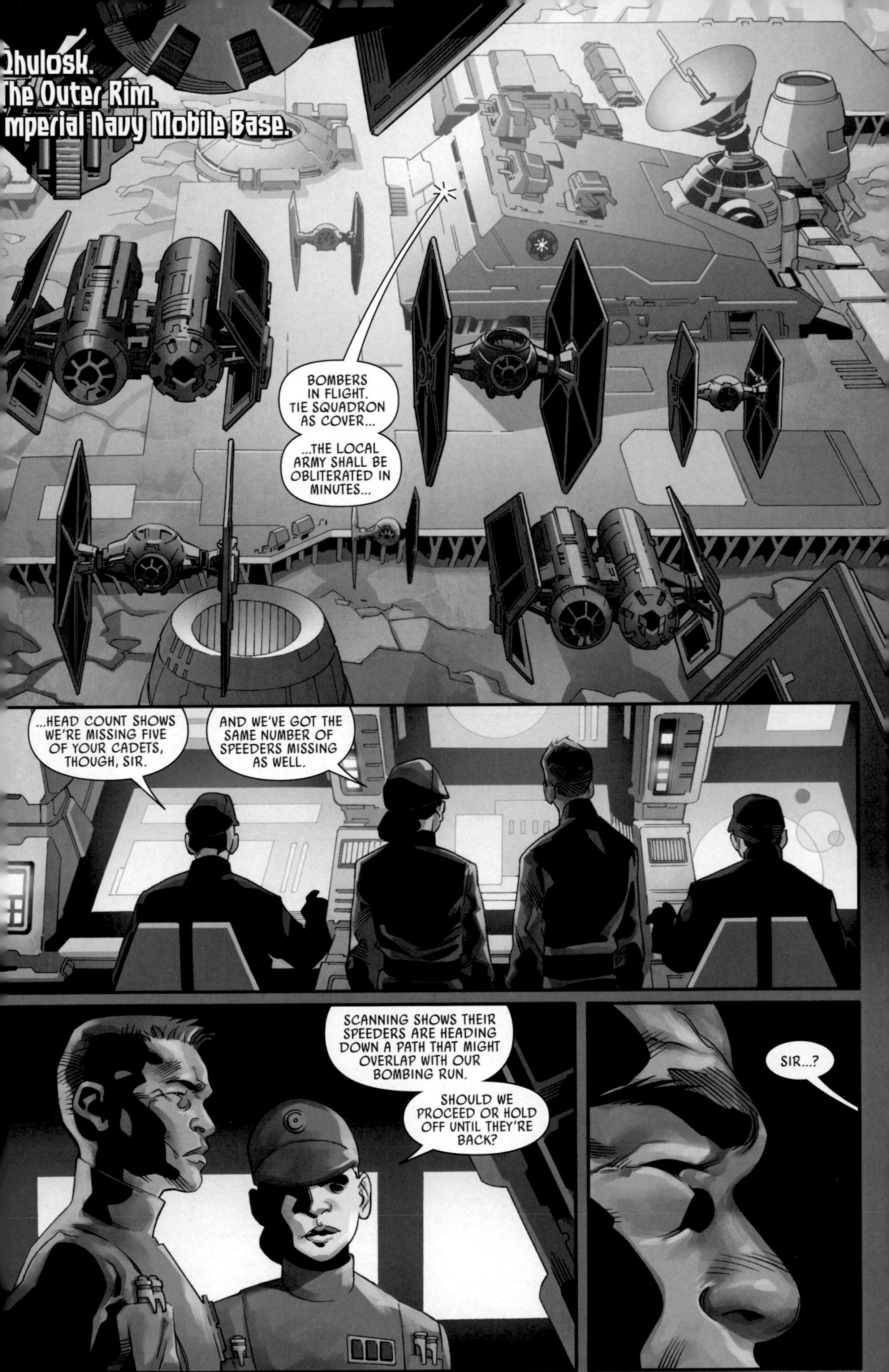
Qhulosk. The Outer Rim. Imperial Navy Mobile Base.
BOMBERS IN FLIGHT. TIE SQUADRON AS COVER...
...THE LOCAL ARMY SHALL BE OBLITERATED IN MINUTES...
...HEAD COUNT SHOWS WE'RE MISSING FIVE OF YOUR CADETS, THOUGH, SIR.
AND WE'VE GOT THE SAME NUMBER OF SPEEDERS MISSING AS WELL.
SCANNING SHOWS THEIR SPEEDERS ARE HEADING DOWN A PATH THAT MIGHT OVERLAP WITH OUR BOMBING RUN.
SHOULD WE PROCEED OR HOLD OFF UNTIL THEY'RE BACK?
SIR...?

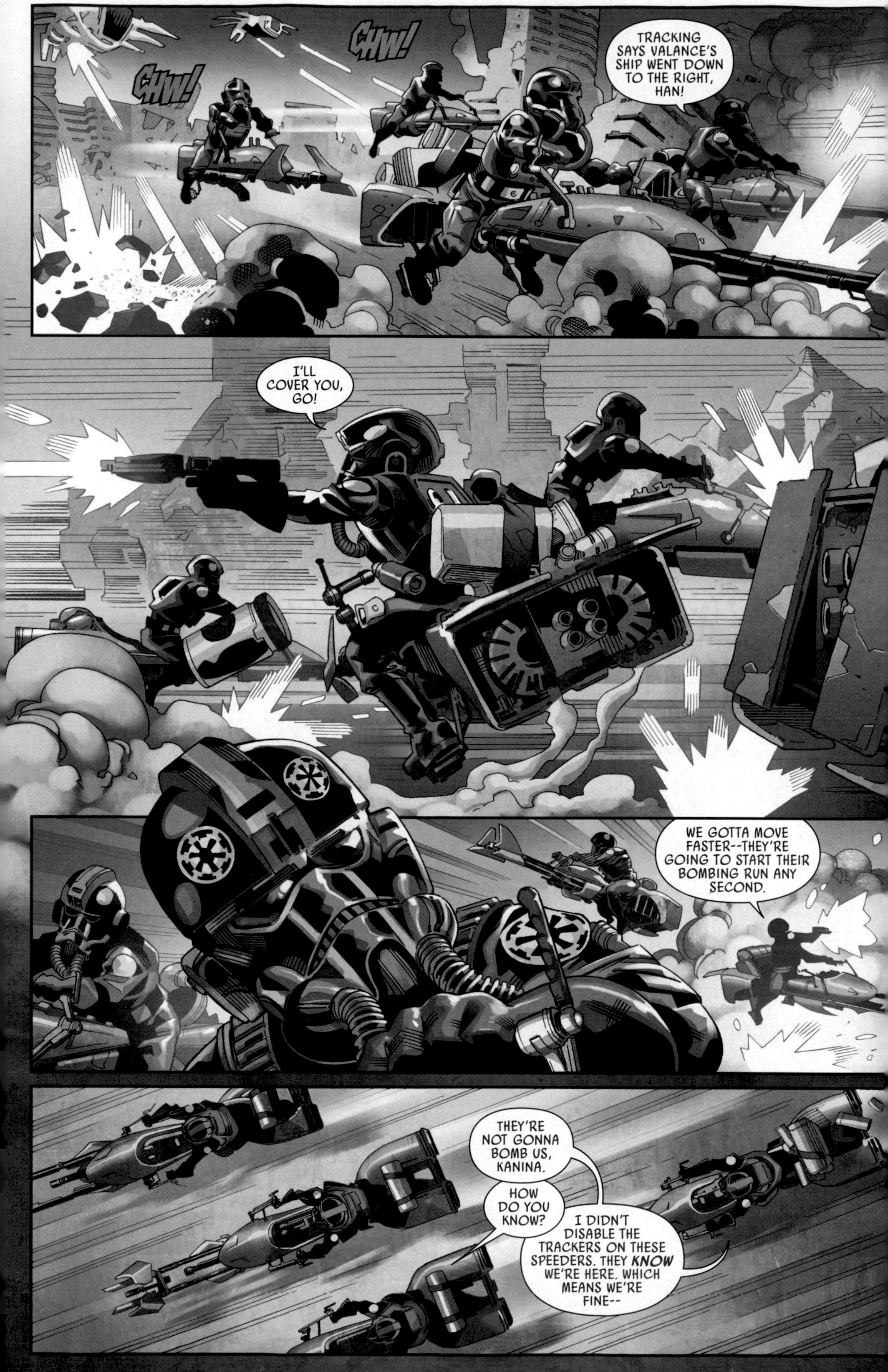

CHW!
CHW!
TRACKING SAYS VALANCE'S SHIP WENT DOWN TO THE RIGHT, HAN!
I'LL COVER YOU, GO!
WE GOTTA MOVE FASTER--THEY'RE GOING TO START THEIR BOMBING RUN ANY SECOND.
THEY'RE NOT GONNA BOMB US, KANINA.
HOW DO YOU KNOW?
I DIDN'T DISABLE THE TRACKERS ON THESE SPEEDERS. THEY KNOW WE'RE HERE. WHICH MEANS WE'RE FINE--

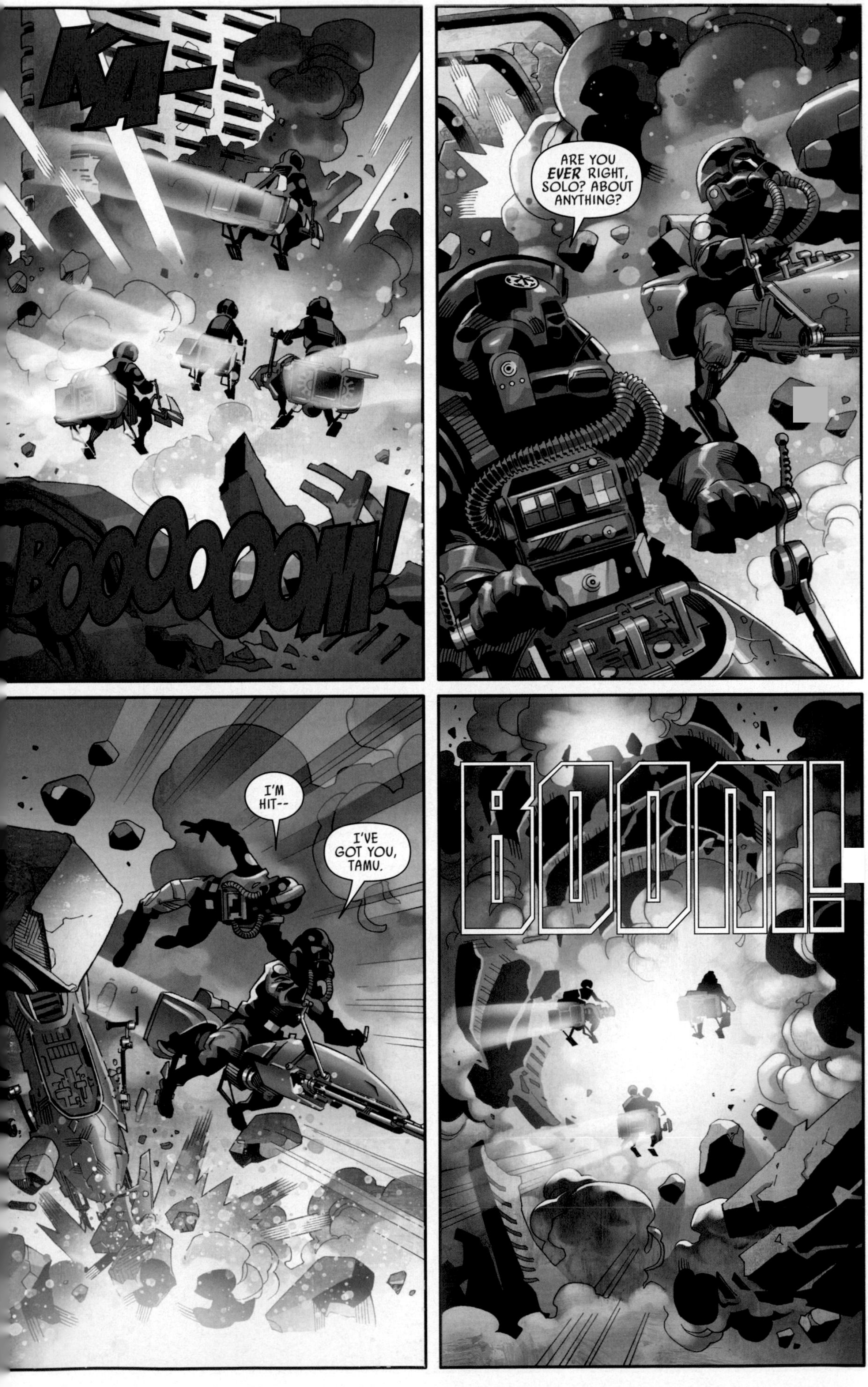
KA-
BOOOOOOM!
ARE YOU EVER RIGHT, SOLO? ABOUT ANYTHING?
I'M HIT--
I'VE GOT YOU, TAMU.
BOOM!

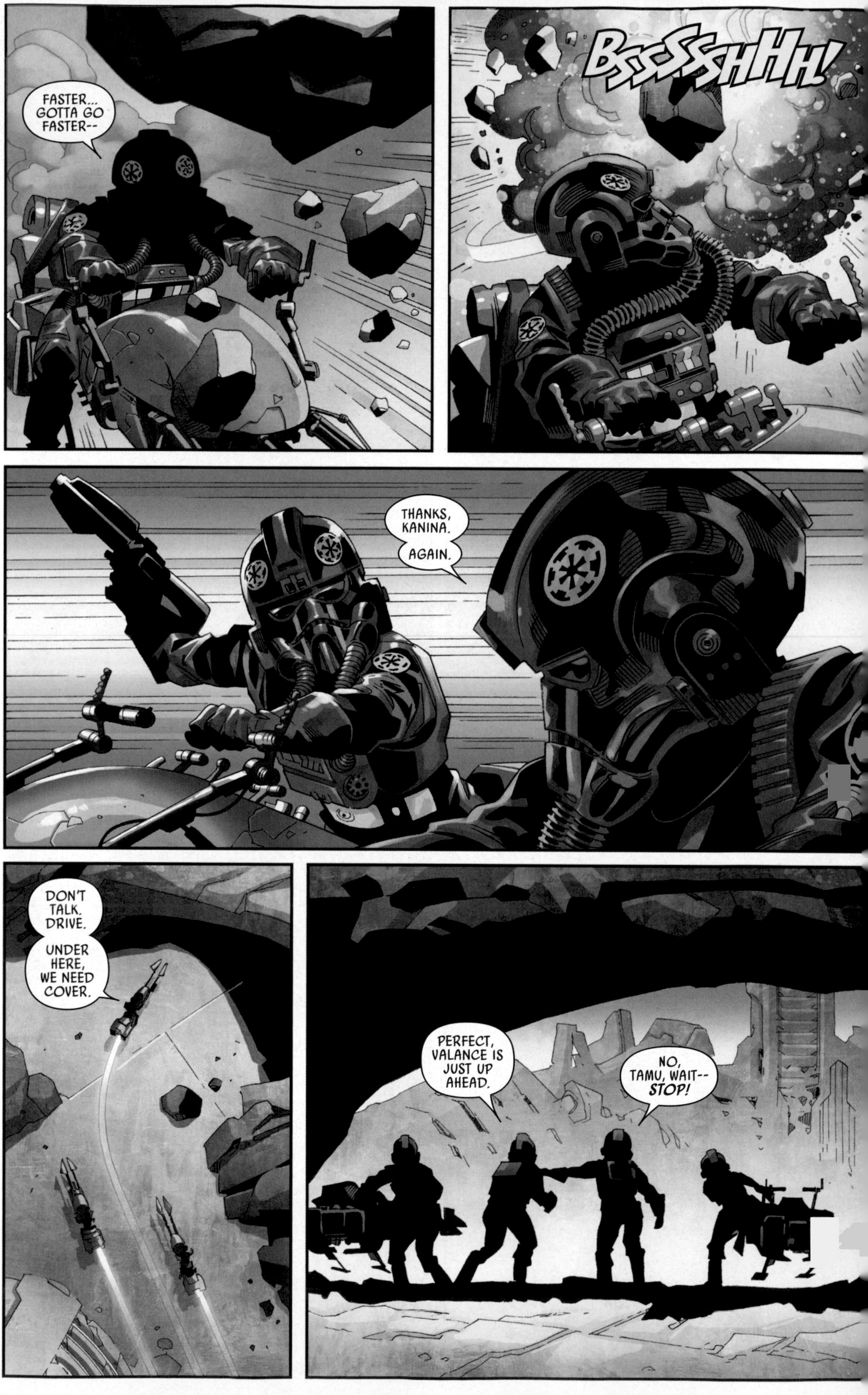
FASTER... GOTTA GO FASTER--
BSSSSHHH!
THANKS, KANINA.
AGAIN.
DON'T TALK. DRIVE.
UNDER HERE, WE NEED COVER.
PERFECT, VALANCE IS JUST UP AHEAD.
NO, TAMU, WAIT-- STOP!

DER DPOFFIAS
ASSAL

VALANCE'S WRECK IS BEHIND THAT BUILDING.

WE WALK FROM HERE.

THIS STRUCTURE IS REINFORCED. OUR BIKES SHOULD BE SAFE.

SHOULD? GREAT. LOVING THIS PLAN SO FAR.

OKAY, WE MOVE TWO BY TWO, I'LL LEAD THE WAY. COVER FORMATION AND--

KANINA LEFT ALREADY, DIDN'T SHE?

YEAH, SHE WENT AHEAD.

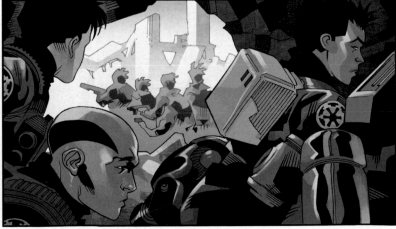

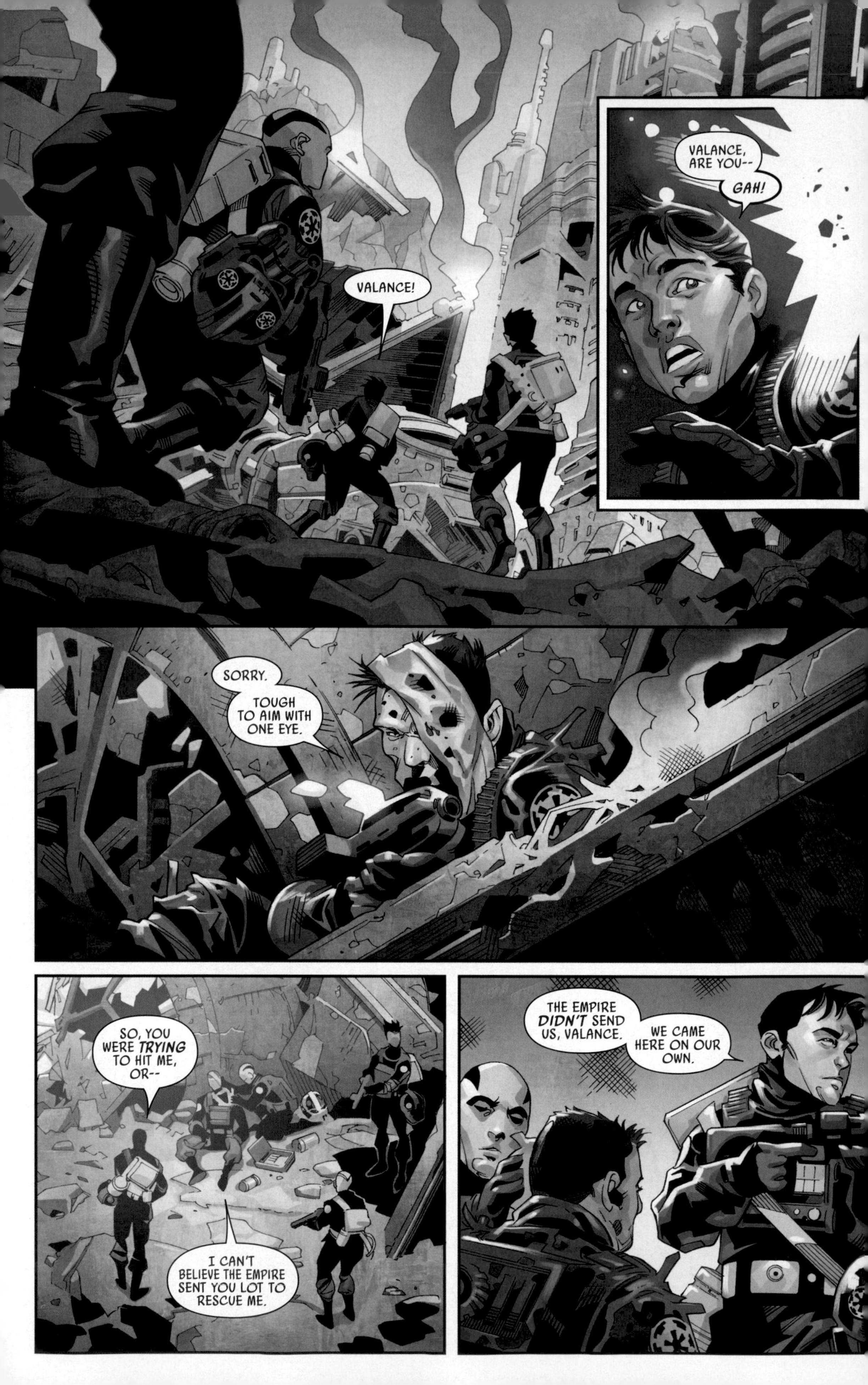
VALANCE!
VALANCE, ARE YOU--
GAH!
SORRY.
TOUGH TO AIM WITH ONE EYE.
SO, YOU WERE *TRYING* TO HIT ME, OR--
I CAN'T BELIEVE THE EMPIRE SENT YOU LOT TO RESCUE ME.
THE EMPIRE *DIDN'T* SEND US, VALANCE.
WE CAME HERE ON OUR OWN.

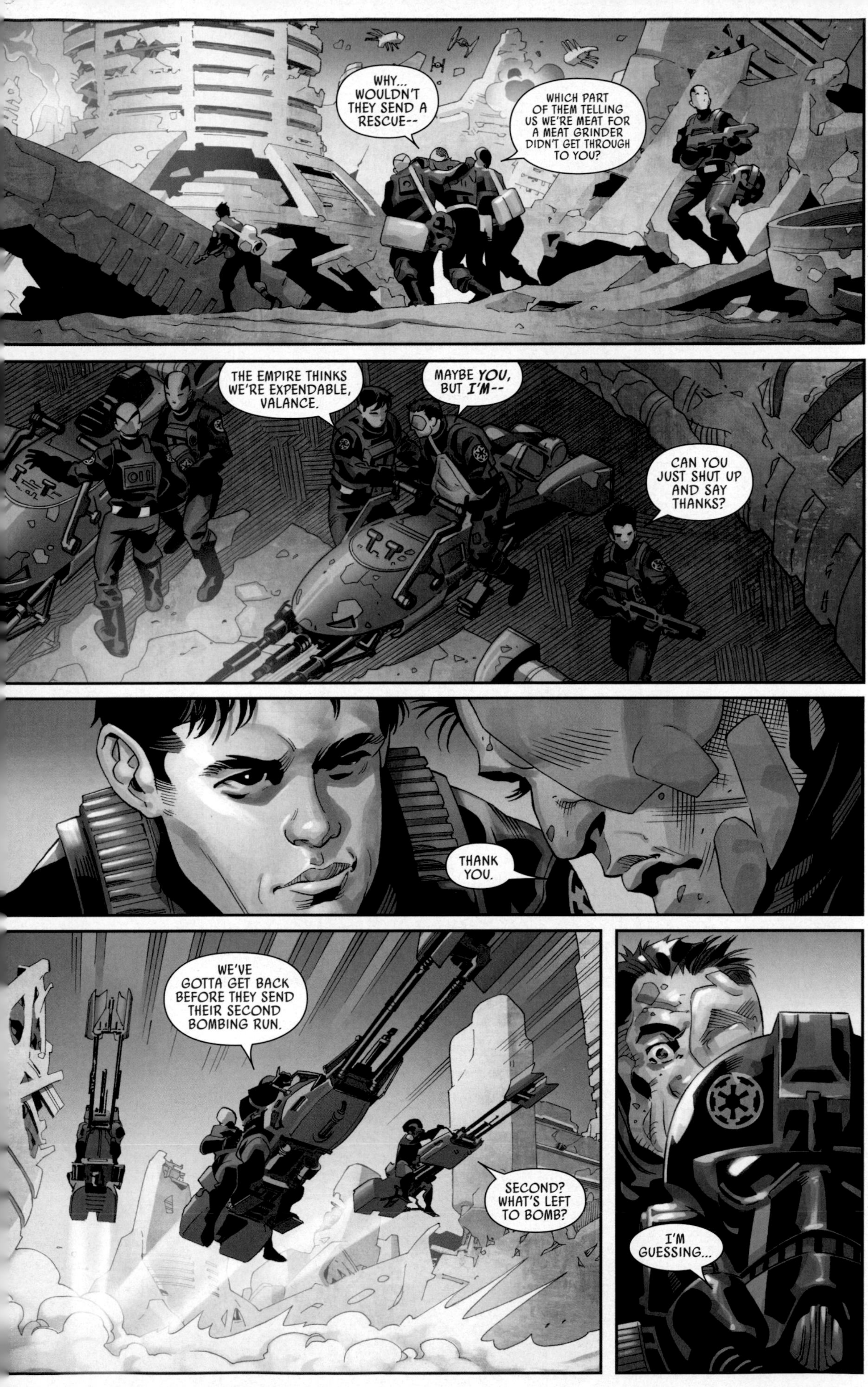
WHY... WOULDN'T THEY SEND A RESCUE--
WHICH PART OF THEM TELLING US WE'RE MEAT FOR A MEAT GRINDER DIDN'T GET THROUGH TO YOU?
THE EMPIRE THINKS WE'RE EXPENDABLE, VALANCE.
MAYBE YOU, BUT I'M--
CAN YOU JUST SHUT UP AND SAY THANKS?
THANK YOU.
WE'VE GOTTA GET BACK BEFORE THEY SEND THEIR SECOND BOMBING RUN.
SECOND? WHAT'S LEFT TO BOMB?
I'M GUESSING...

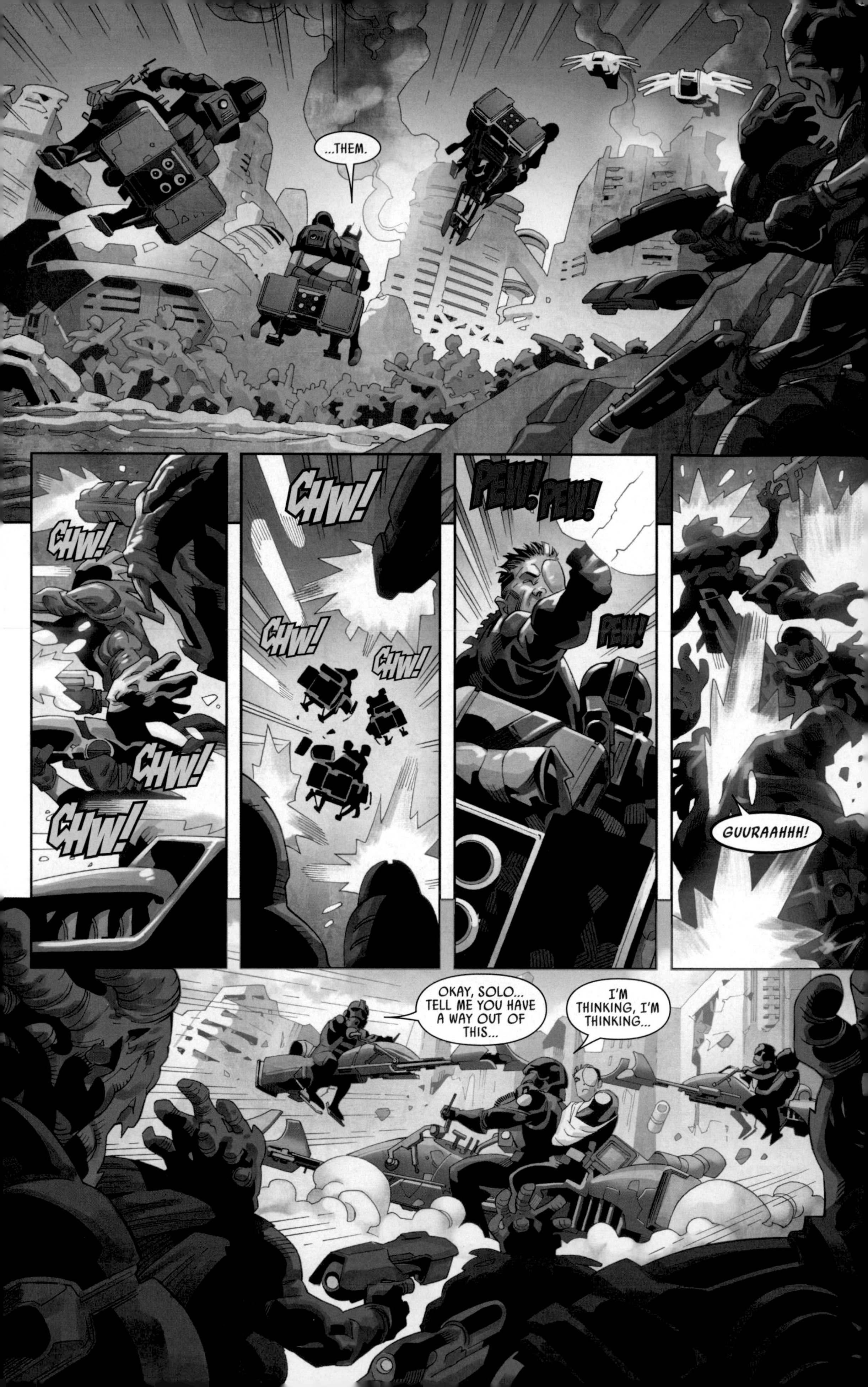
...THEM.
CHW!
CHW!
CHW!
CHW!
CHW!
CHW!
PEW! PEW!
PEW!
GUURAAHHH!
OKAY, SOLO... TELL ME YOU HAVE A WAY OUT OF THIS...
I'M THINKING, I'M THINKING...

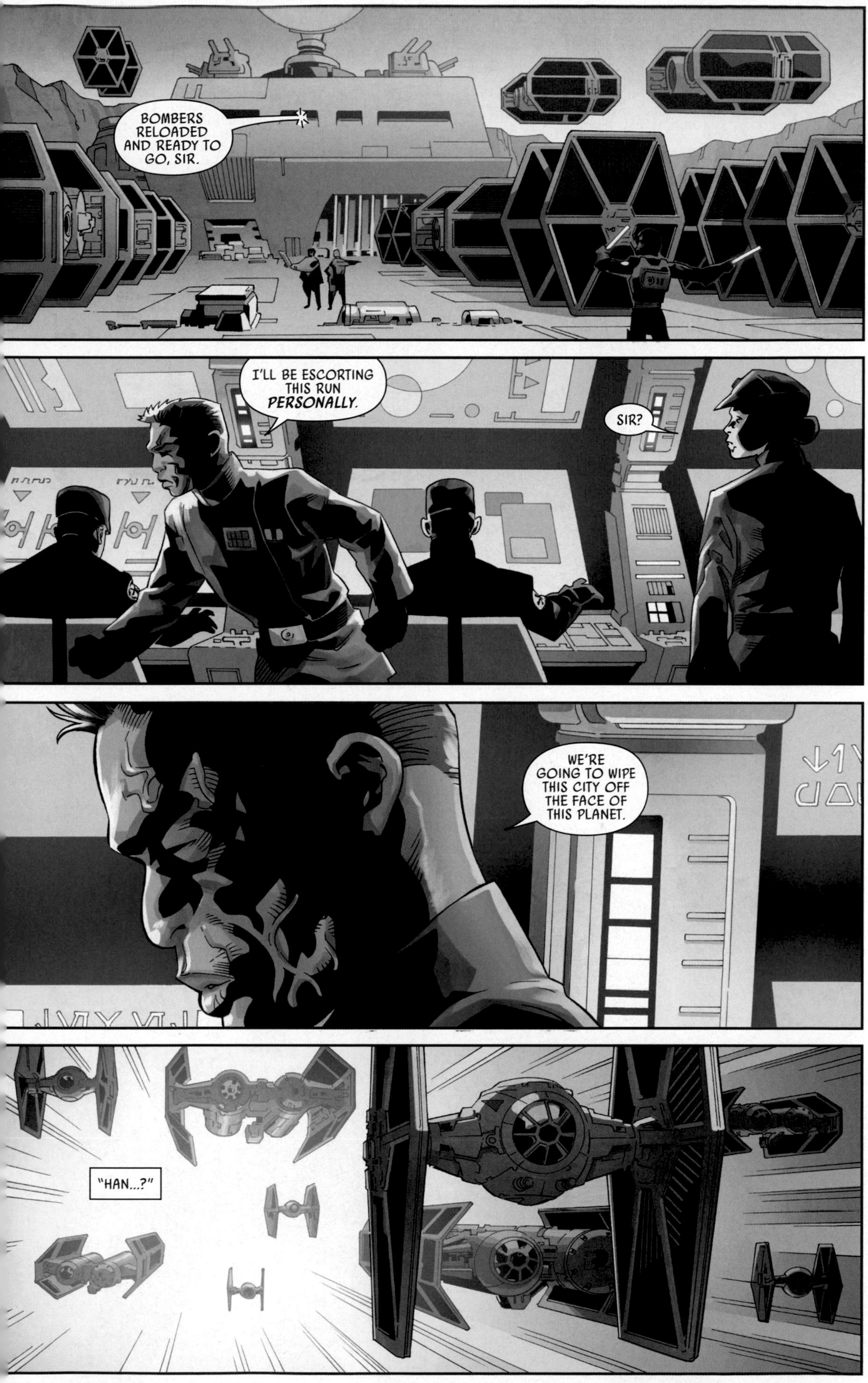
BOMBERS RELOADED AND READY TO GO, SIR.
I'LL BE ESCORTING THIS RUN PERSONALLY.
SIR?
WE'RE GOING TO WIPE THIS CITY OFF THE FACE OF THIS PLANET.
"HAN...?"

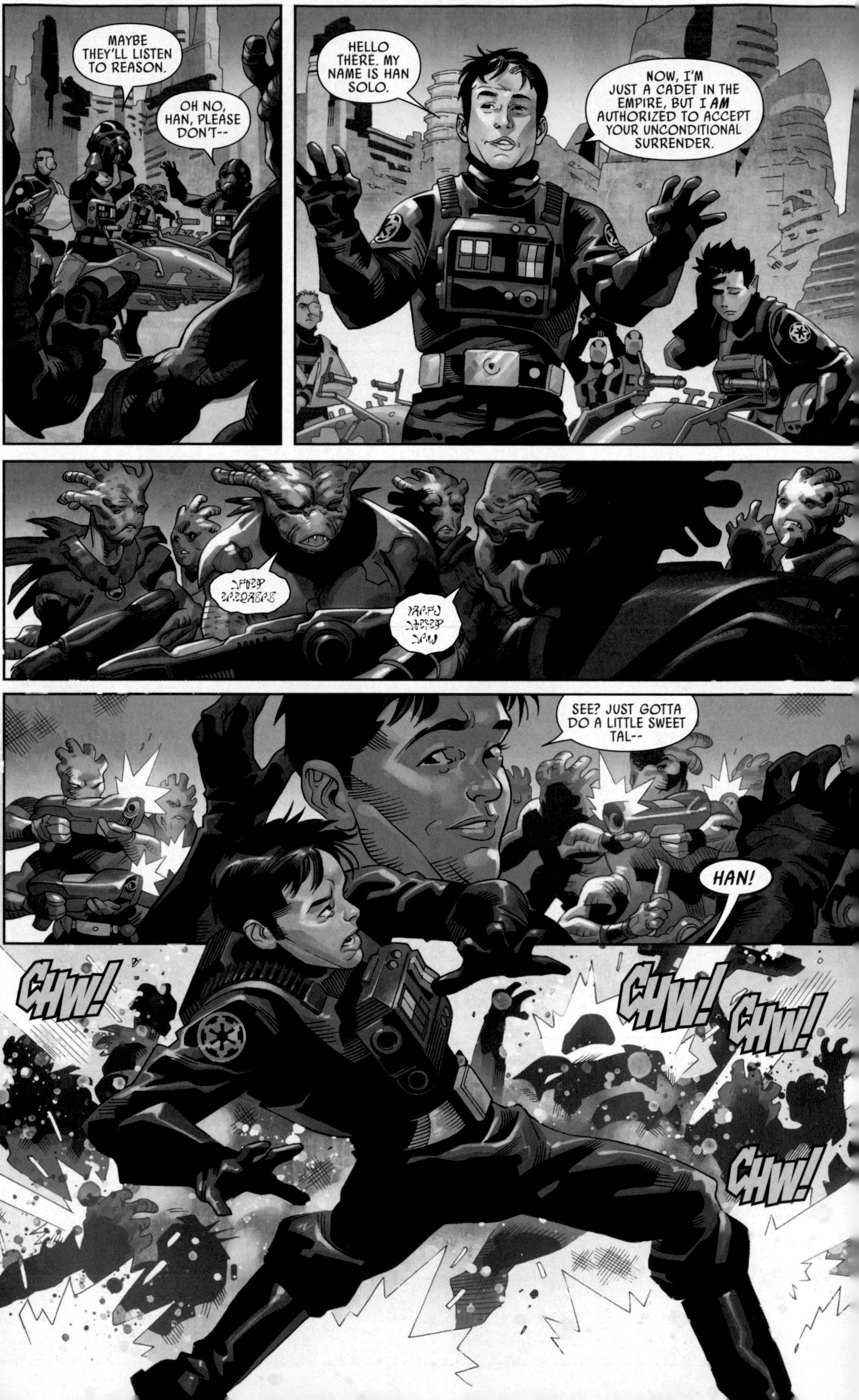
MAYBE THEY'LL LISTEN TO REASON.
OH NO, HAN, PLEASE DON'T--
HELLO THERE. MY NAME IS HAN SOLO.
NOW, I'M JUST A CADET IN THE EMPIRE, BUT I *AM* AUTHORIZED TO ACCEPT YOUR UNCONDITIONAL SURRENDER.
SEE? JUST GOTTA DO A LITTLE SWEET TAL--
HAN!
CHW!
CHW!
CHW!
CHW!

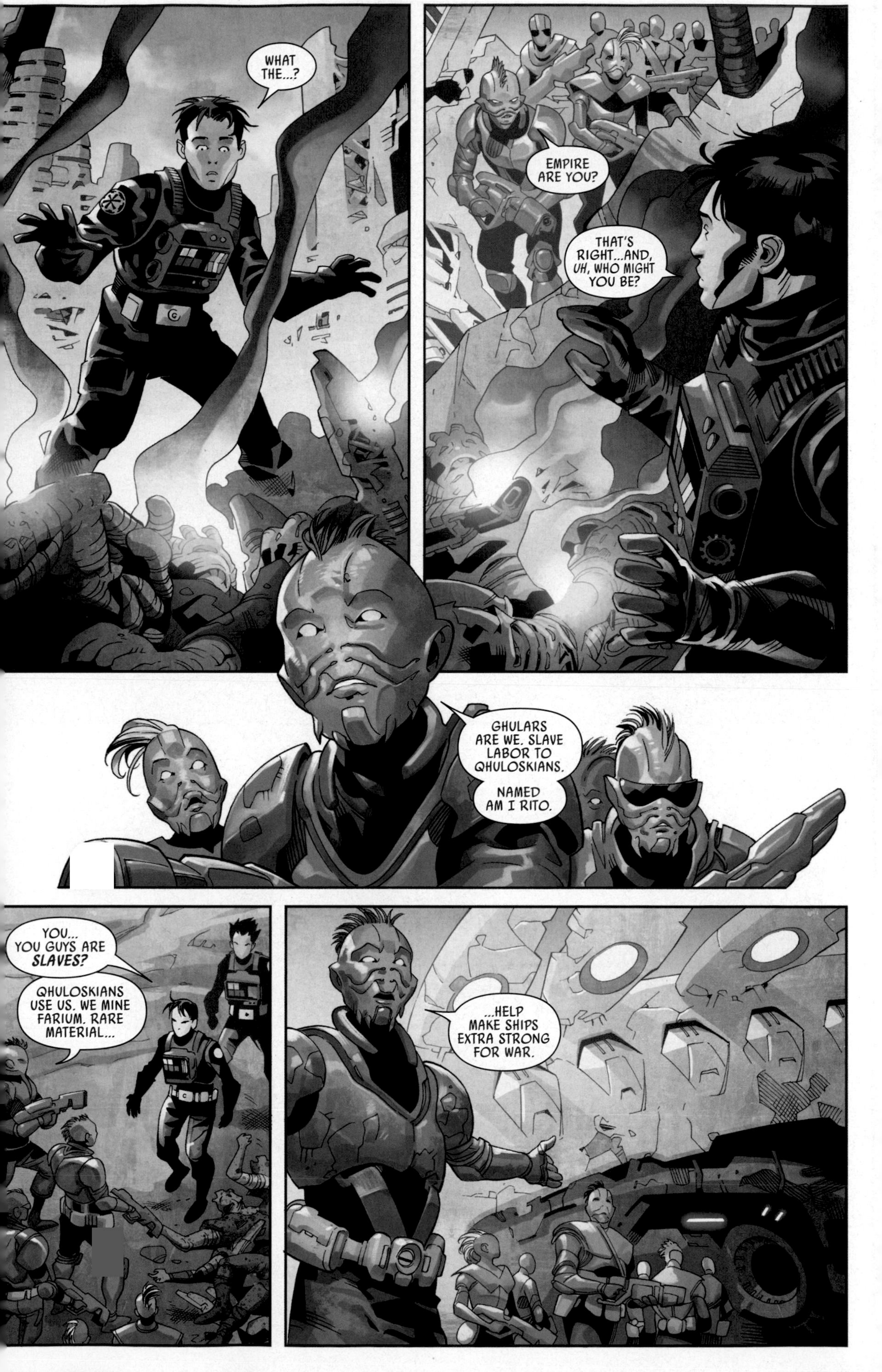
WHAT THE...?
EMPIRE ARE YOU?
THAT'S RIGHT...AND, UH, WHO MIGHT YOU BE?
GHULARS ARE WE. SLAVE LABOR TO QHULOSKIANS.
NAMED AM I RITO.
YOU... YOU GUYS ARE SLAVES?
QHULOSKIANS USE US. WE MINE FARIUM. RARE MATERIAL...
...HELP MAKE SHIPS EXTRA STRONG FOR WAR.

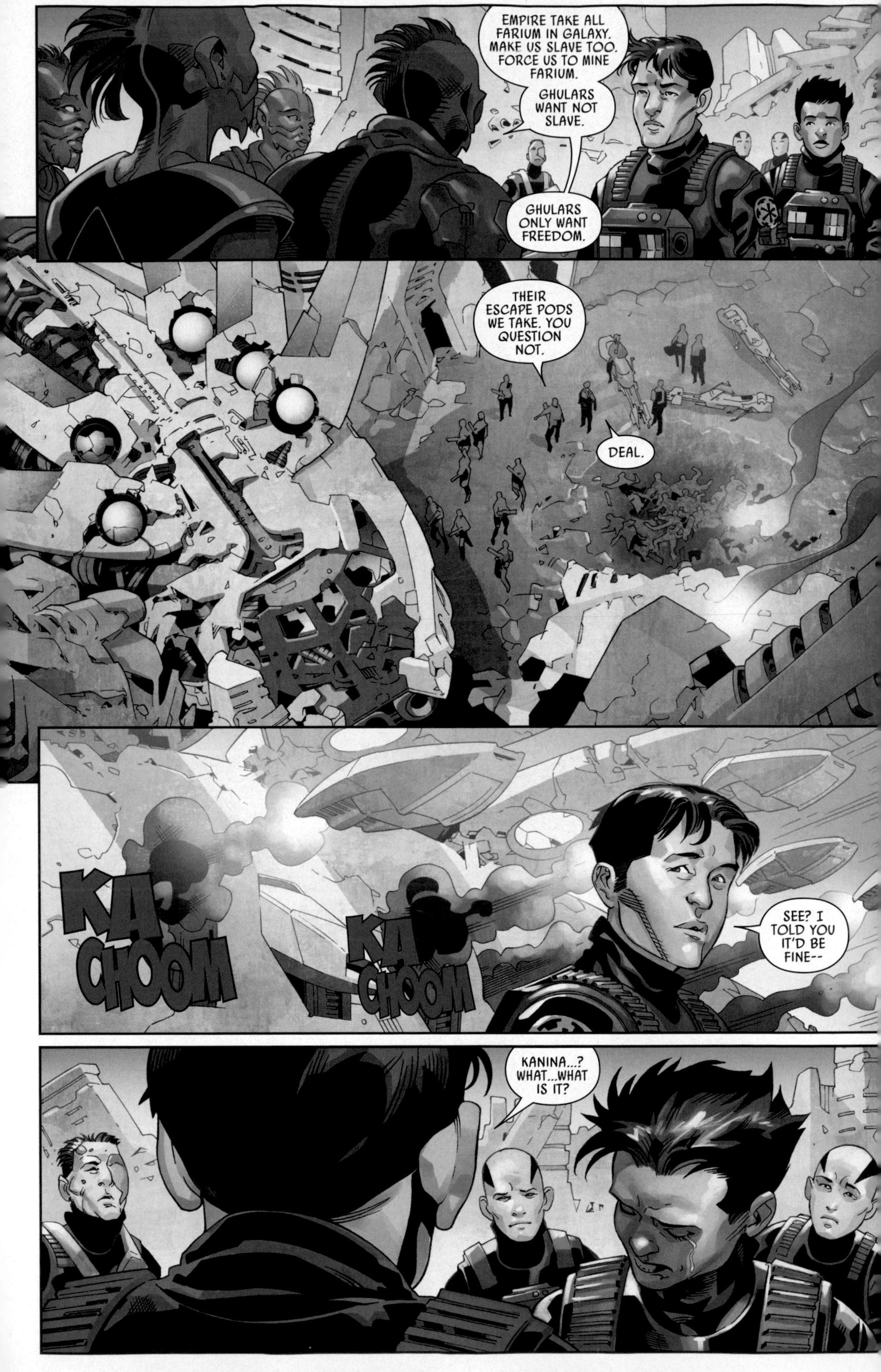
EMPIRE TAKE ALL FARIUM IN GALAXY. MAKE US SLAVE TOO. FORCE US TO MINE FARIUM.
GHULARS WANT NOT SLAVE.
GHULARS ONLY WANT FREEDOM.
THEIR ESCAPE PODS WE TAKE. YOU QUESTION NOT.
DEAL.
KA CHOOM
KA CHOOM
SEE? I TOLD YOU IT'D BE FINE--
KANINA...? WHAT...WHAT IS IT?

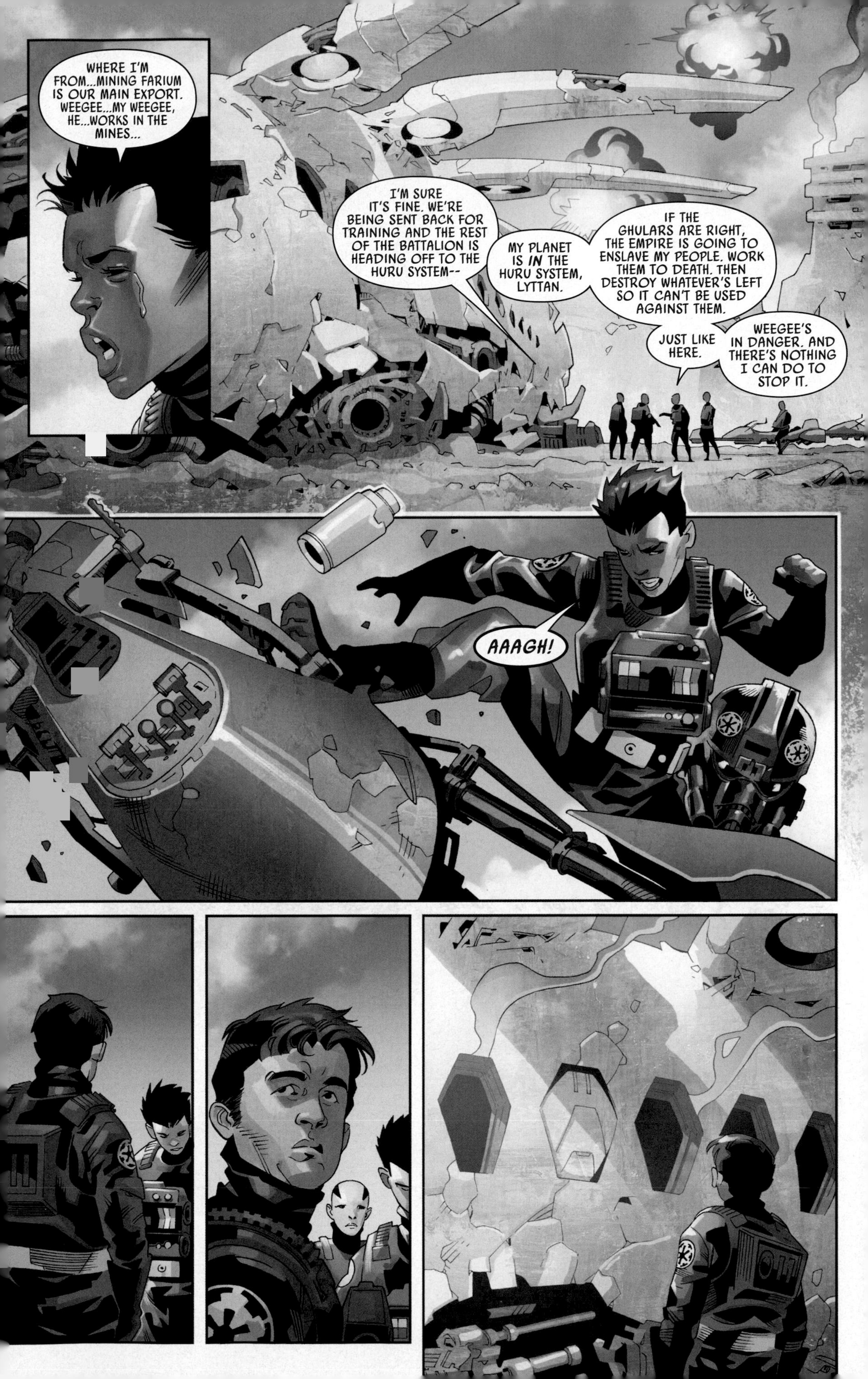
WHERE I'M FROM...MINING FARIUM IS OUR MAIN EXPORT. WEEGEE...MY WEEGEE, HE...WORKS IN THE MINES...
I'M SURE IT'S FINE. WE'RE BEING SENT BACK FOR TRAINING AND THE REST OF THE BATTALION IS HEADING OFF TO THE HURU SYSTEM--
MY PLANET IS *IN* THE HURU SYSTEM, LYTTAN.
IF THE GHULARS ARE RIGHT, THE EMPIRE IS GOING TO ENSLAVE MY PEOPLE. WORK THEM TO DEATH. THEN DESTROY WHATEVER'S LEFT SO IT CAN'T BE USED AGAINST THEM.
JUST LIKE HERE.
WEEGEE'S IN DANGER. AND THERE'S NOTHING I CAN DO TO STOP IT.
AAAGH!

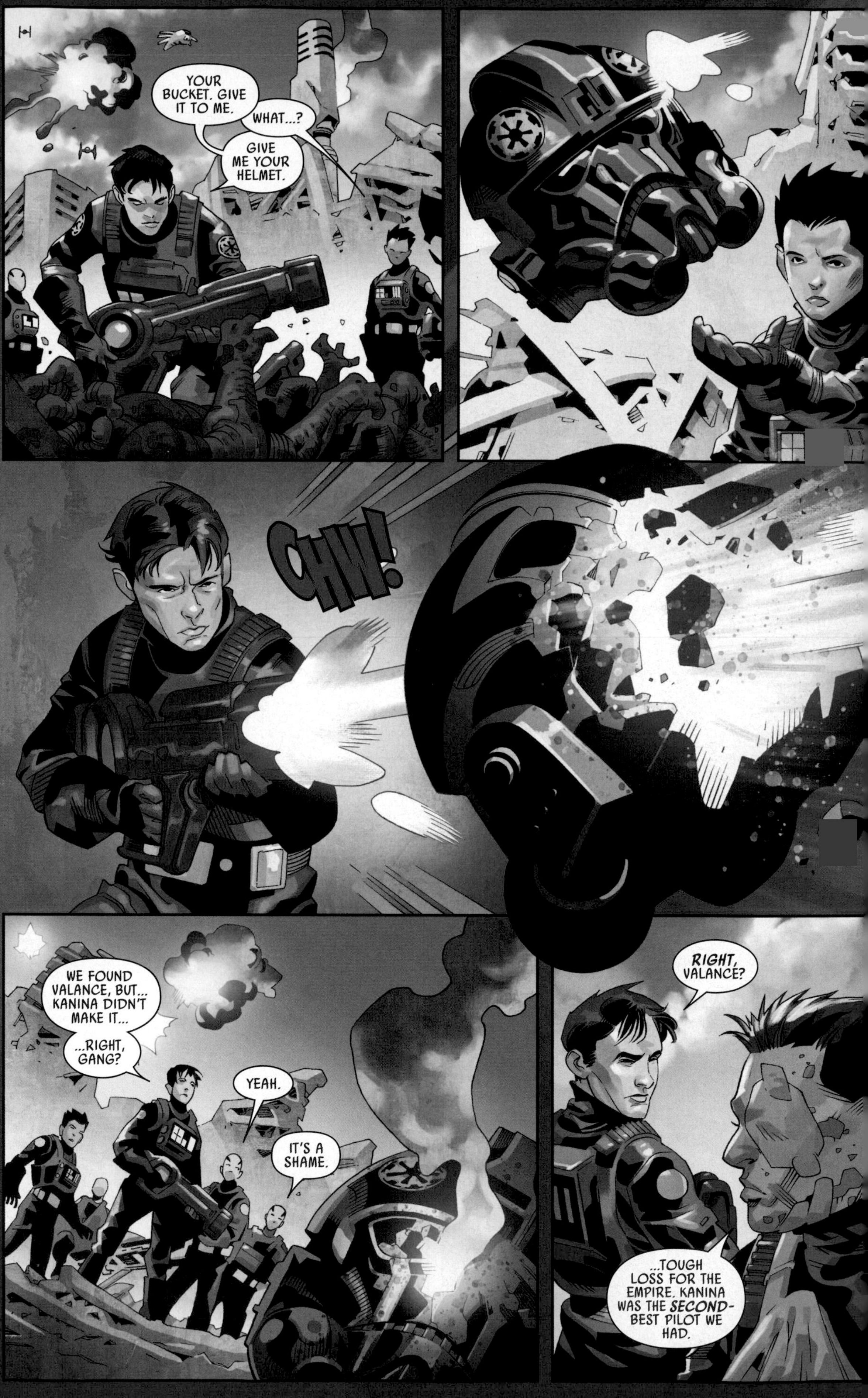
YOUR BUCKET. GIVE IT TO ME.
WHAT...?
GIVE ME YOUR HELMET.
CHW!
WE FOUND VALANCE, BUT... KANINA DIDN'T MAKE IT...
...RIGHT, GANG?
YEAH.
IT'S A SHAME.
RIGHT, VALANCE?
...TOUGH LOSS FOR THE EMPIRE. KANINA WAS THE SECOND-BEST PILOT WE HAD.

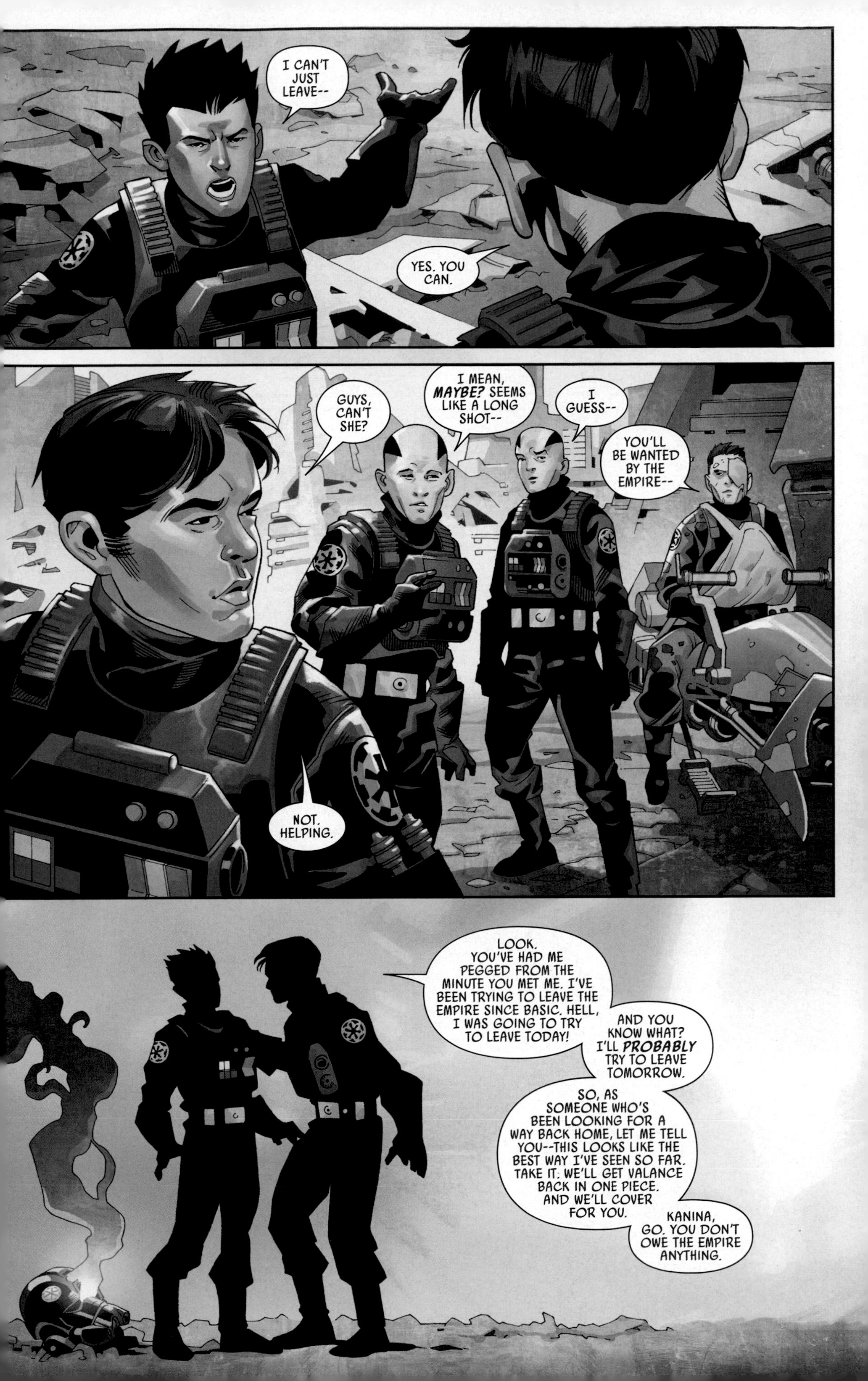
I CAN'T JUST LEAVE--
YES. YOU CAN.
GUYS, CAN'T SHE?
I MEAN, *MAYBE?* SEEMS LIKE A LONG SHOT--
I GUESS--
YOU'LL BE WANTED BY THE EMPIRE--
NOT. HELPING.
LOOK. YOU'VE HAD ME PEGGED FROM THE MINUTE YOU MET ME. I'VE BEEN TRYING TO LEAVE THE EMPIRE SINCE BASIC. HELL, I WAS GOING TO TRY TO LEAVE TODAY!
AND YOU KNOW WHAT? I'LL ***PROBABLY*** TRY TO LEAVE TOMORROW.
SO, AS SOMEONE WHO'S BEEN LOOKING FOR A WAY BACK HOME, LET ME TELL YOU--THIS LOOKS LIKE THE BEST WAY I'VE SEEN SO FAR. TAKE IT. WE'LL GET VALANCE BACK IN ONE PIECE. AND WE'LL COVER FOR YOU.
KANINA, GO. YOU DON'T OWE THE EMPIRE ANYTHING.

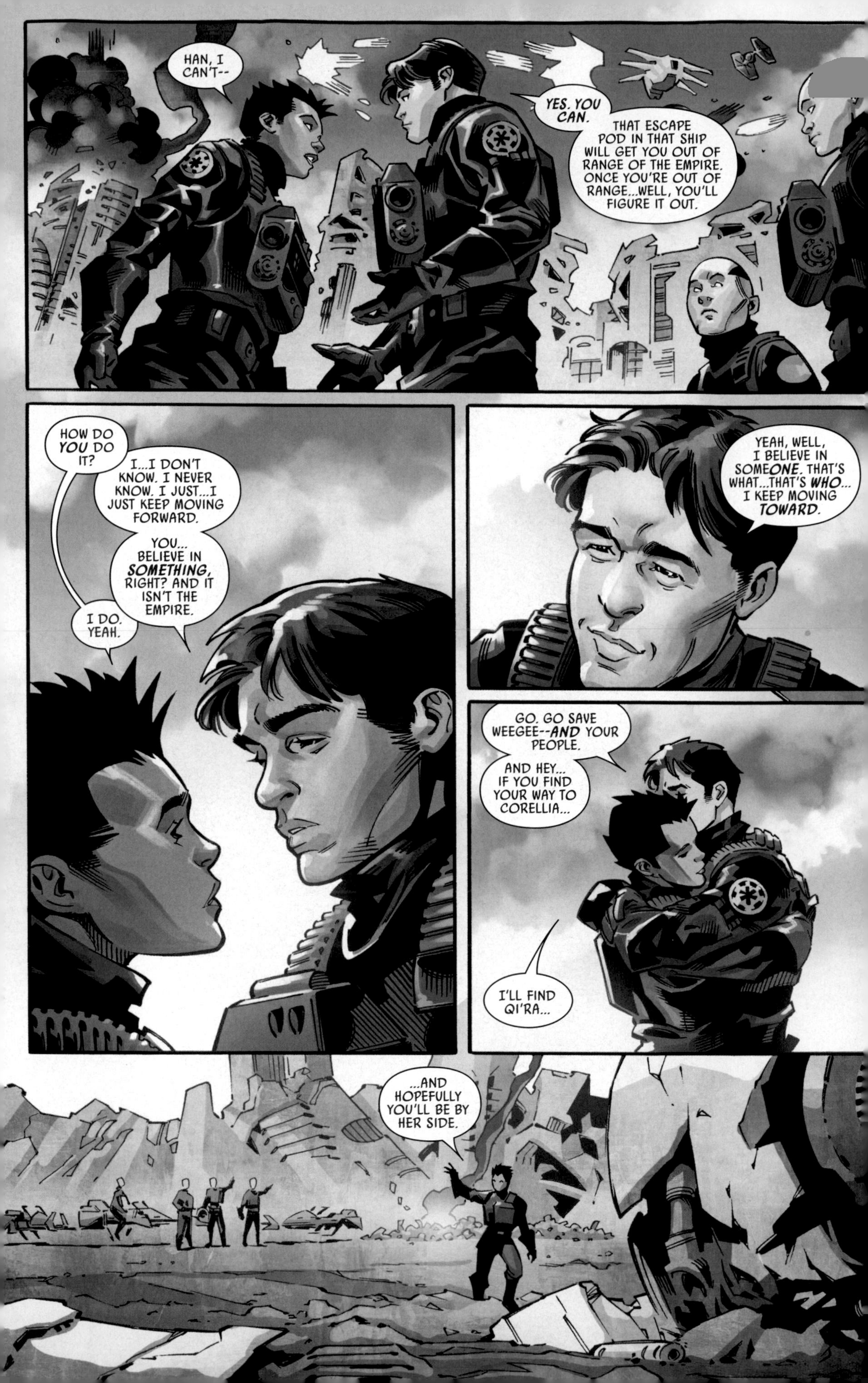
HAN, I CAN'T--
YES. YOU CAN.
THAT ESCAPE POD IN THAT SHIP WILL GET YOU OUT OF RANGE OF THE EMPIRE. ONCE YOU'RE OUT OF RANGE...WELL, YOU'LL FIGURE IT OUT.
HOW DO YOU DO IT?
I...I DON'T KNOW. I NEVER KNOW. I JUST...I JUST KEEP MOVING FORWARD.
YOU... BELIEVE IN SOMETHING, RIGHT? AND IT ISN'T THE EMPIRE.
I DO. YEAH.
YEAH, WELL, I BELIEVE IN SOMEONE. THAT'S WHAT...THAT'S WHO... I KEEP MOVING TOWARD.
GO. GO SAVE WEEGEE--AND YOUR PEOPLE.
AND HEY... IF YOU FIND YOUR WAY TO CORELLIA...
I'LL FIND QI'RA...
...AND HOPEFULLY YOU'LL BE BY HER SIDE.

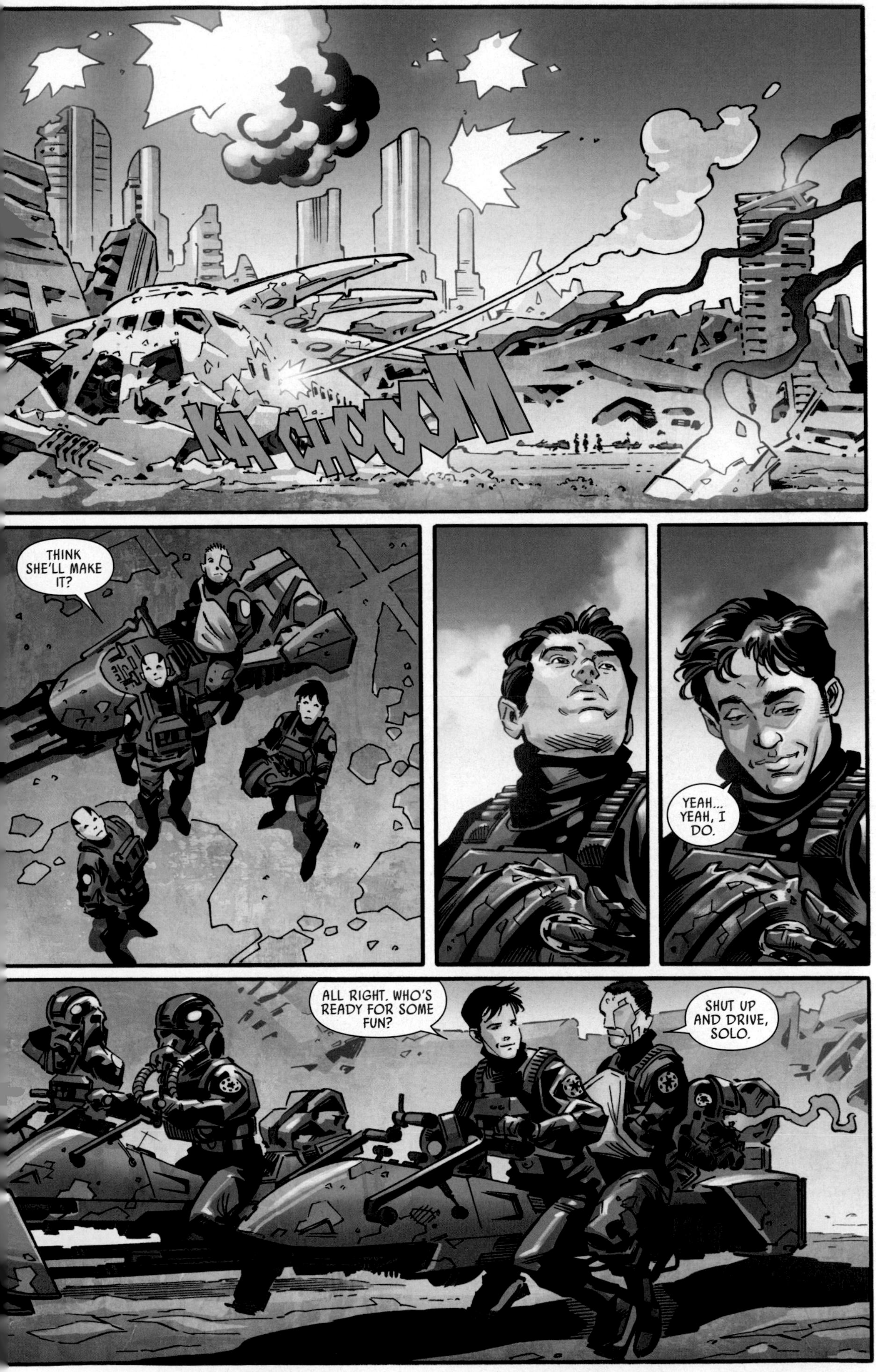
KA CHOOOM
THINK SHE'LL MAKE IT?
YEAH... YEAH, I DO.
ALL RIGHT. WHO'S READY FOR SOME FUN?
SHUT UP AND DRIVE, SOLO.

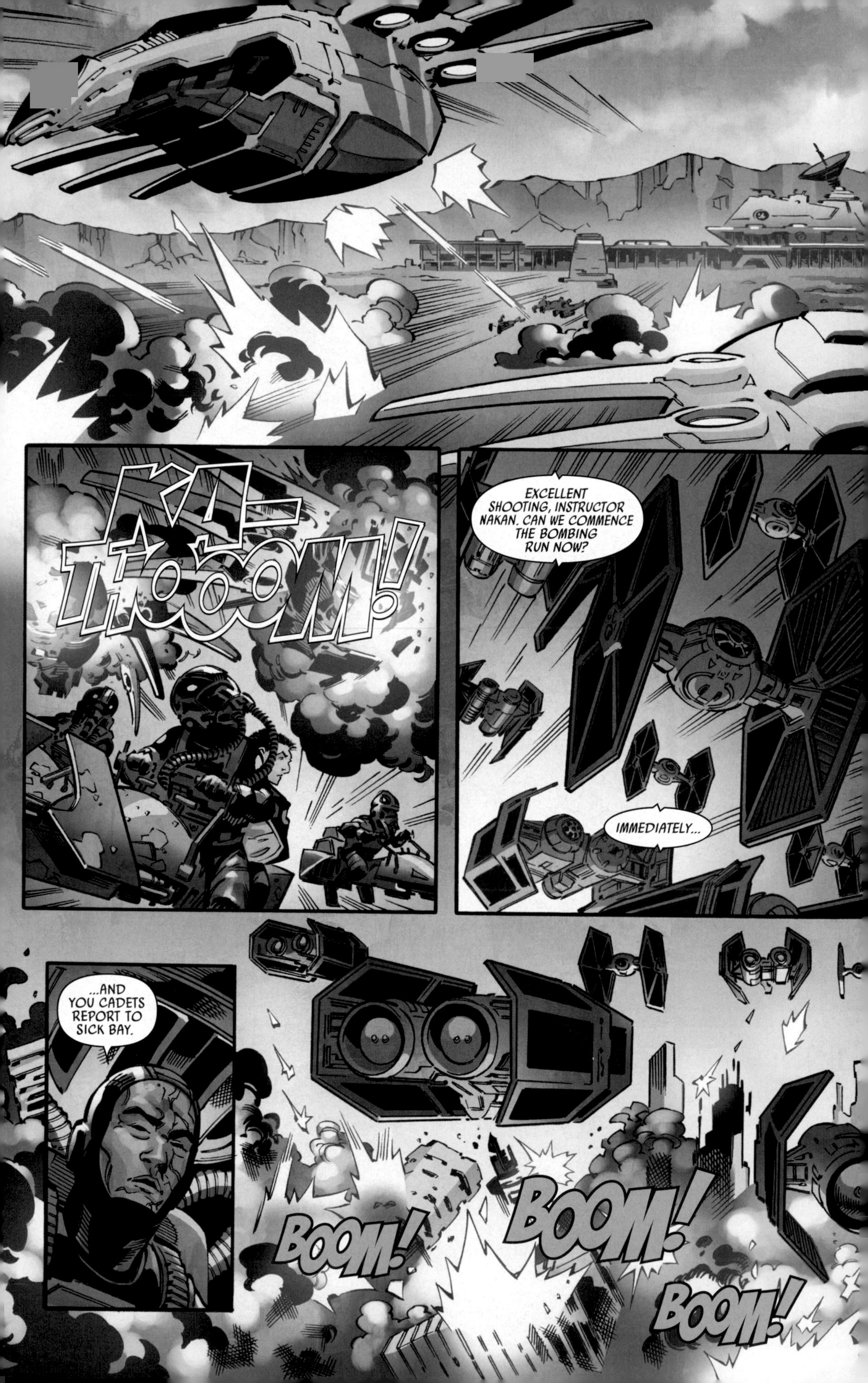
KA-THOOOM!
EXCELLENT SHOOTING, INSTRUCTOR NAKAN. CAN WE COMMENCE THE BOMBING RUN NOW?
IMMEDIATELY...
...AND YOU CADETS REPORT TO SICK BAY.
BOOM!
BOOM!
BOOM!

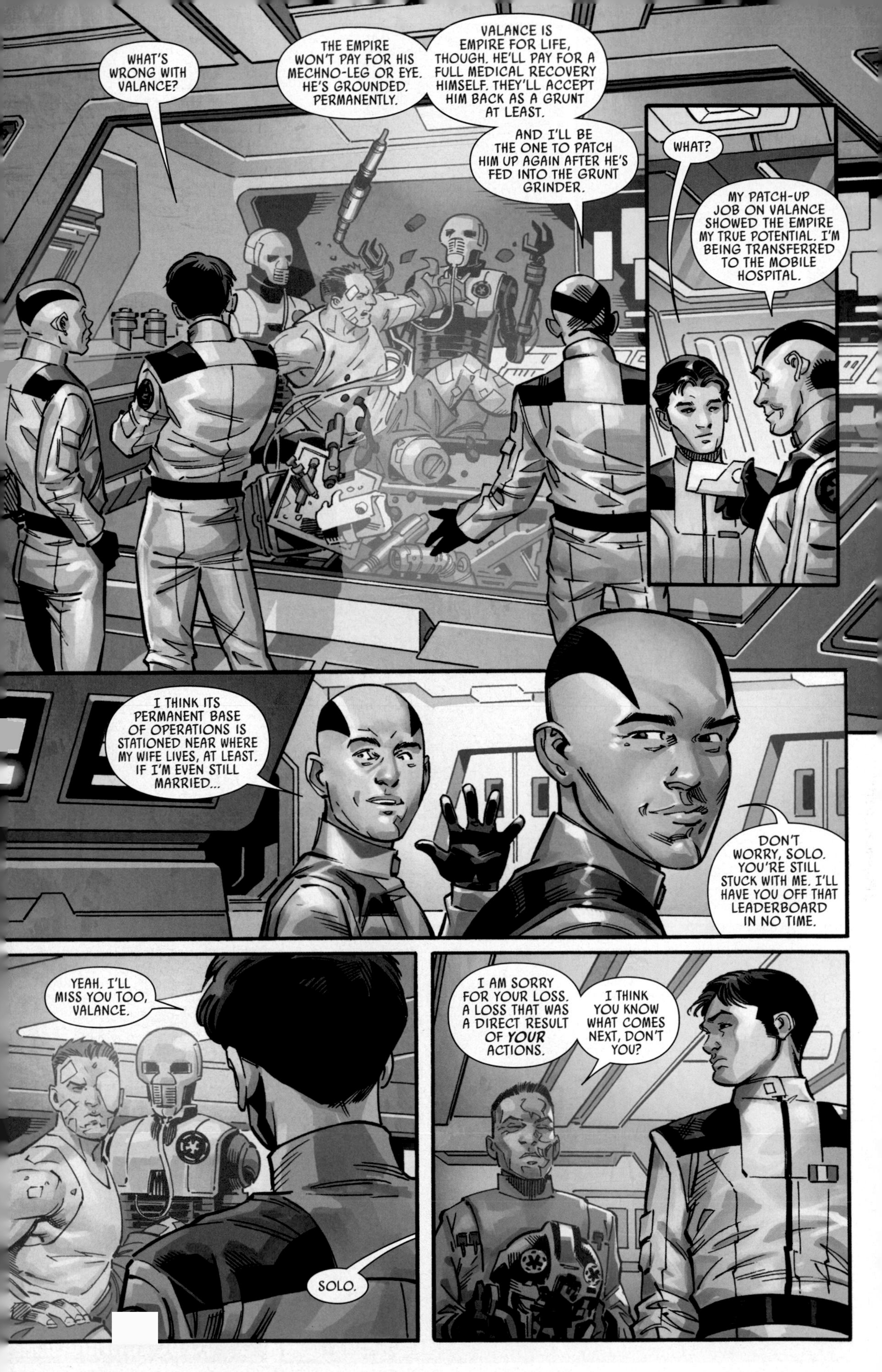
WHAT'S WRONG WITH VALANCE?
THE EMPIRE WON'T PAY FOR HIS MECHNO-LEG OR EYE. HE'S GROUNDED. PERMANENTLY.
VALANCE IS EMPIRE FOR LIFE, THOUGH. HE'LL PAY FOR A FULL MEDICAL RECOVERY HIMSELF. THEY'LL ACCEPT HIM BACK AS A GRUNT AT LEAST.
AND I'LL BE THE ONE TO PATCH HIM UP AGAIN AFTER HE'S FED INTO THE GRUNT GRINDER.
WHAT?
MY PATCH-UP JOB ON VALANCE SHOWED THE EMPIRE MY TRUE POTENTIAL. I'M BEING TRANSFERRED TO THE MOBILE HOSPITAL.
I THINK ITS PERMANENT BASE OF OPERATIONS IS STATIONED NEAR WHERE MY WIFE LIVES, AT LEAST. IF I'M EVEN STILL MARRIED...
DON'T WORRY, SOLO. YOU'RE STILL STUCK WITH ME. I'LL HAVE YOU OFF THAT LEADERBOARD IN NO TIME.
YEAH. I'LL MISS YOU TOO, VALANCE.
SOLO.
I AM SORRY FOR YOUR LOSS. A LOSS THAT WAS A DIRECT RESULT OF *YOUR* ACTIONS.
I THINK YOU KNOW WHAT COMES NEXT, DON'T YOU?

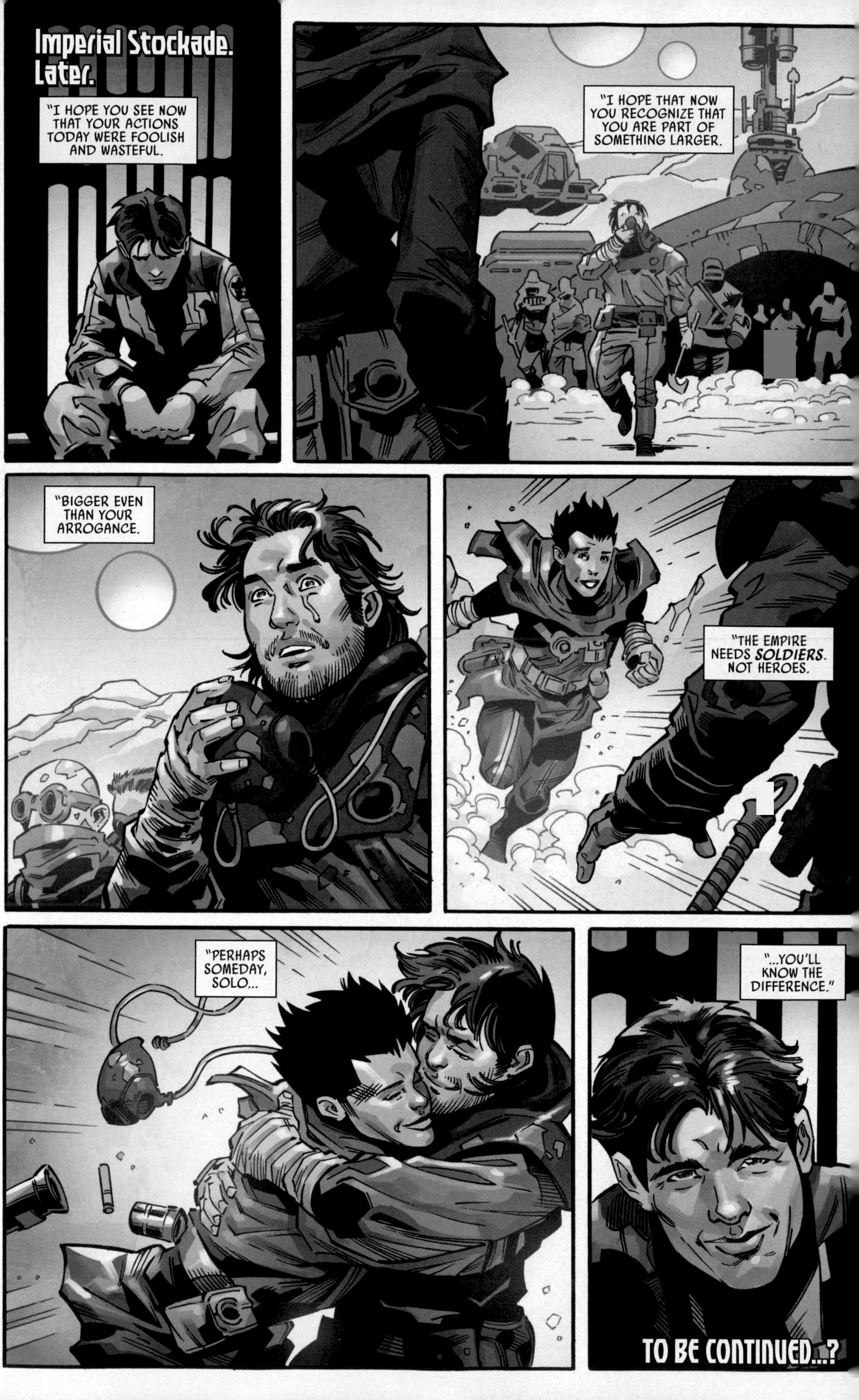
Imperial Stockade.
Later.
"I HOPE YOU SEE NOW THAT YOUR ACTIONS TODAY WERE FOOLISH AND WASTEFUL.
"I HOPE THAT NOW YOU RECOGNIZE THAT YOU ARE PART OF SOMETHING LARGER.
"BIGGER EVEN THAN YOUR ARROGANCE.
"THE EMPIRE NEEDS SOLDIERS. NOT HEROES.
"PERHAPS SOMEDAY, SOLO...
"...YOU'LL KNOW THE DIFFERENCE."
TO BE CONTINUED...?

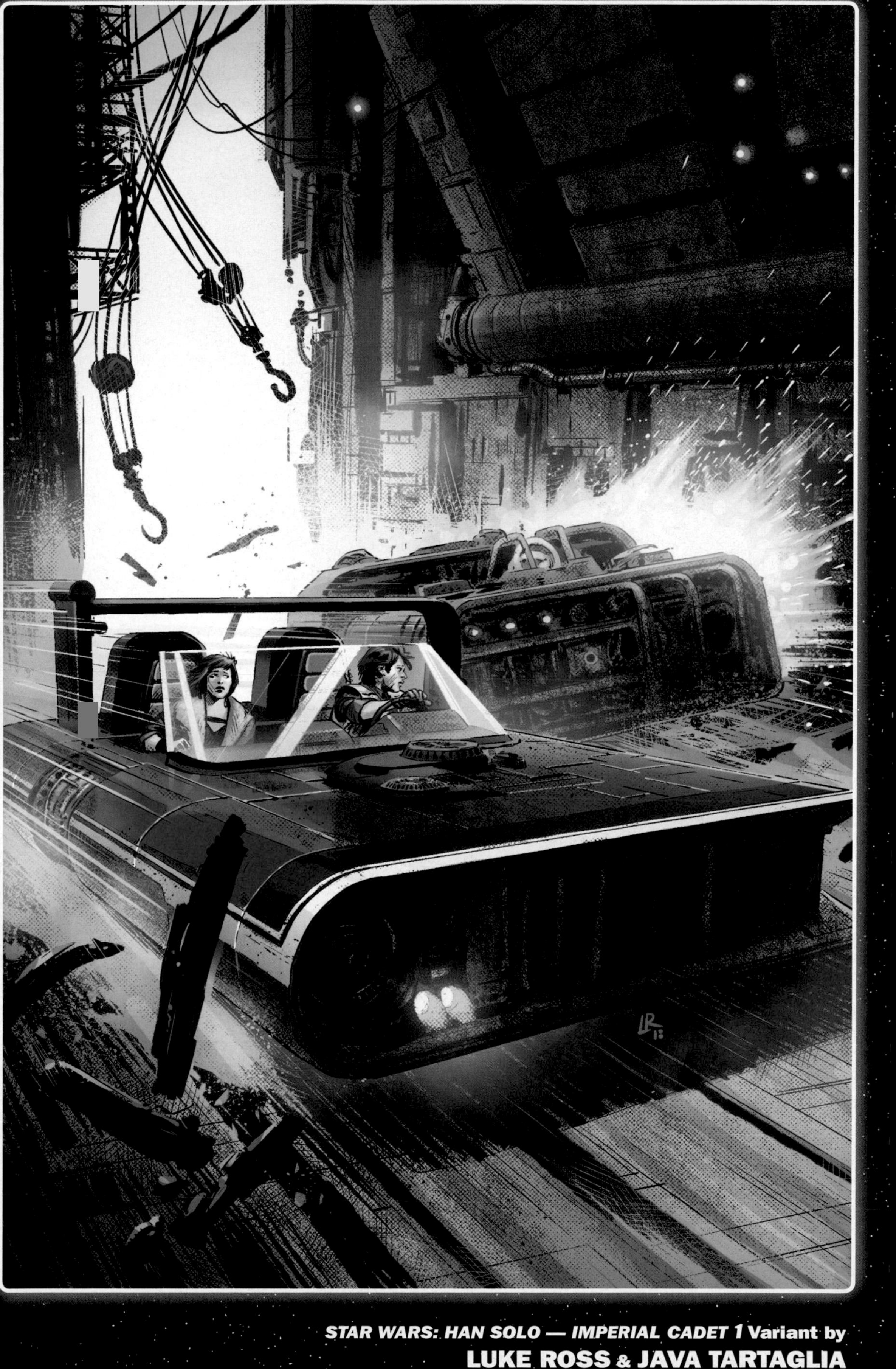

STAR WARS: HAN SOLO — IMPERIAL CADET 1 **Variant by**
LUKE ROSS & JAVA TARTAGLIA

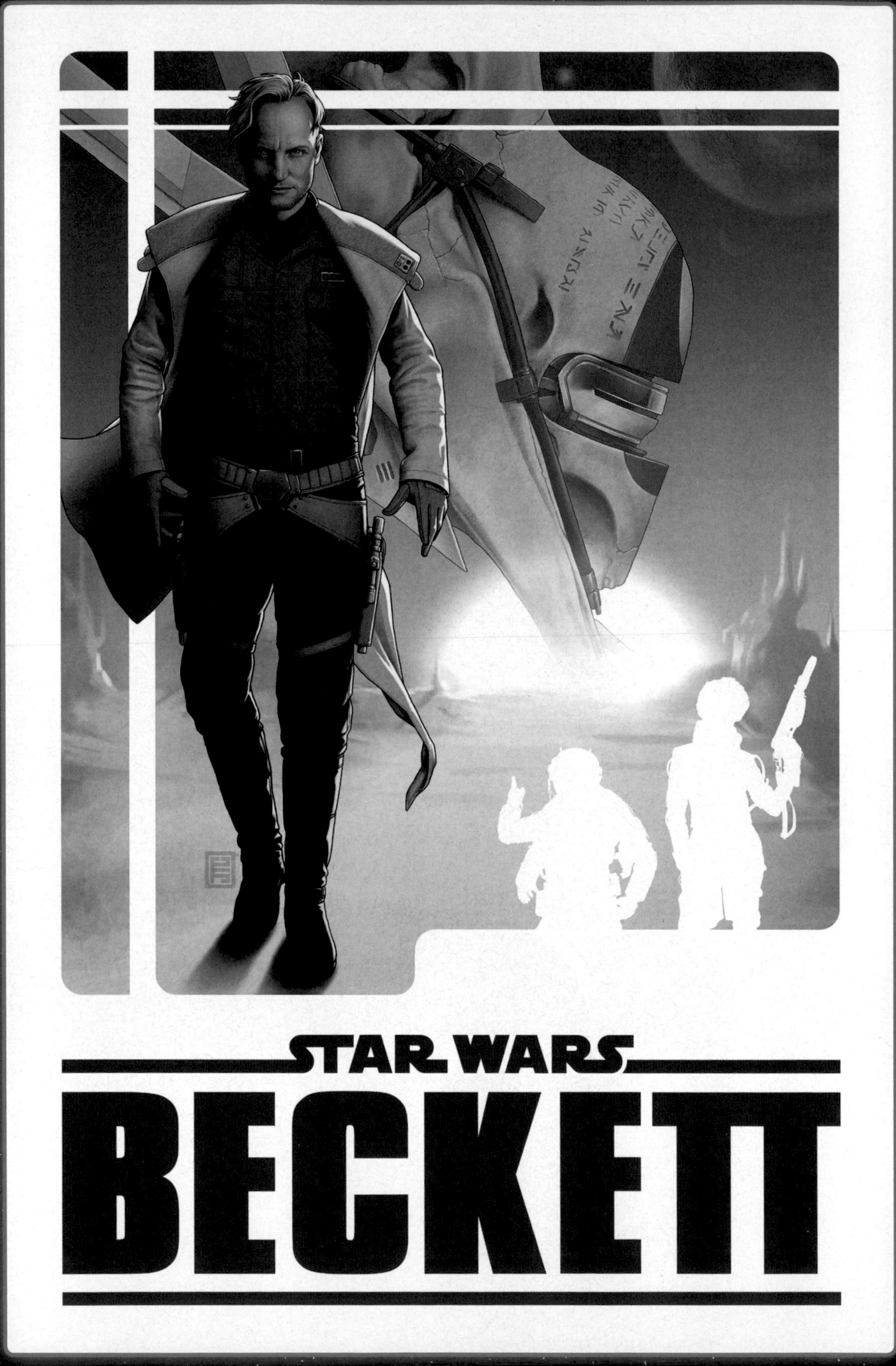
STAR WARS
BECKETT

BECKETT 1

WANTED

TOBIAS BECKETT

Human male. Notorious thief and leader of his own highly dangerous gang of outlaws.

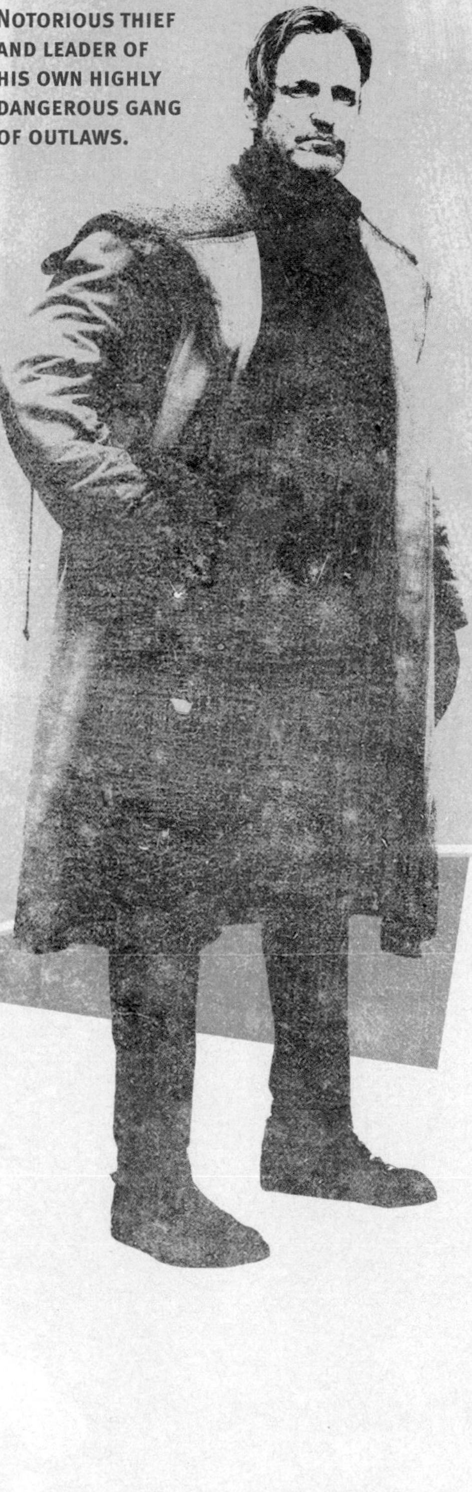

Beckett's crew of scoundrels is heavily armed and extremely lethal. There is no job too dangerous or scheme too risky for Beckett and his thugs. Their alleged illicit activities may involve known criminal syndicates.

Information on Beckett's whereabouts or recent dealings should be immediately reported to your local authorities.

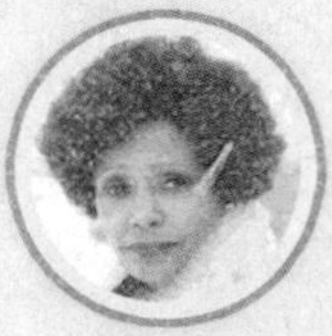

VAL

Human female. Weapons expert in Beckett's gang. Extremely skilled with a blaster rifle.

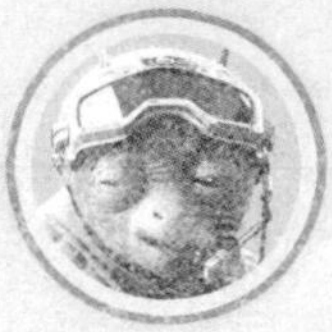

RIO DURANT

Ardennian male. Pilot of Beckett's gang. Veteran of Freedom's Sons.

Chapter One

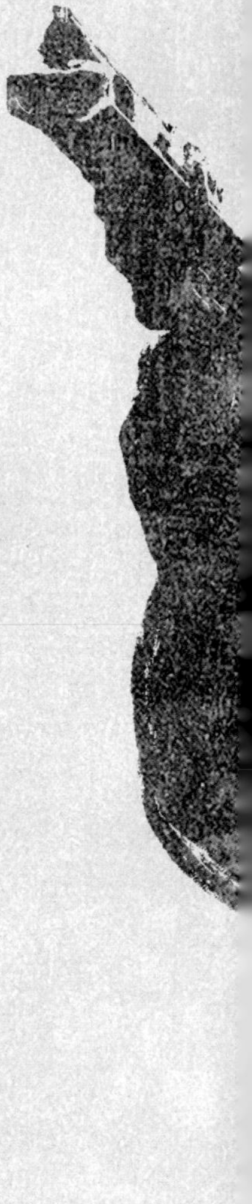

The Man in Black

Illustrated by Edgar Salazar

1

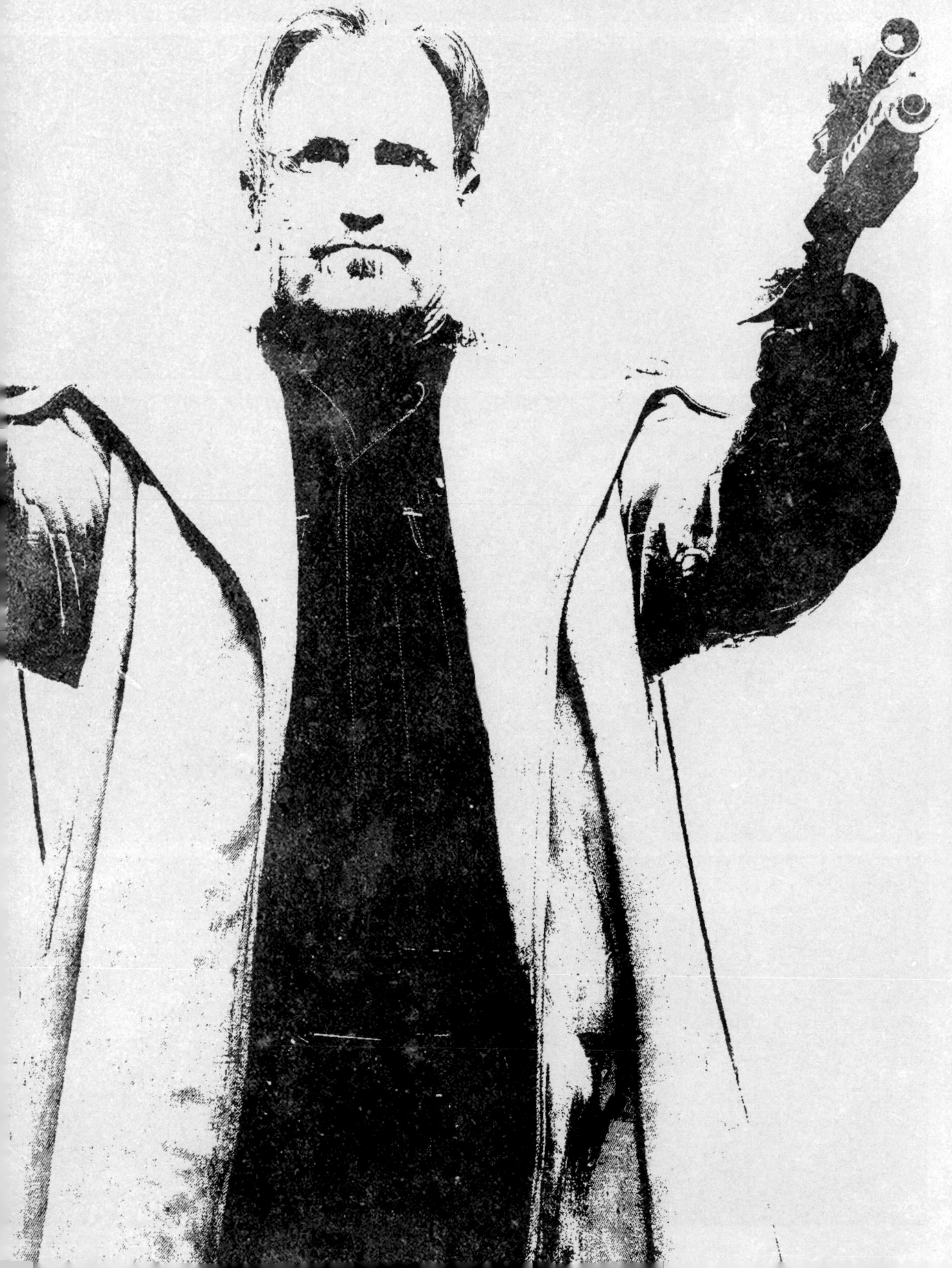

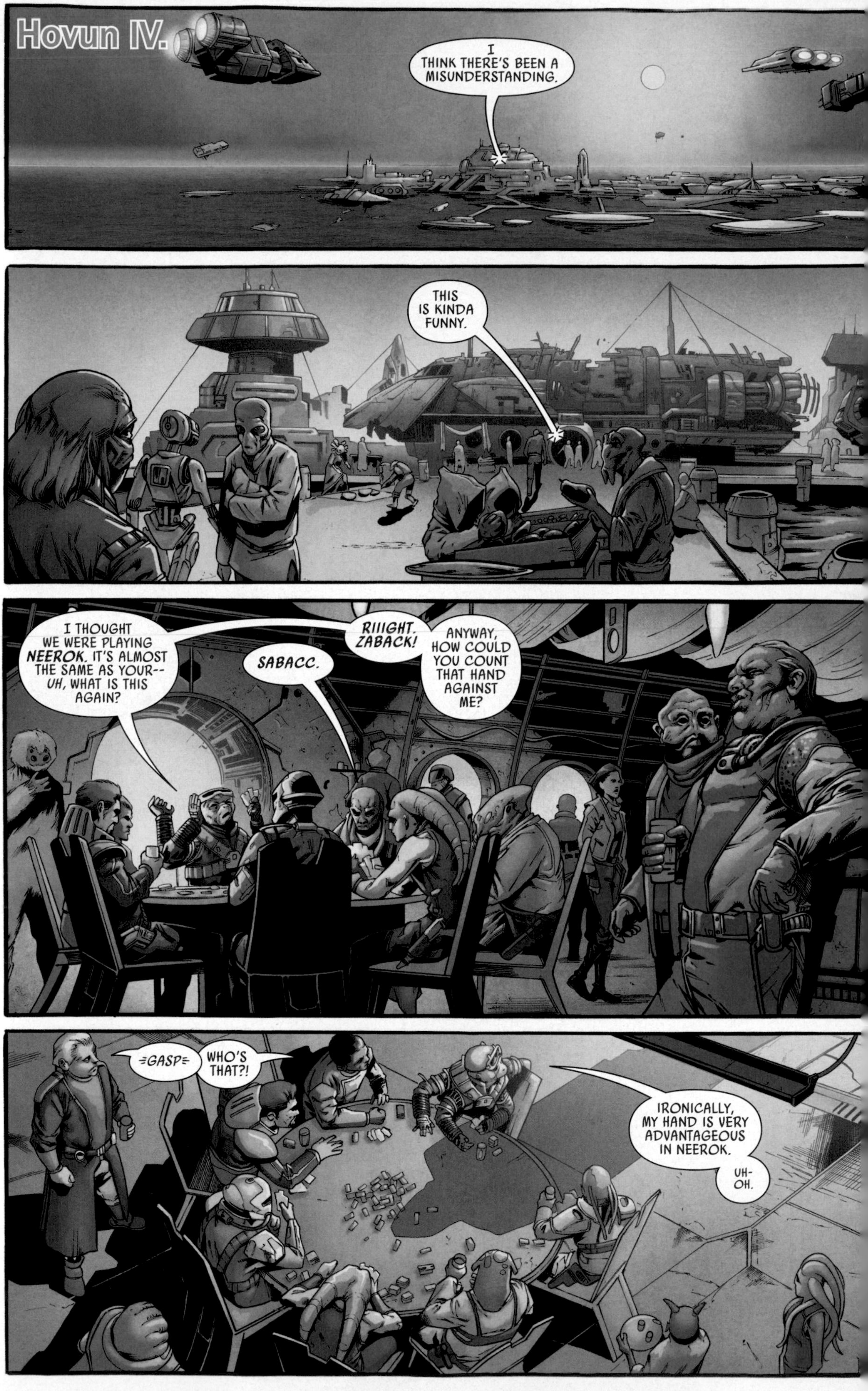
Hovun IV.
I THINK THERE'S BEEN A MISUNDERSTANDING.
THIS IS KINDA FUNNY.
I THOUGHT WE WERE PLAYING NEEROK. IT'S ALMOST THE SAME AS YOUR-- UH, WHAT IS THIS AGAIN?
SABACC.
RIIIGHT. ZABACK!
ANYWAY, HOW COULD YOU COUNT THAT HAND AGAINST ME?
=GASP=
WHO'S THAT?!
IRONICALLY, MY HAND IS VERY ADVANTAGEOUS IN NEEROK.
UH-OH.

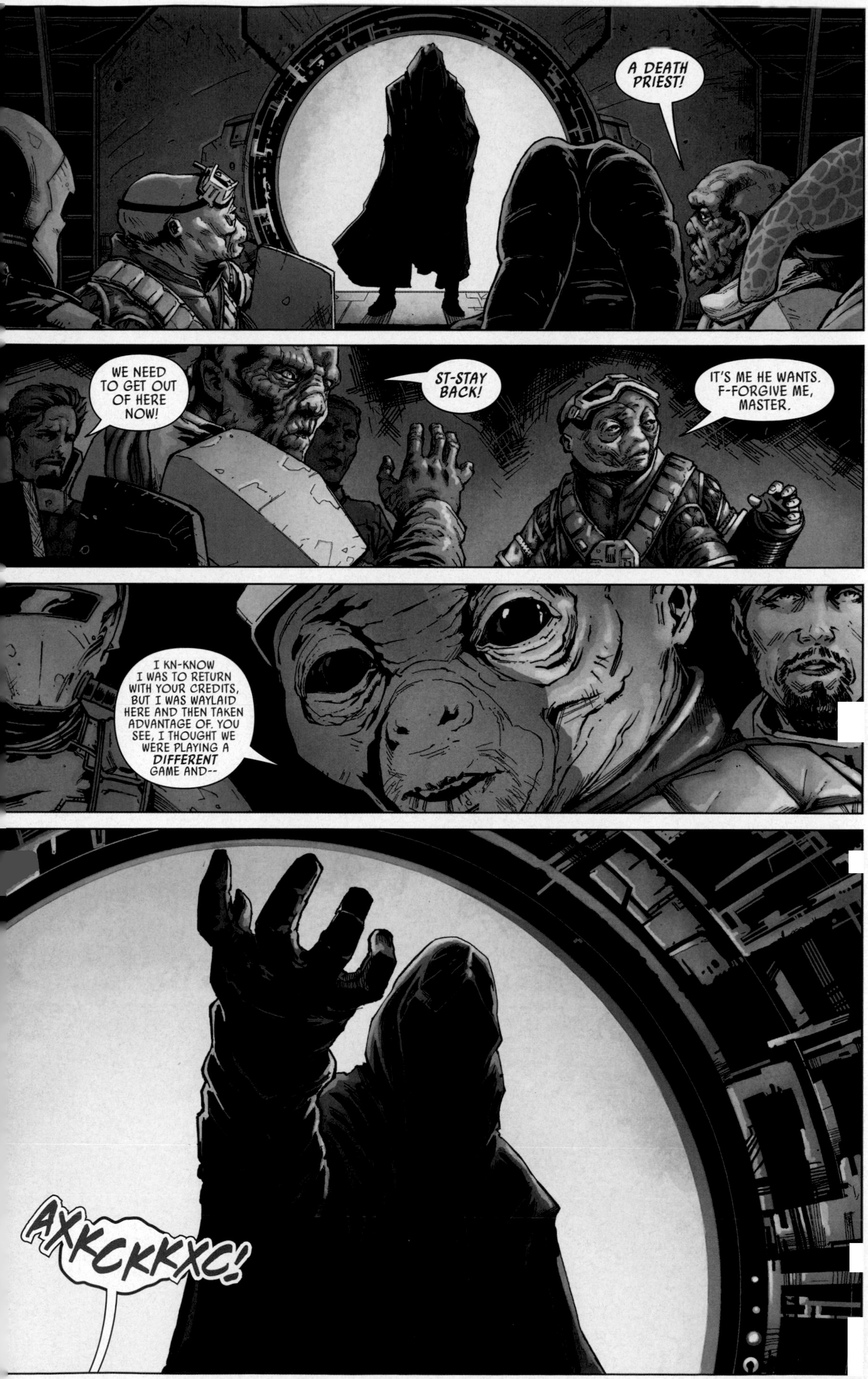

A DEATH PRIEST!
WE NEED TO GET OUT OF HERE NOW!
ST-STAY BACK!
IT'S ME HE WANTS. F-FORGIVE ME, MASTER.
I KN-KNOW I WAS TO RETURN WITH YOUR CREDITS, BUT I WAS WAYLAID HERE AND THEN TAKEN ADVANTAGE OF. YOU SEE, I THOUGHT WE WERE PLAYING A *DIFFERENT* GAME AND--
AXKCKKXC!

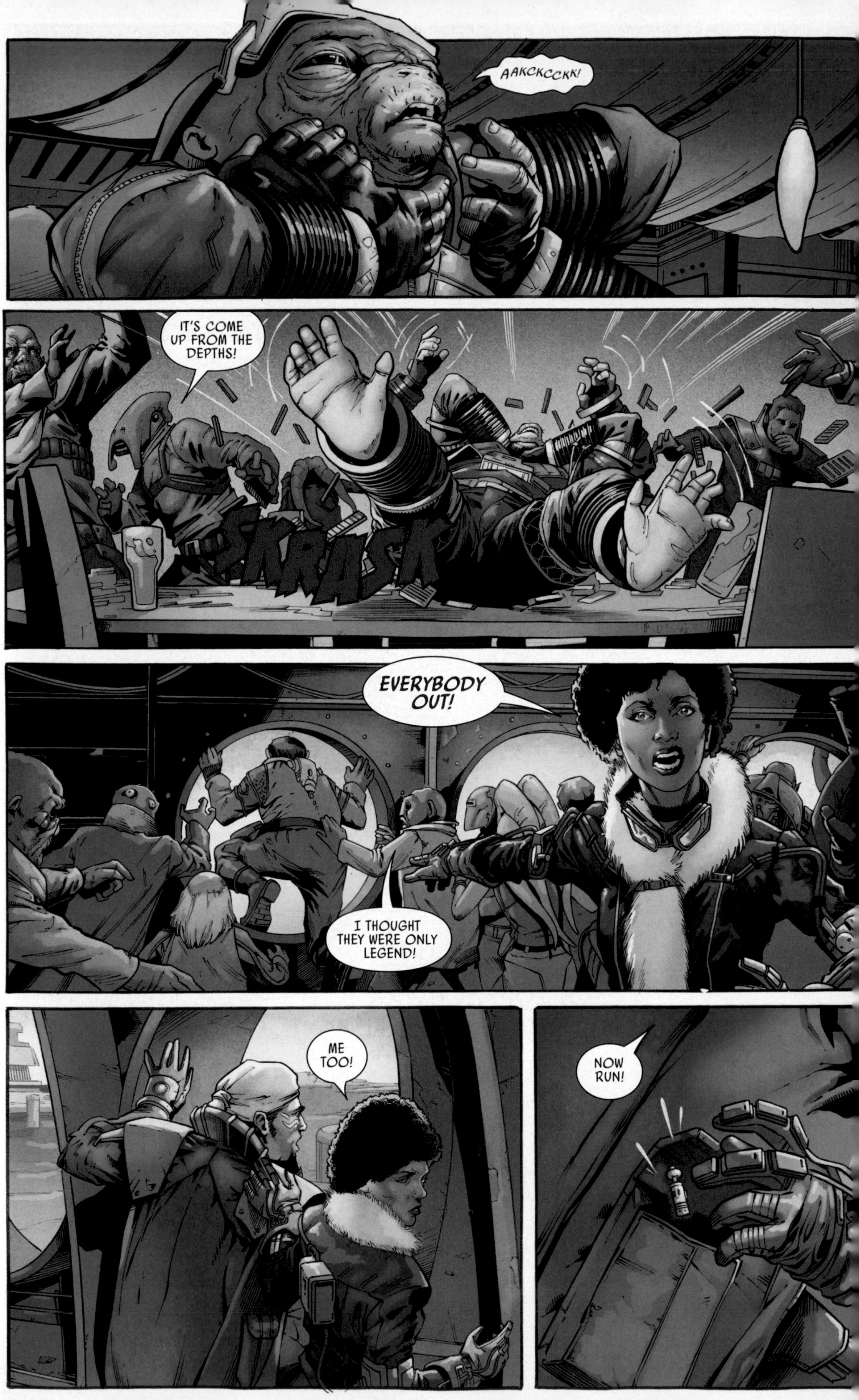
AAKCKCCKK!
IT'S COME UP FROM THE DEPTHS!
SKRASK
EVERYBODY OUT!
I THOUGHT THEY WERE ONLY LEGEND!
ME TOO!
NOW RUN!

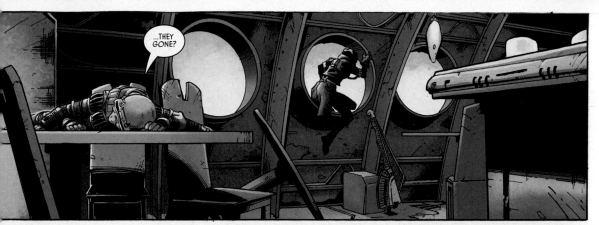

...THEY GONE?

NOBODY DIES LIKE YOU, RIO.

WHY DO YOU ALWAYS GET TO PLAY THE EVIL WIZARD, BECKETT?

'CAUSE I'VE GOT MORE CHARISMA THAN YOU DO. AND YOU'VE GOT MORE ARMS TO SCOOP UP THE TAKE. HOW'D WE DO, BY THE WAY?

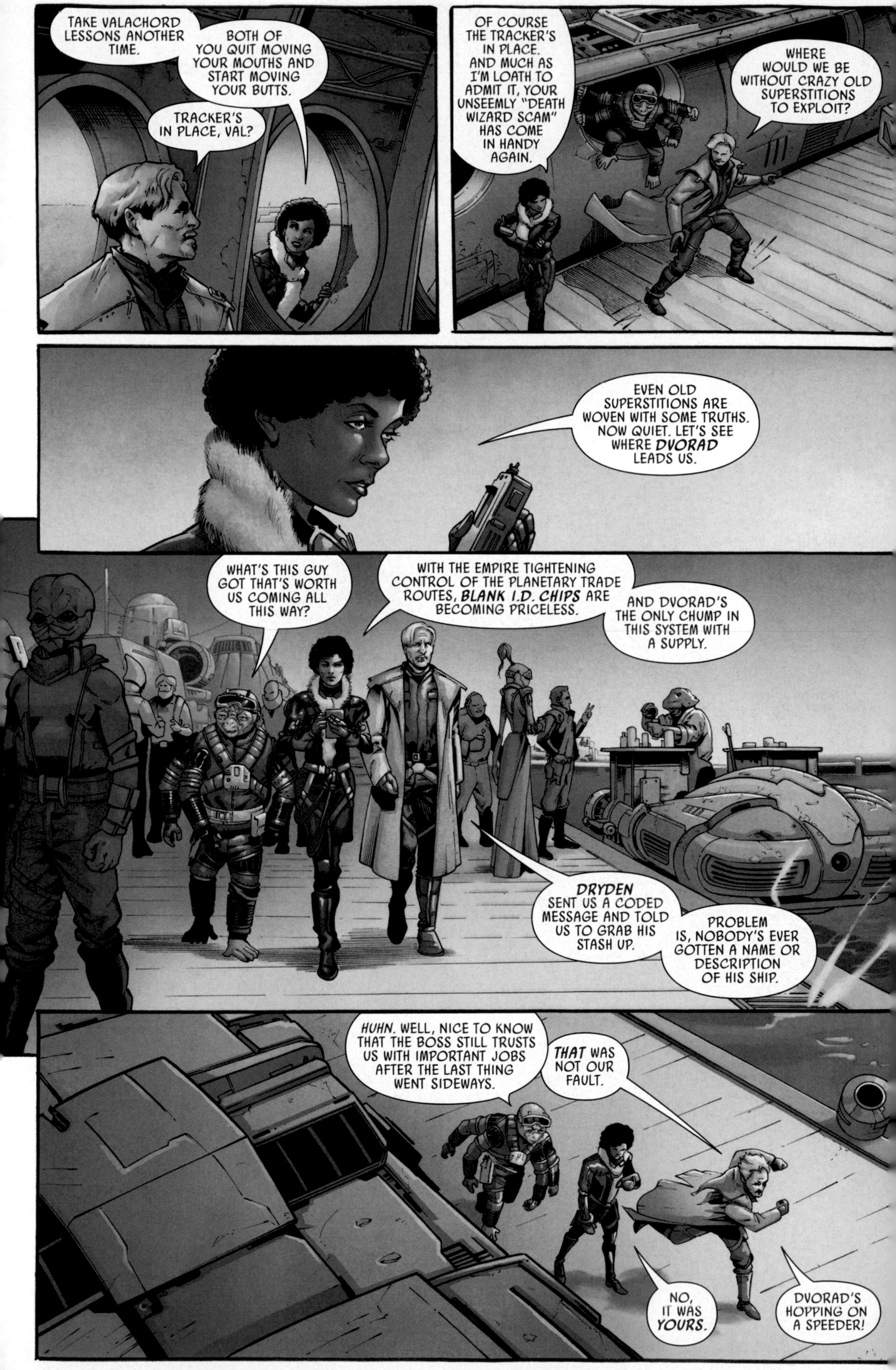
TAKE VALACHORD LESSONS ANOTHER TIME.
BOTH OF YOU QUIT MOVING YOUR MOUTHS AND START MOVING YOUR BUTTS.
TRACKER'S IN PLACE, VAL?
OF COURSE THE TRACKER'S IN PLACE. AND MUCH AS I'M LOATH TO ADMIT IT, YOUR UNSEEMLY "DEATH WIZARD SCAM" HAS COME IN HANDY AGAIN.
WHERE WOULD WE BE WITHOUT CRAZY OLD SUPERSTITIONS TO EXPLOIT?
EVEN OLD SUPERSTITIONS ARE WOVEN WITH SOME TRUTHS. NOW QUIET. LET'S SEE WHERE *DVORAD* LEADS US.
WHAT'S THIS GUY GOT THAT'S WORTH US COMING ALL THIS WAY?
WITH THE EMPIRE TIGHTENING CONTROL OF THE PLANETARY TRADE ROUTES, *BLANK I.D. CHIPS* ARE BECOMING PRICELESS.
AND DVORAD'S THE ONLY CHUMP IN THIS SYSTEM WITH A SUPPLY.
DRYDEN SENT US A CODED MESSAGE AND TOLD US TO GRAB HIS STASH UP.
PROBLEM IS, NOBODY'S EVER GOTTEN A NAME OR DESCRIPTION OF HIS SHIP.
HUHN. WELL, NICE TO KNOW THAT THE BOSS STILL TRUSTS US WITH IMPORTANT JOBS AFTER THE LAST THING WENT SIDEWAYS.
THAT WAS NOT OUR FAULT.
NO, IT WAS *YOURS.*
DVORAD'S HOPPING ON A SPEEDER!

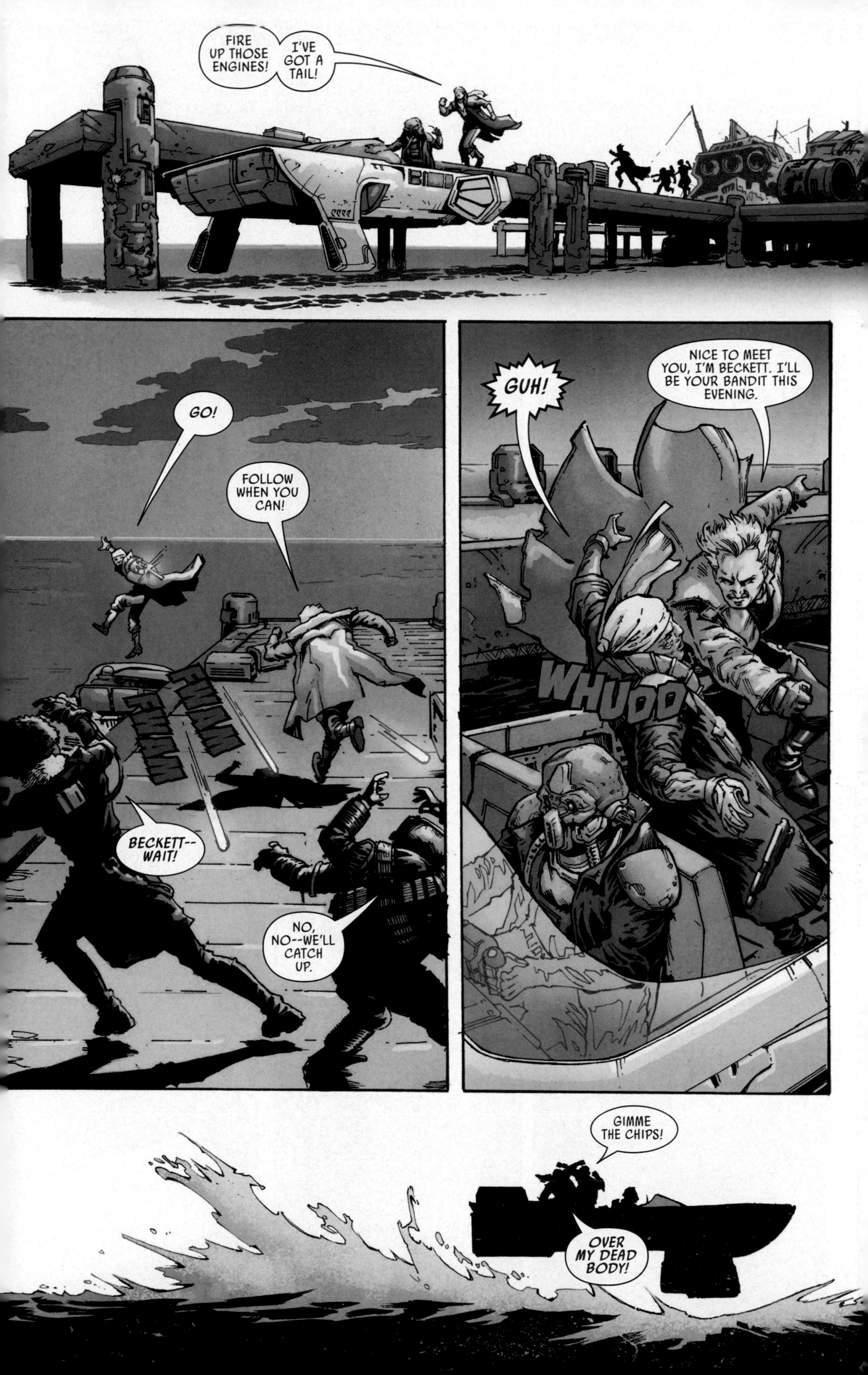
FIRE UP THOSE ENGINES!
I'VE GOT A TAIL!
GO!
FOLLOW WHEN YOU CAN!
FWAM
FWAM
FWAM
BECKETT--WAIT!
NO, NO--WE'LL CATCH UP.
GUH!
NICE TO MEET YOU, I'M BECKETT. I'LL BE YOUR BANDIT THIS EVENING.
WHUDD
GIMME THE CHIPS!
OVER MY DEAD BODY!

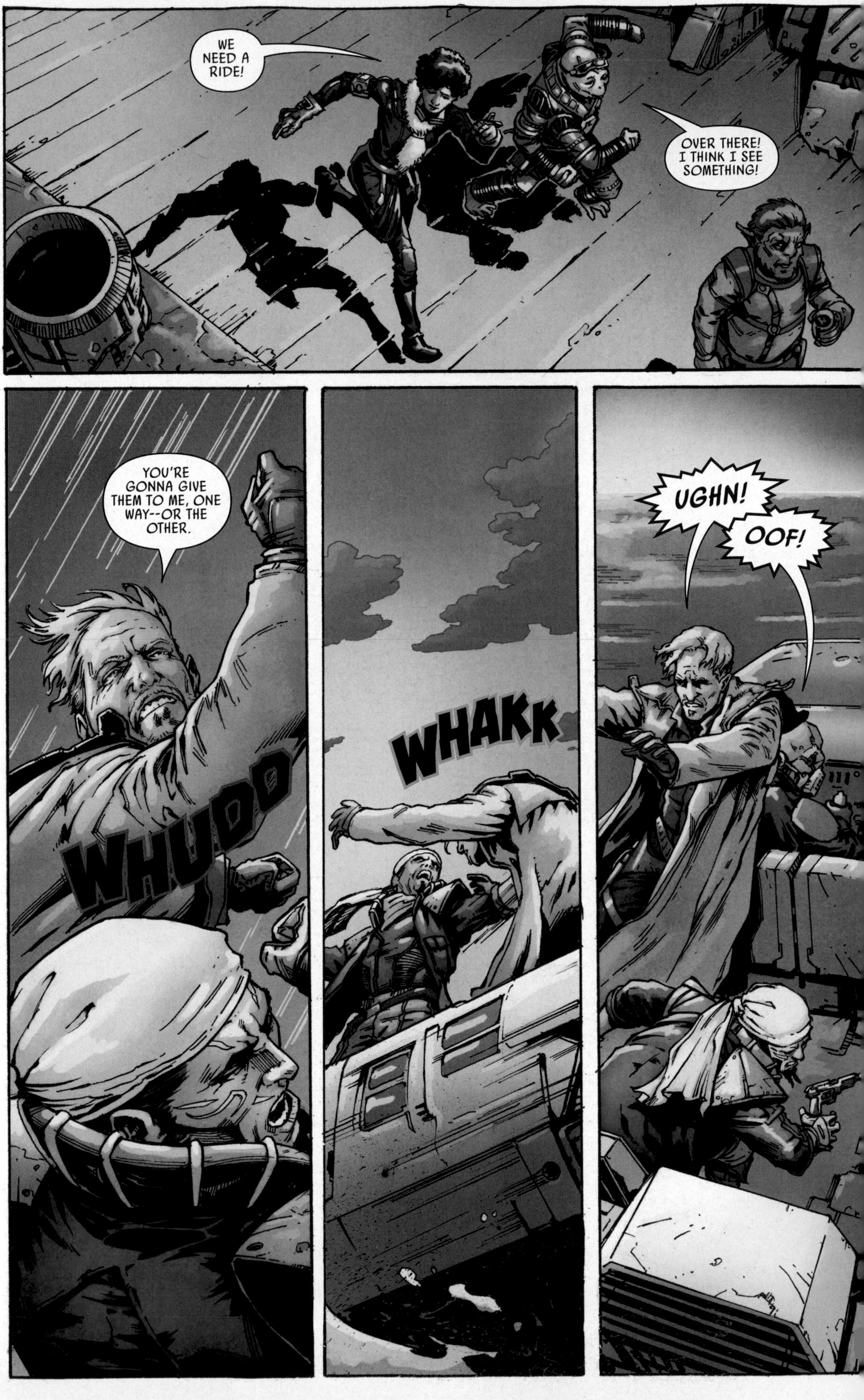
WE NEED A RIDE!
OVER THERE! I THINK I SEE SOMETHING!
YOU'RE GONNA GIVE THEM TO ME, ONE WAY--OR THE OTHER.
WHUDD
WHAKK
UGHN!
OOF!

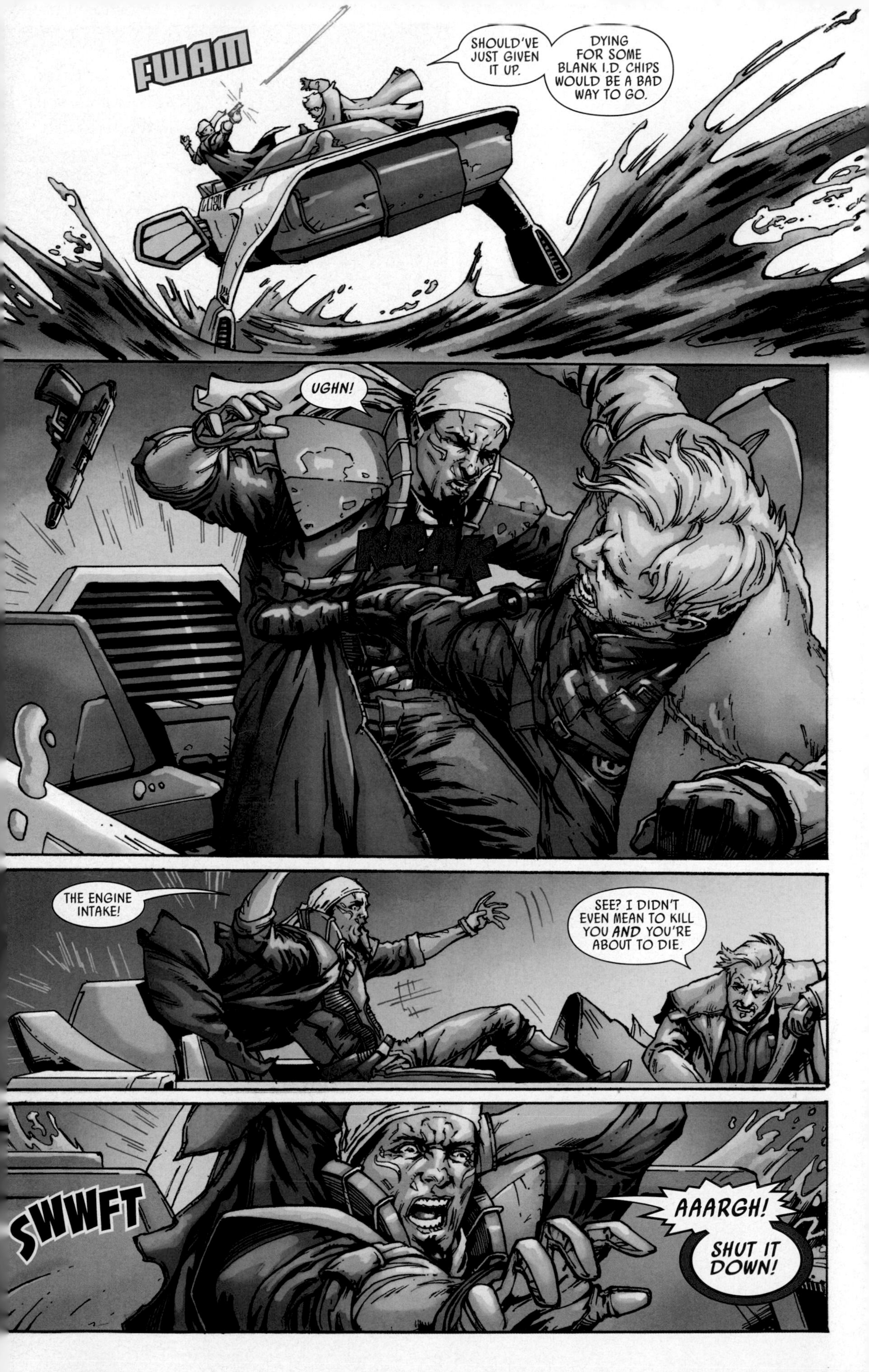
FWAM
SHOULD'VE JUST GIVEN IT UP.
DYING FOR SOME BLANK I.D. CHIPS WOULD BE A BAD WAY TO GO.
UGHN!
THE ENGINE INTAKE!
SEE? I DIDN'T EVEN MEAN TO KILL YOU AND YOU'RE ABOUT TO DIE.
SWWFT
AAARGH!
SHUT IT DOWN!

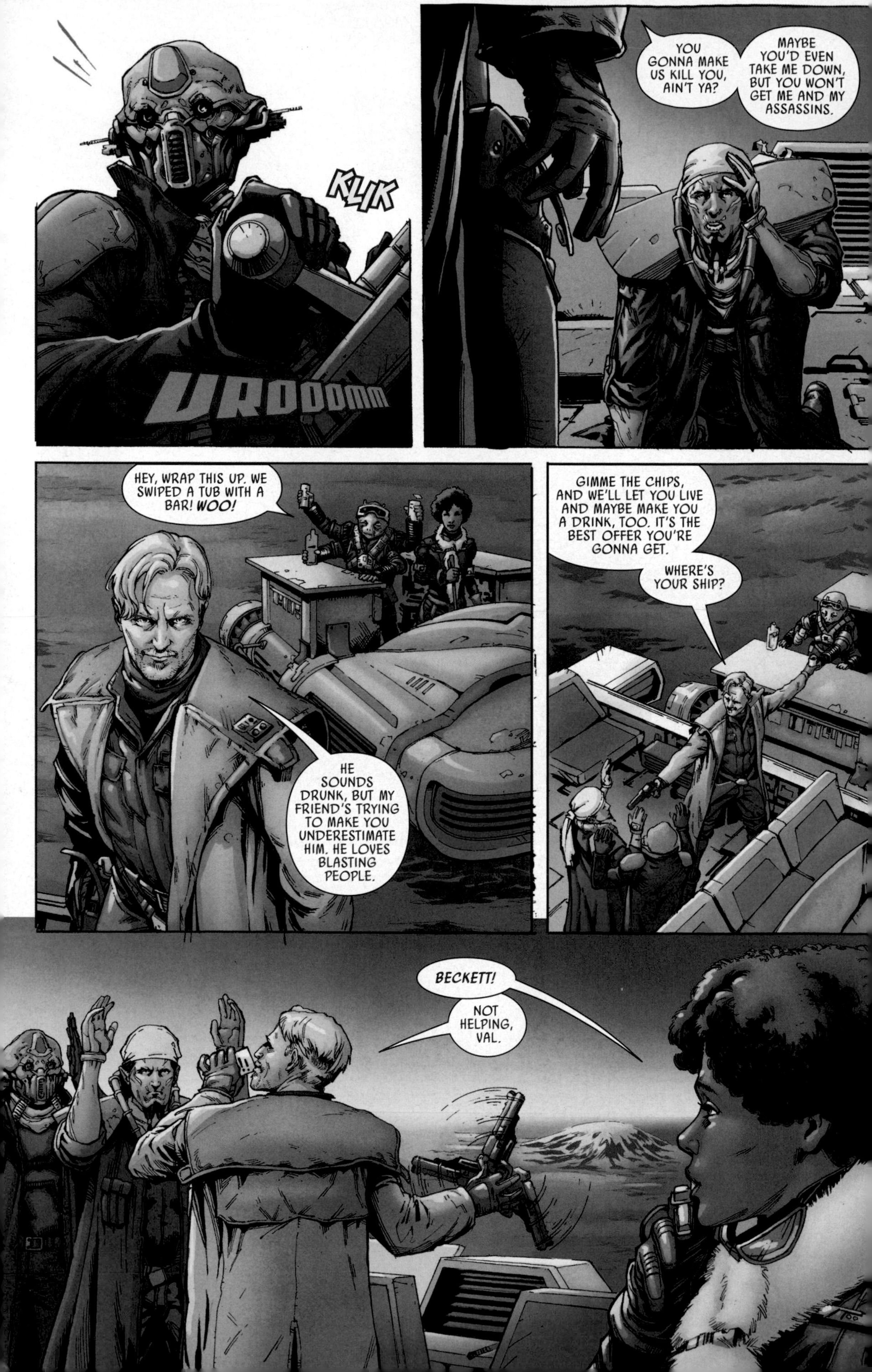
KLIK
VROOOMM
YOU GONNA MAKE US KILL YOU, AIN'T YA?
MAYBE YOU'D EVEN TAKE ME DOWN, BUT YOU WON'T GET ME AND MY ASSASSINS.
HEY, WRAP THIS UP. WE SWIPED A TUB WITH A BAR! WOO!
HE SOUNDS DRUNK, BUT MY FRIEND'S TRYING TO MAKE YOU UNDERESTIMATE HIM. HE LOVES BLASTING PEOPLE.
GIMME THE CHIPS, AND WE'LL LET YOU LIVE AND MAYBE MAKE YOU A DRINK, TOO. IT'S THE BEST OFFER YOU'RE GONNA GET.
WHERE'S YOUR SHIP?
BECKETT!
NOT HELPING, VAL.

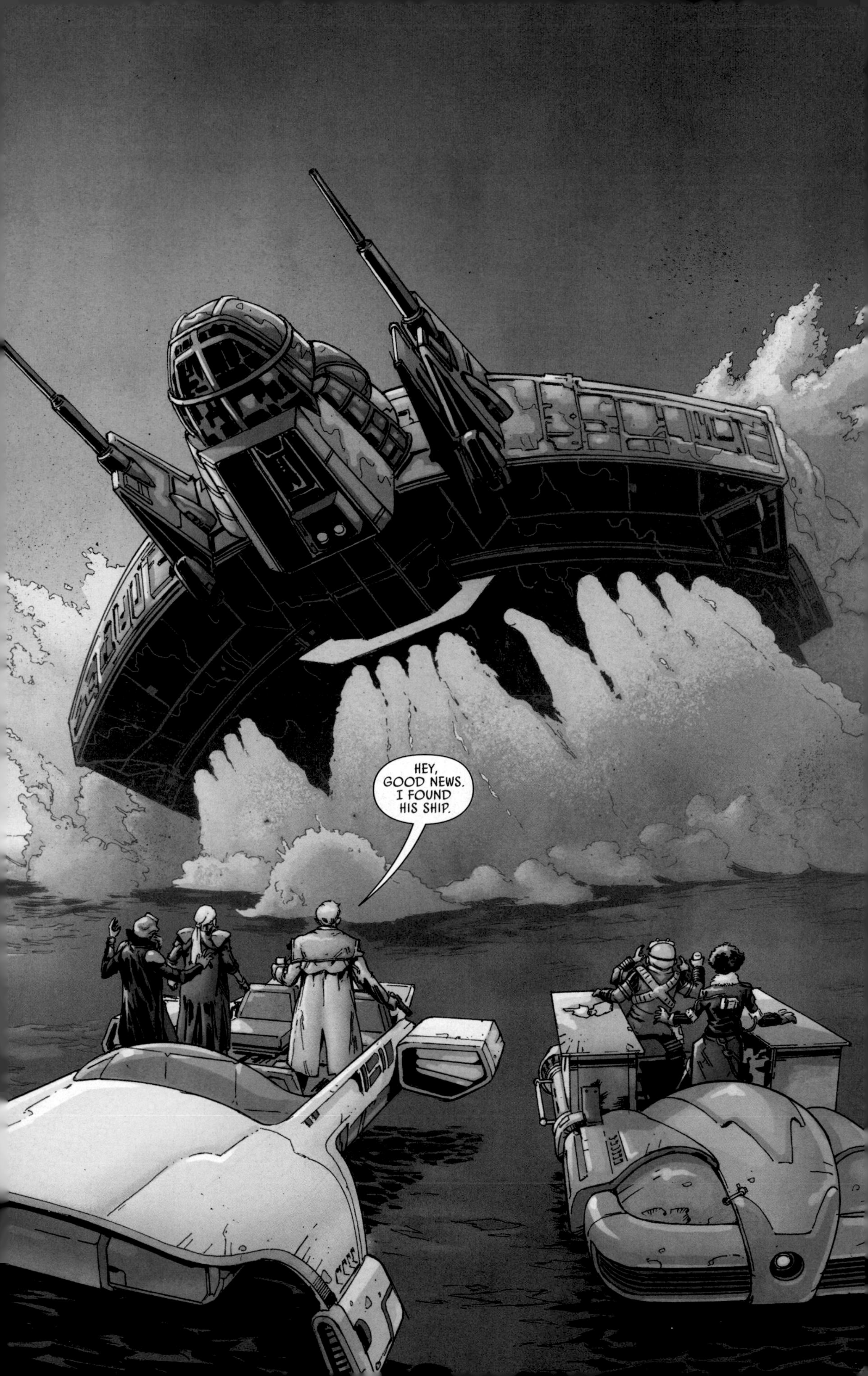
HEY, GOOD NEWS. I FOUND HIS SHIP.

Chapter Two

To Live
and Die
On Hovun IV

Illustrated by Marc Laming

2

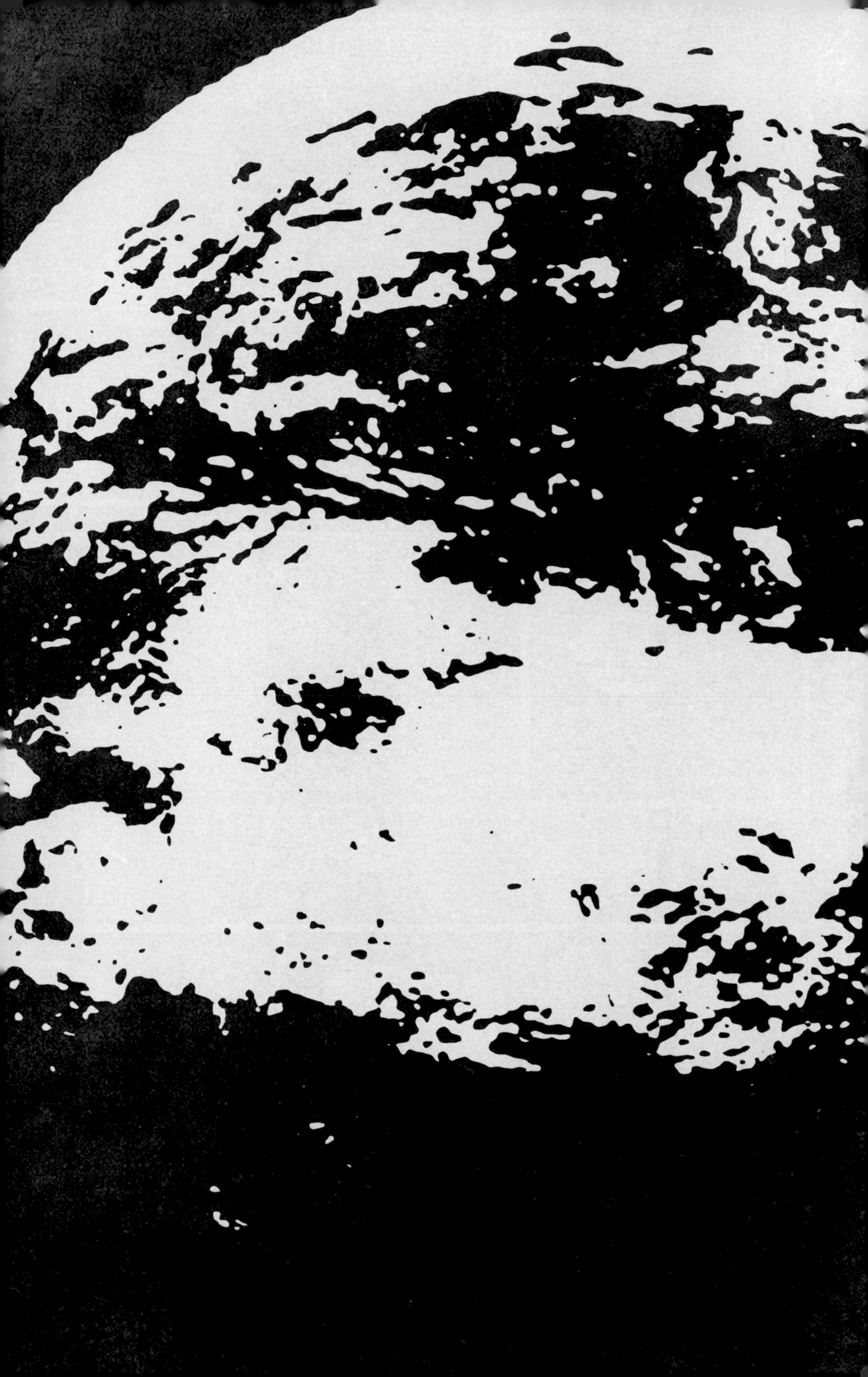

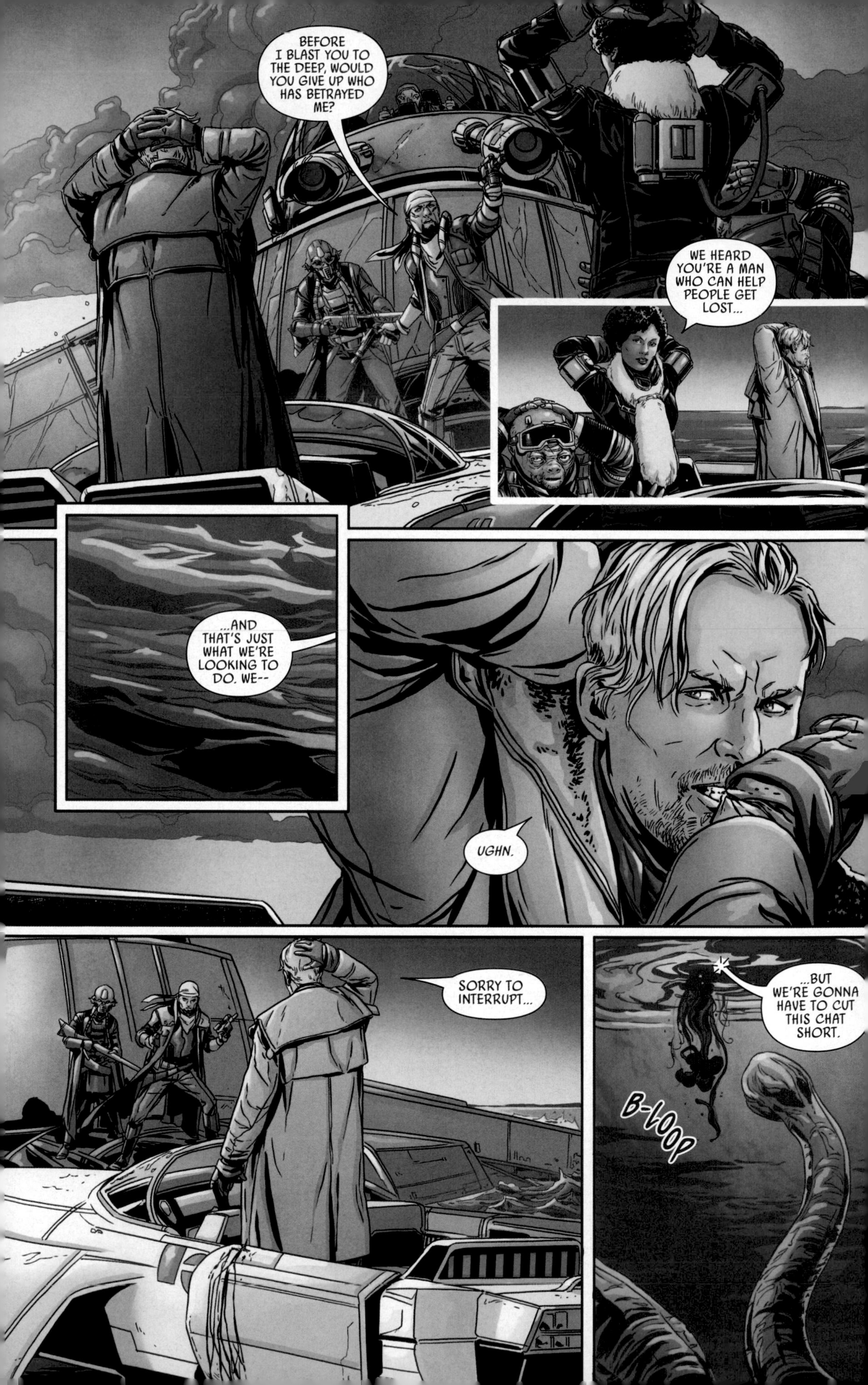
BEFORE I BLAST YOU TO THE DEEP, WOULD YOU GIVE UP WHO HAS BETRAYED ME?
WE HEARD YOU'RE A MAN WHO CAN HELP PEOPLE GET LOST...
...AND THAT'S JUST WHAT WE'RE LOOKING TO DO. WE--
UGHN.
SORRY TO INTERRUPT...
...BUT WE'RE GONNA HAVE TO CUT THIS CHAT SHORT.
B-LOOP

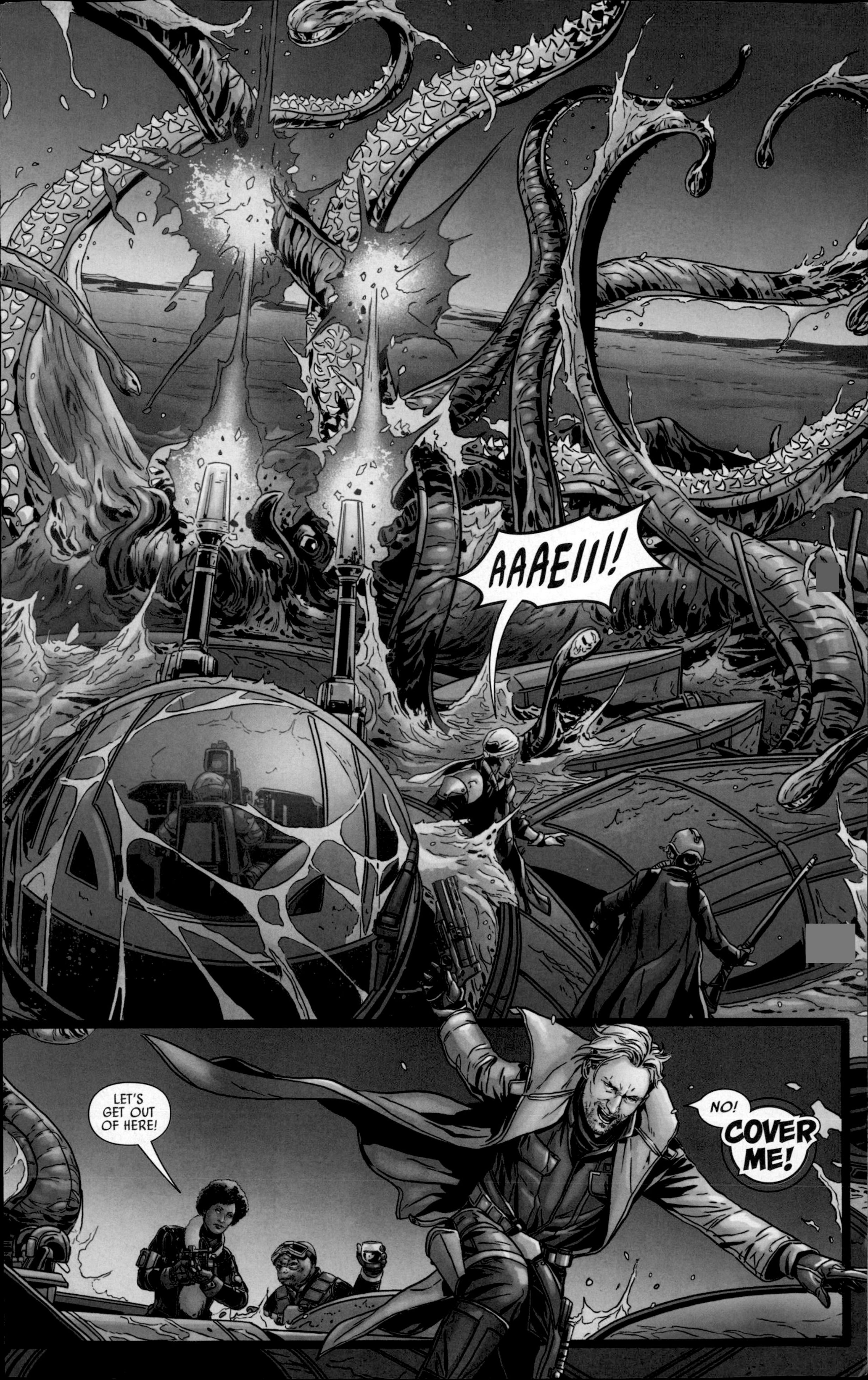
AAAEIII!
LET'S GET OUT OF HERE!
NO! COVER ME!

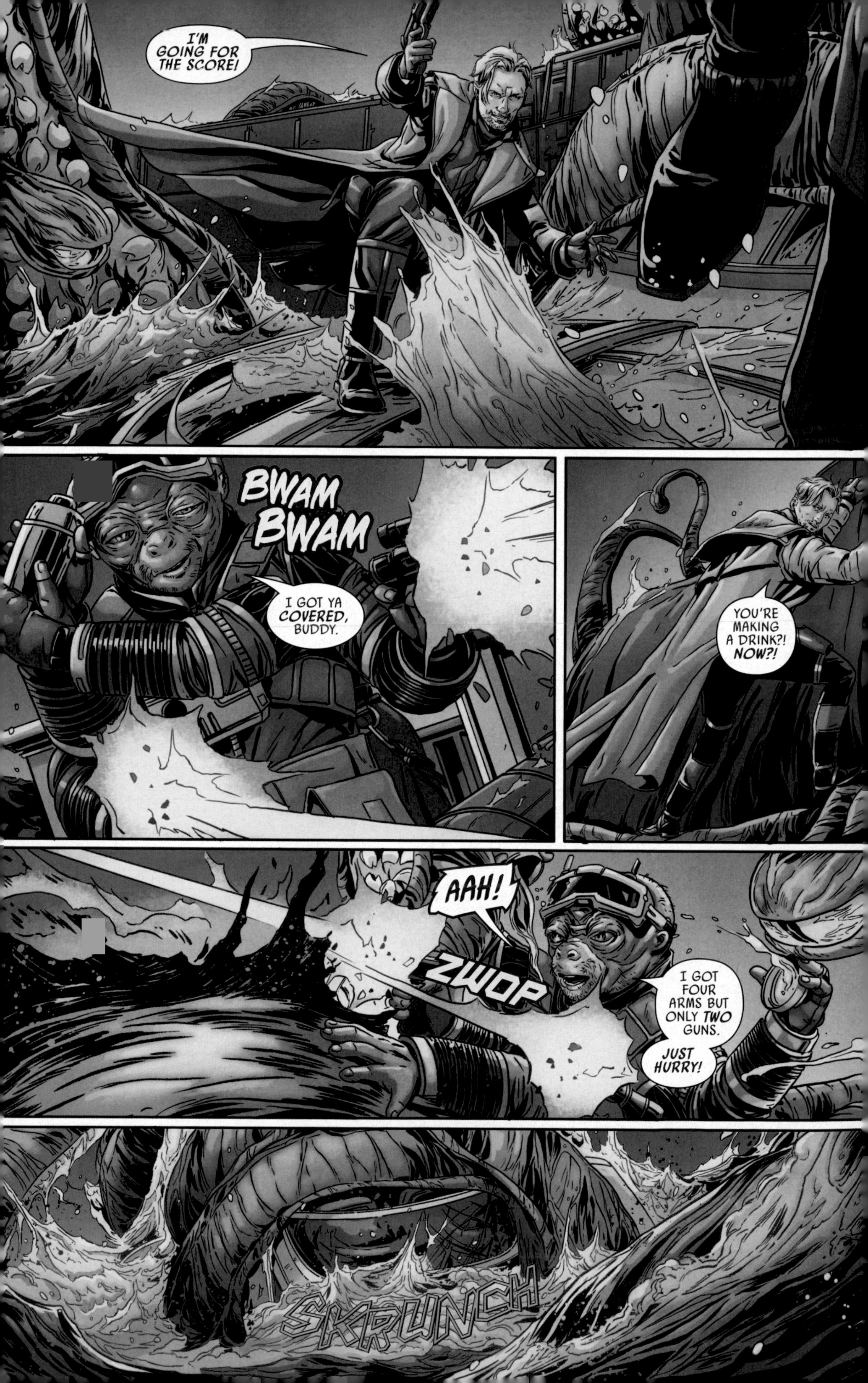
I'M GOING FOR THE SCORE!
BWAM BWAM
I GOT YA COVERED, BUDDY.
YOU'RE MAKING A DRINK?! NOW?!
AAH!
ZWOP
I GOT FOUR ARMS BUT ONLY TWO GUNS.
JUST HURRY!
SKRUNCH

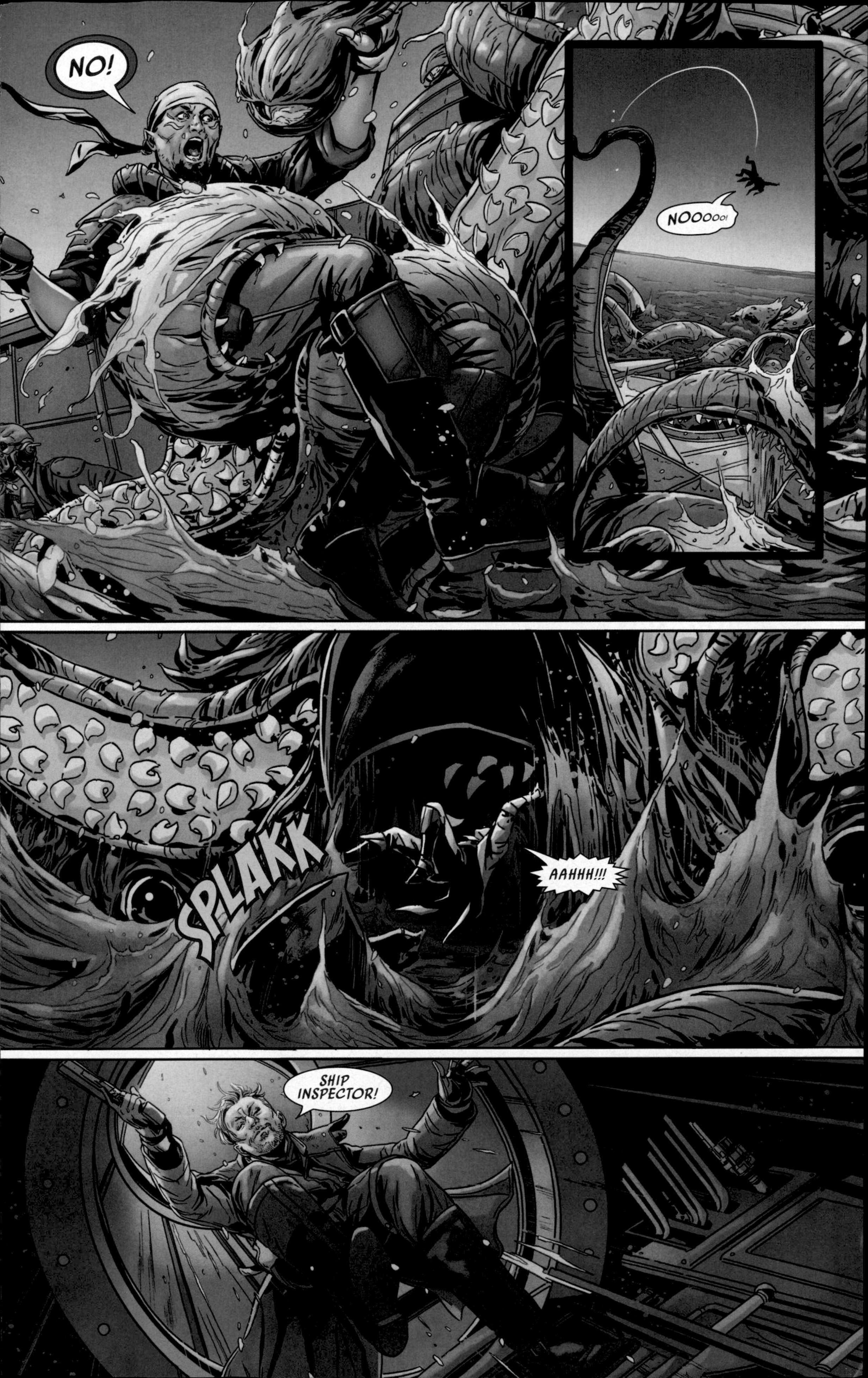
NO!
NOOooo!
SPLAKK
AAHHH!!!
SHIP INSPECTOR!

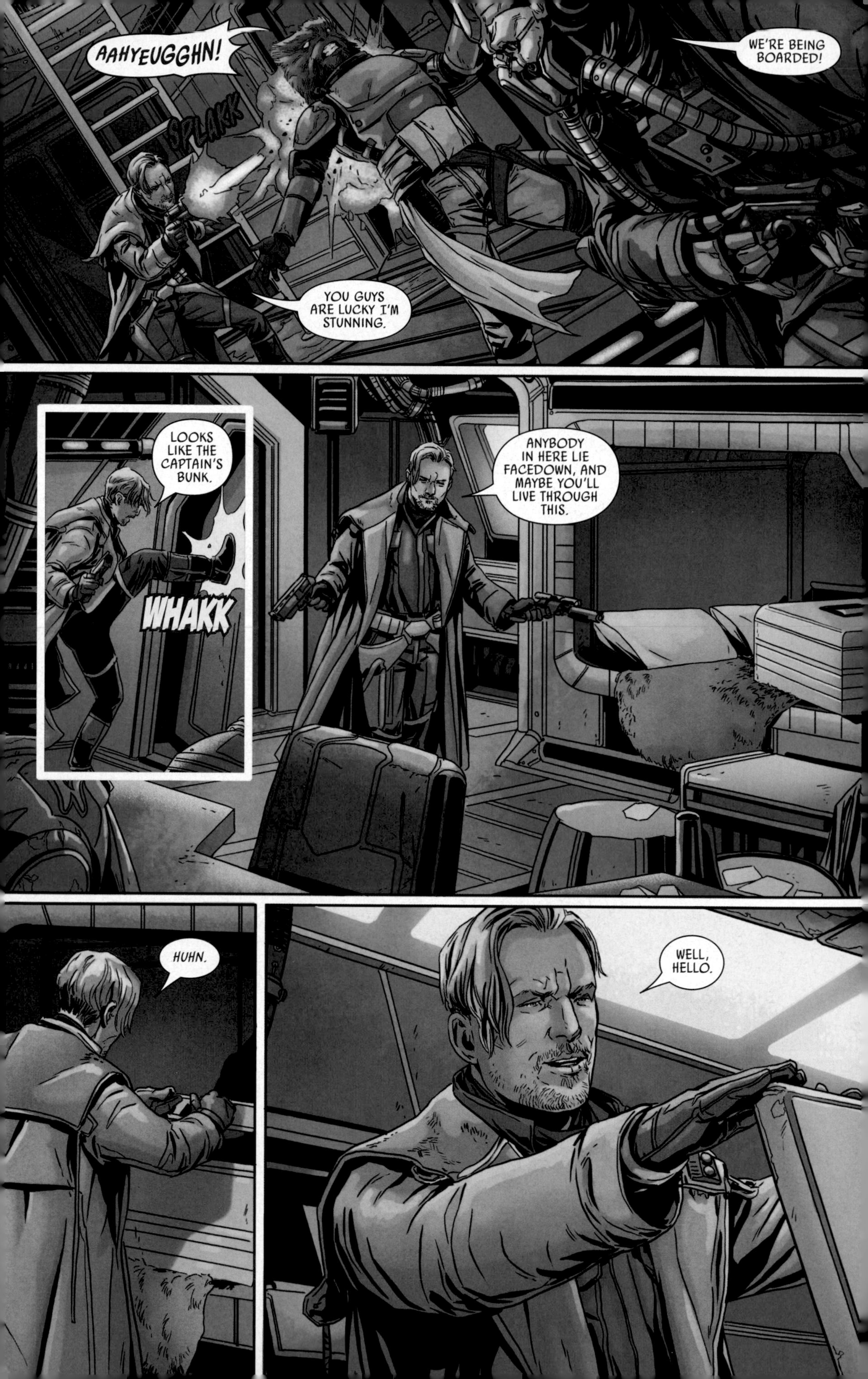
AAHYEUGGHN!
SPLAKK
WE'RE BEING BOARDED!
YOU GUYS ARE LUCKY I'M STUNNING.
LOOKS LIKE THE CAPTAIN'S BUNK.
WHAKK
ANYBODY IN HERE LIE FACEDOWN, AND MAYBE YOU'LL LIVE THROUGH THIS.
HUHN.
WELL, HELLO.

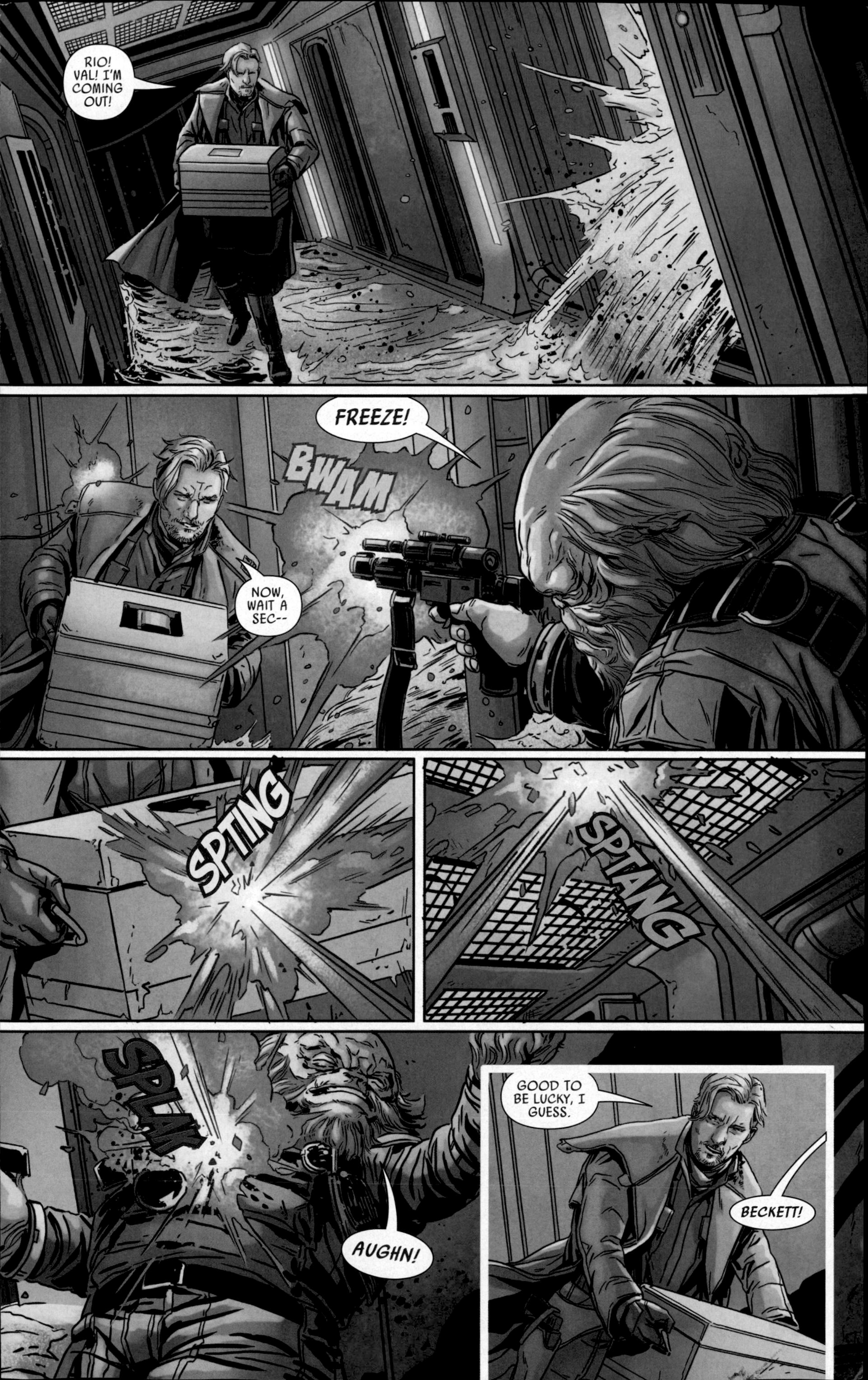
RIO! VAL! I'M COMING OUT!
FREEZE!
BWAM
NOW, WAIT A SEC--
SPTING
SPTANG
SPLAK
AUGHN!
GOOD TO BE LUCKY, I GUESS.
BECKETT!

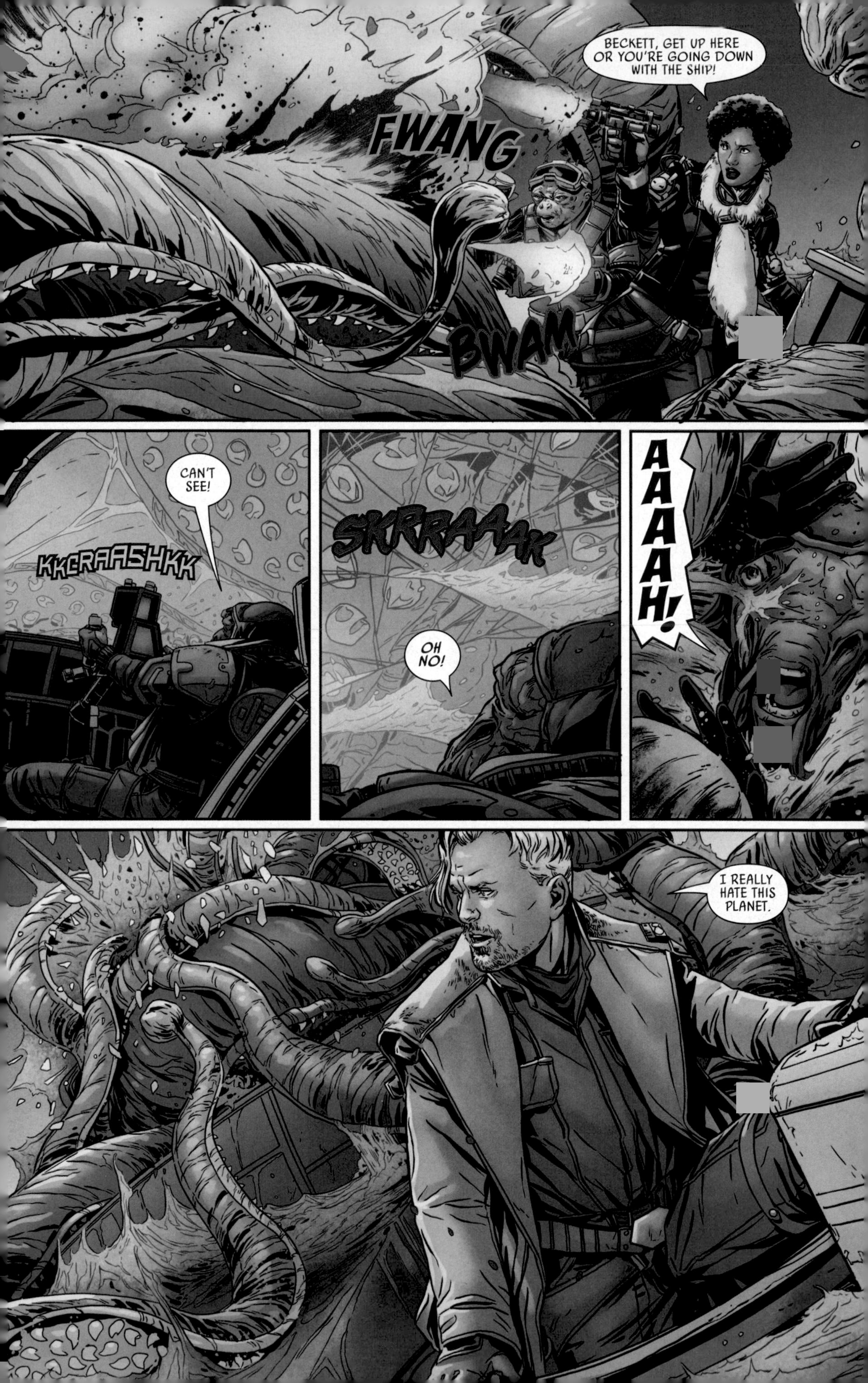
BECKETT, GET UP HERE OR YOU'RE GOING DOWN WITH THE SHIP!
FWANG
BWAM
CAN'T SEE!
KKCRAASHKK
SKRRAAAAK
OH NO!
AAAAAH!
I REALLY HATE THIS PLANET.

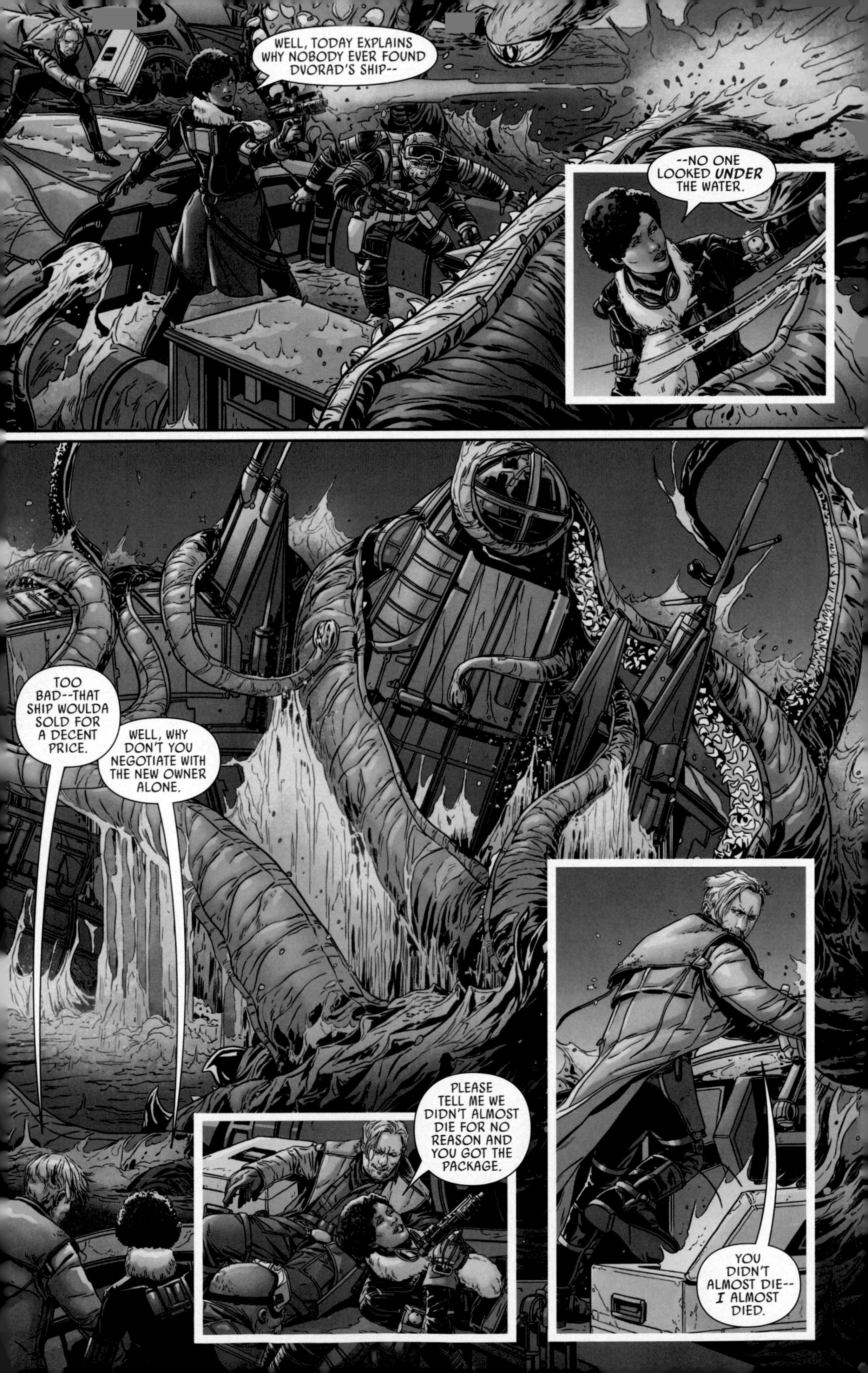
WELL, TODAY EXPLAINS WHY NOBODY EVER FOUND DVORAD'S SHIP--
--NO ONE LOOKED UNDER THE WATER.
TOO BAD--THAT SHIP WOULDA SOLD FOR A DECENT PRICE.
WELL, WHY DON'T YOU NEGOTIATE WITH THE NEW OWNER ALONE.
PLEASE TELL ME WE DIDN'T ALMOST DIE FOR NO REASON AND YOU GOT THE PACKAGE.
YOU DIDN'T ALMOST DIE-- I ALMOST DIED.

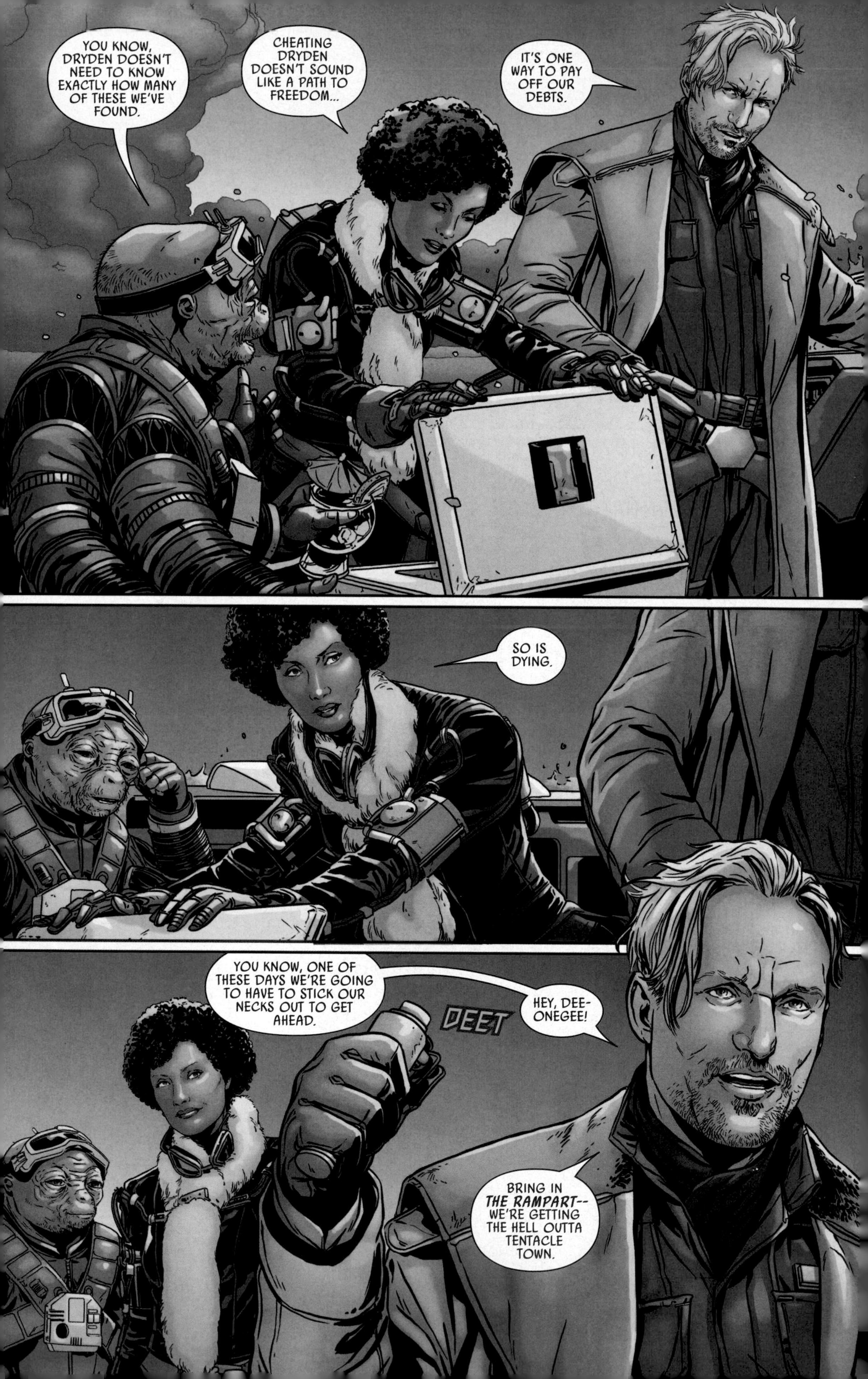
YOU KNOW, DRYDEN DOESN'T NEED TO KNOW EXACTLY HOW MANY OF THESE WE'VE FOUND.
CHEATING DRYDEN DOESN'T SOUND LIKE A PATH TO FREEDOM...
IT'S ONE WAY TO PAY OFF OUR DEBTS.
SO IS DYING.
YOU KNOW, ONE OF THESE DAYS WE'RE GOING TO HAVE TO STICK OUR NECKS OUT TO GET AHEAD.
DEET
HEY, DEE-ONEGEE!
BRING IN *THE RAMPART*-- WE'RE GETTING THE HELL OUTTA TENTACLE TOWN.

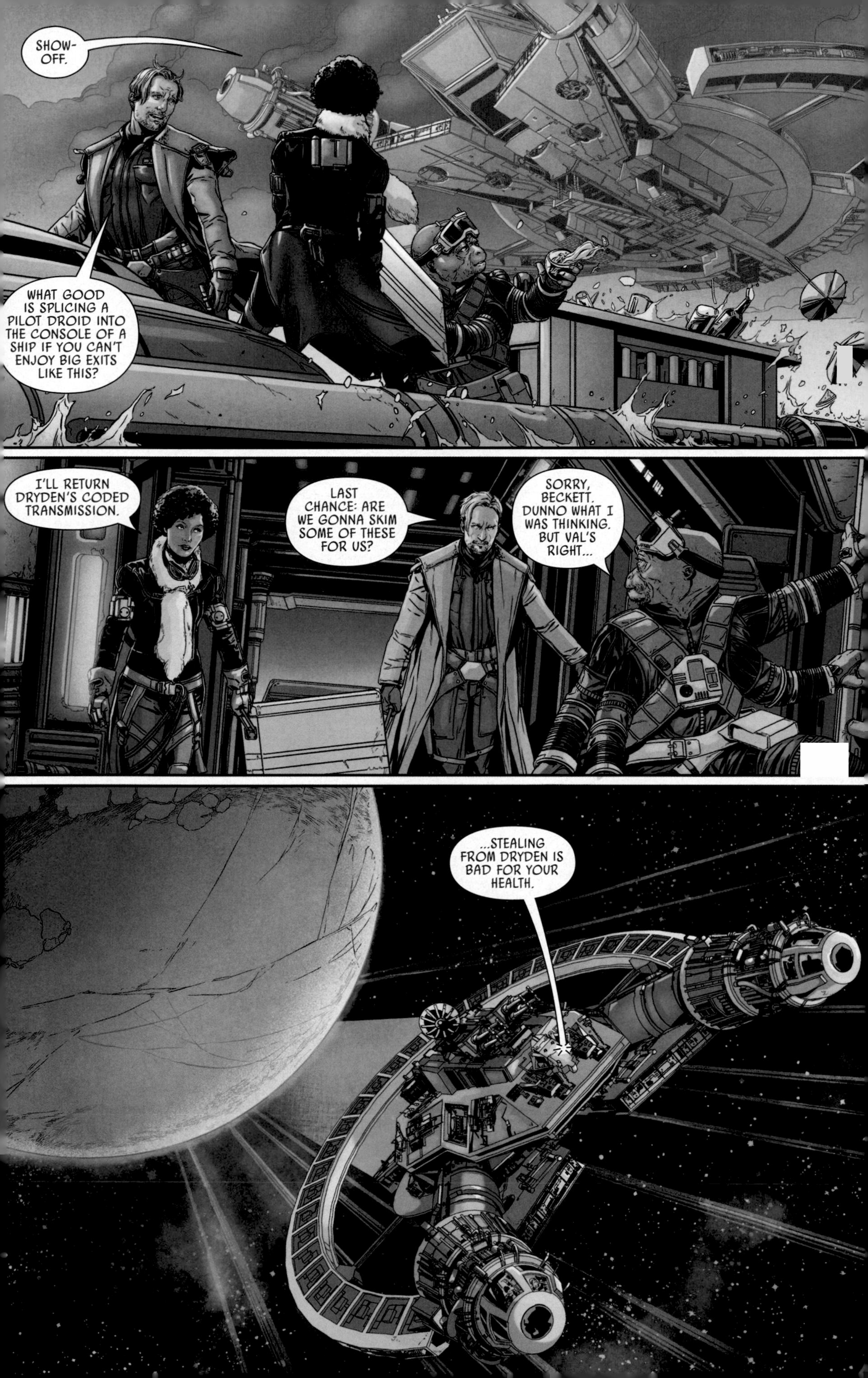
SHOW-OFF.
WHAT GOOD IS SPLICING A PILOT DROID INTO THE CONSOLE OF A SHIP IF YOU CAN'T ENJOY BIG EXITS LIKE THIS?
I'LL RETURN DRYDEN'S CODED TRANSMISSION.
LAST CHANCE: ARE WE GONNA SKIM SOME OF THESE FOR US?
SORRY, BECKETT. DUNNO WHAT I WAS THINKING. BUT VAL'S RIGHT...
...STEALING FROM DRYDEN IS BAD FOR YOUR HEALTH.

Chapter Three

You and the Bantha You Rode In On

Illustrated by Will Sliney

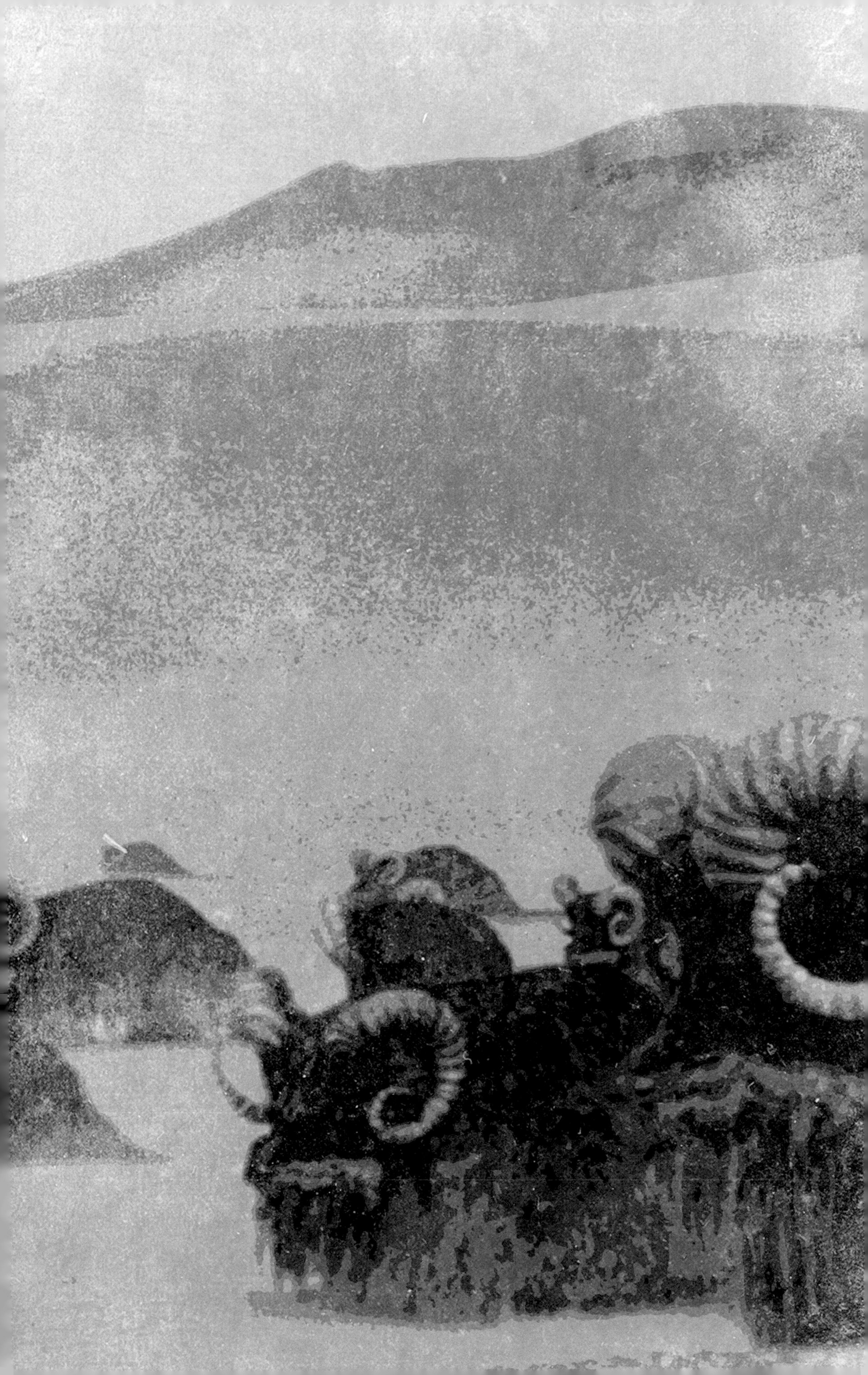

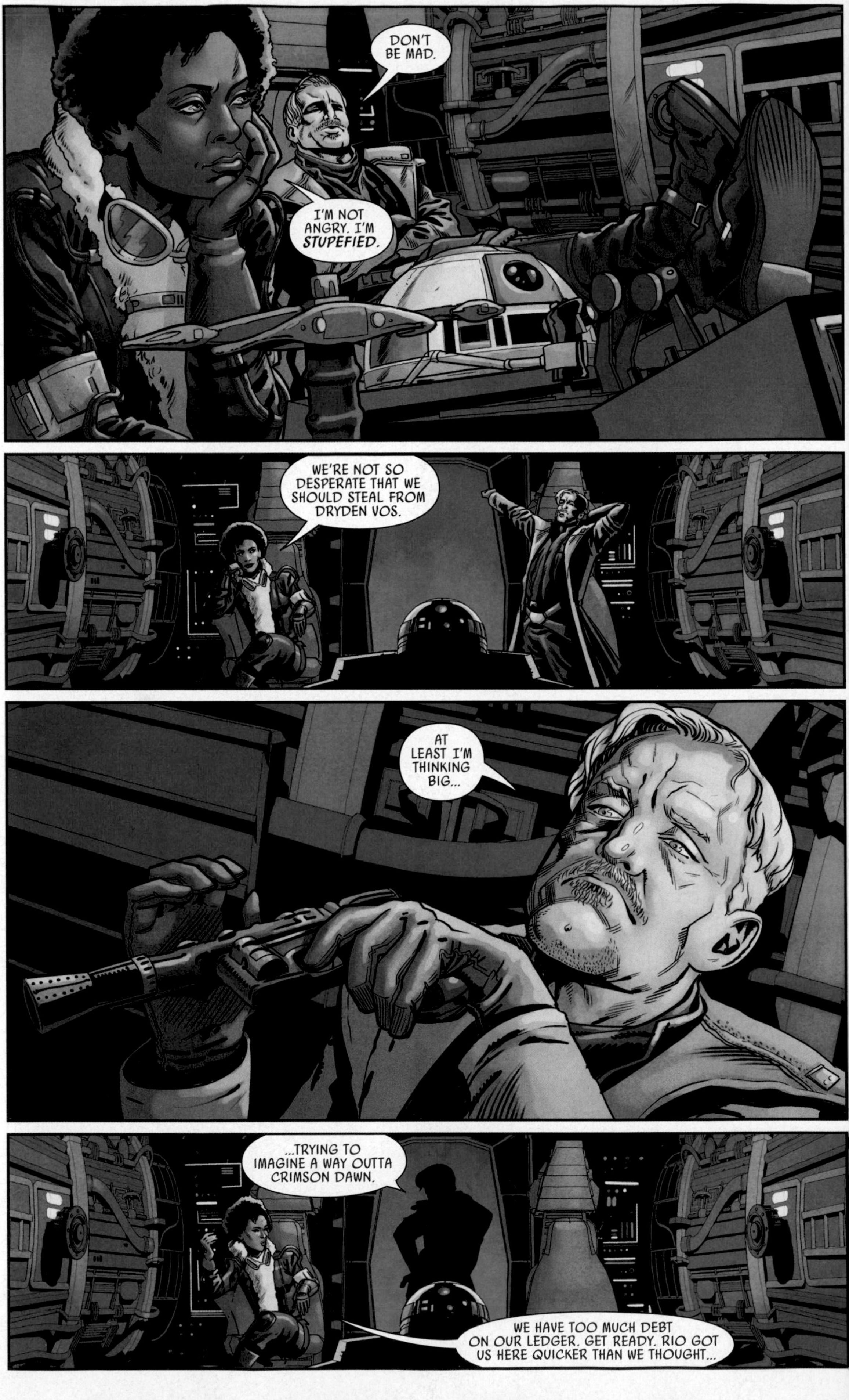
DON'T BE MAD.
I'M NOT ANGRY. I'M STUPEFIED.
WE'RE NOT SO DESPERATE THAT WE SHOULD STEAL FROM DRYDEN VOS.
AT LEAST I'M THINKING BIG...
...TRYING TO IMAGINE A WAY OUTTA CRIMSON DAWN.
WE HAVE TOO MUCH DEBT ON OUR LEDGER. GET READY. RIO GOT US HERE QUICKER THAN WE THOUGHT...

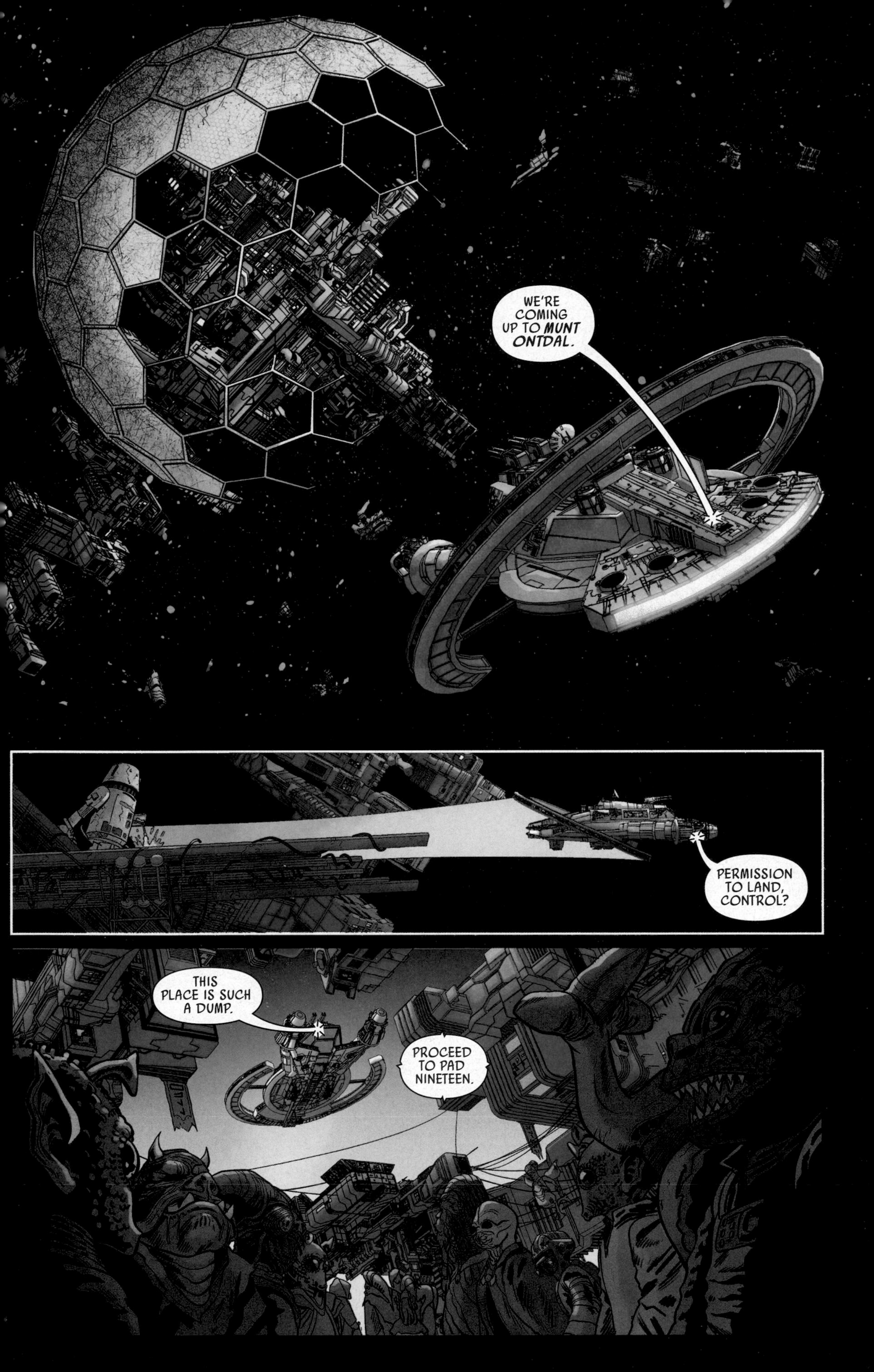
WE'RE COMING UP TO MUNT ONTDAL.
PERMISSION TO LAND, CONTROL?
THIS PLACE IS SUCH A DUMP.
PROCEED TO PAD NINETEEN.

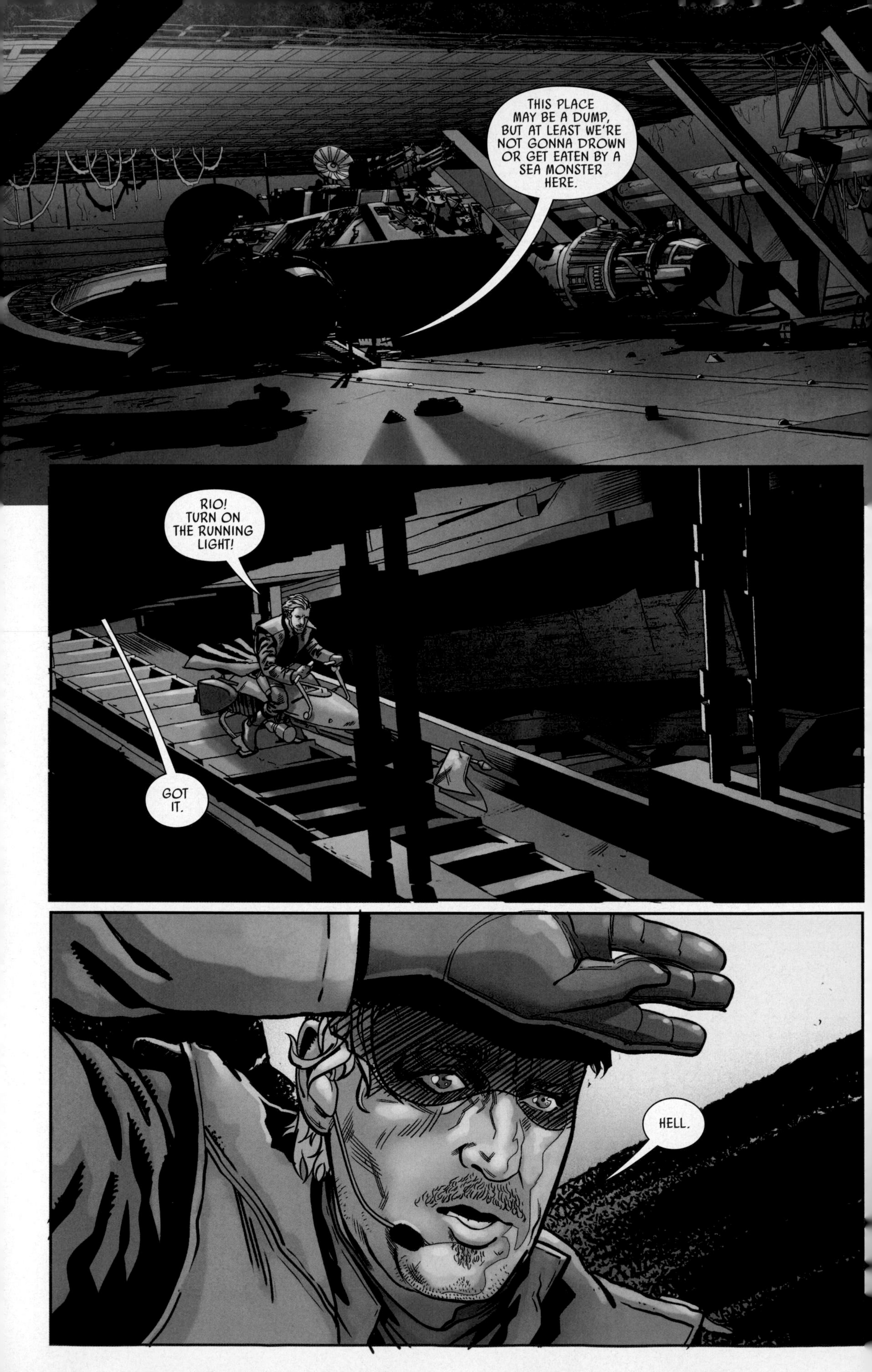
THIS PLACE MAY BE A DUMP, BUT AT LEAST WE'RE NOT GONNA DROWN OR GET EATEN BY A SEA MONSTER HERE.
RIO! TURN ON THE RUNNING LIGHT!
GOT IT.
HELL.

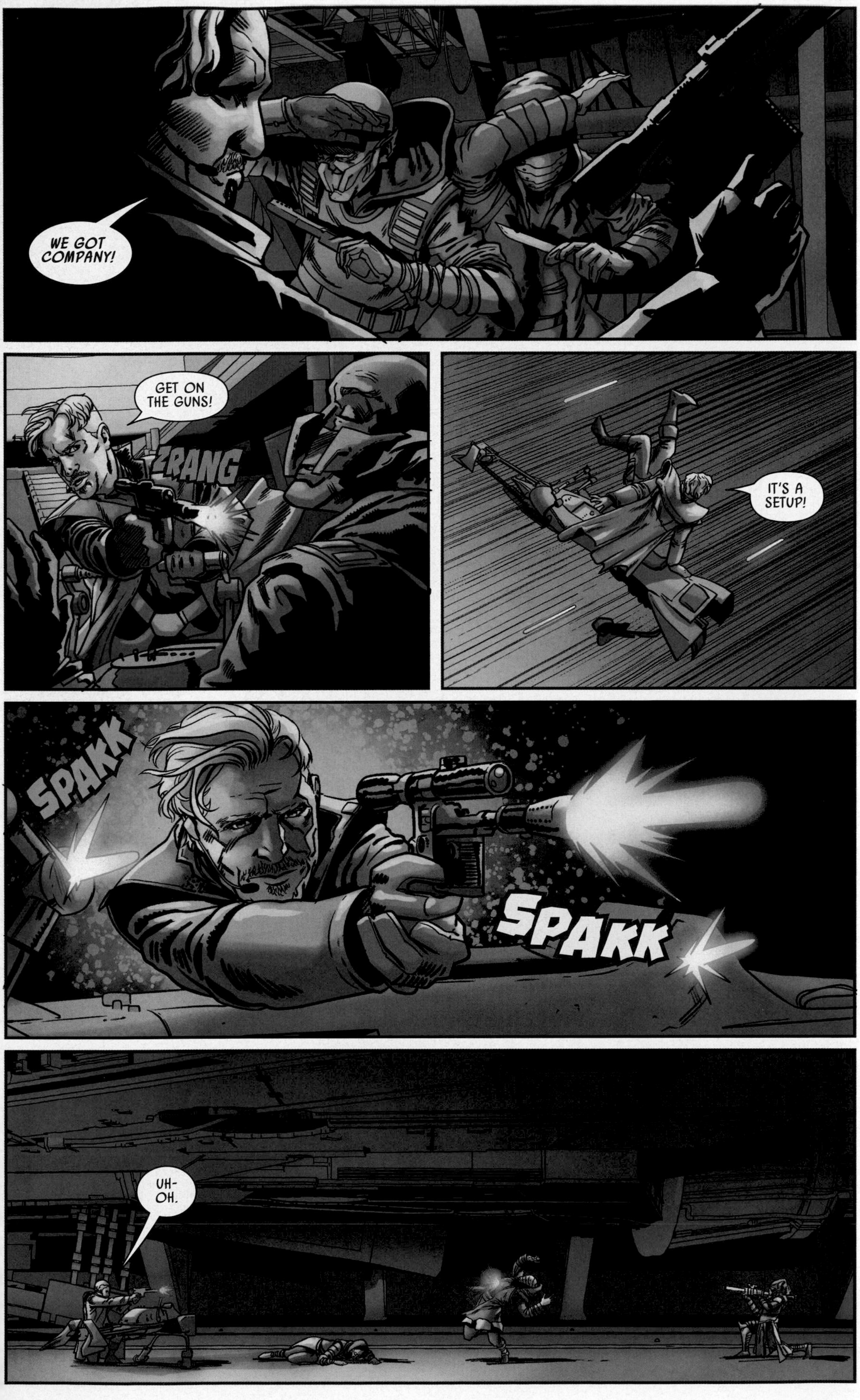
WE GOT COMPANY!
GET ON THE GUNS!
ZRANG
IT'S A SETUP!
SPAKK
SPAKK
UH-OH.

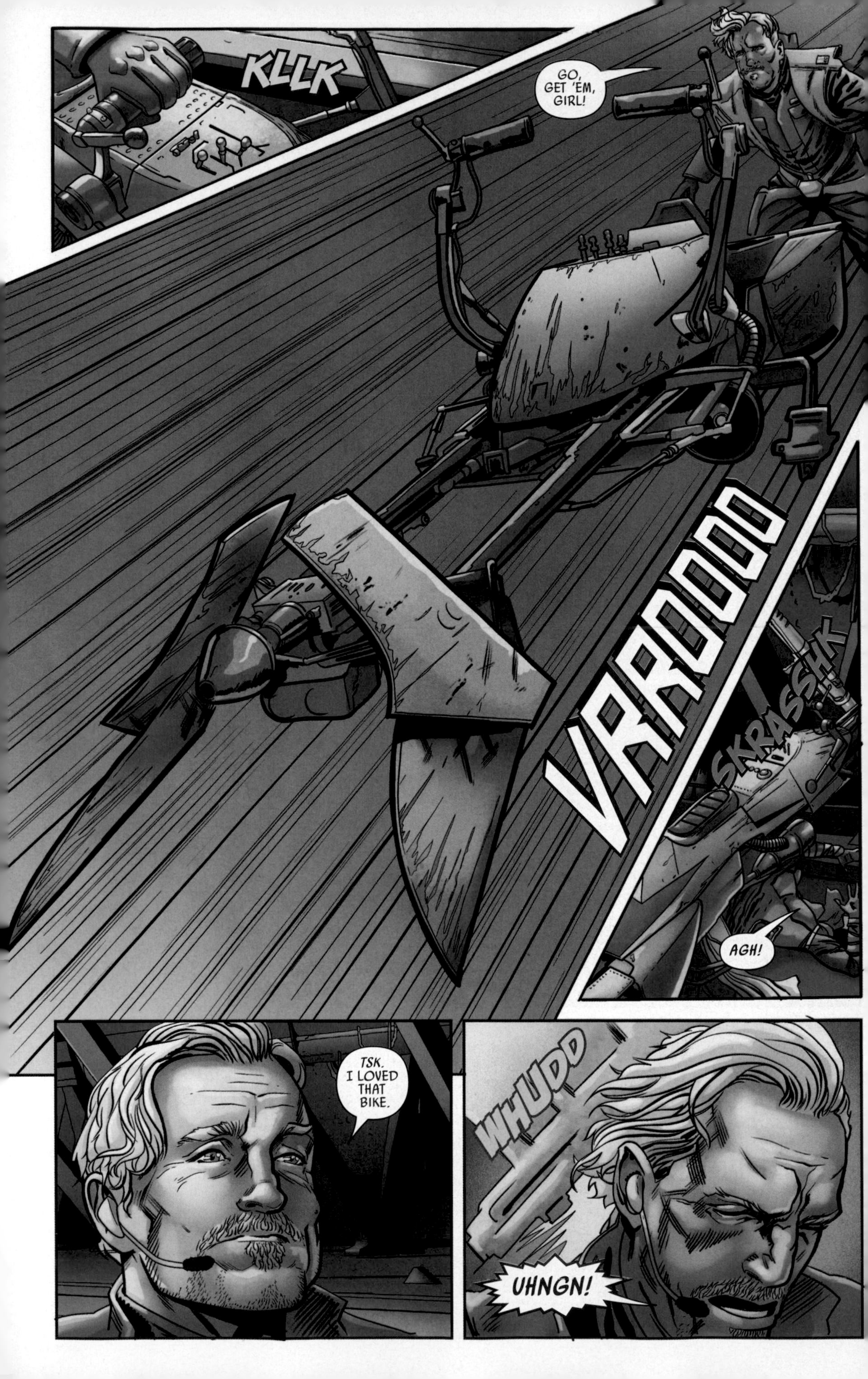
KLLK
GO, GET 'EM, GIRL!
VRROOOO
SKRASSHK
AGH!
TSK. I LOVED THAT BIKE.
WHUDD
UHNGN!

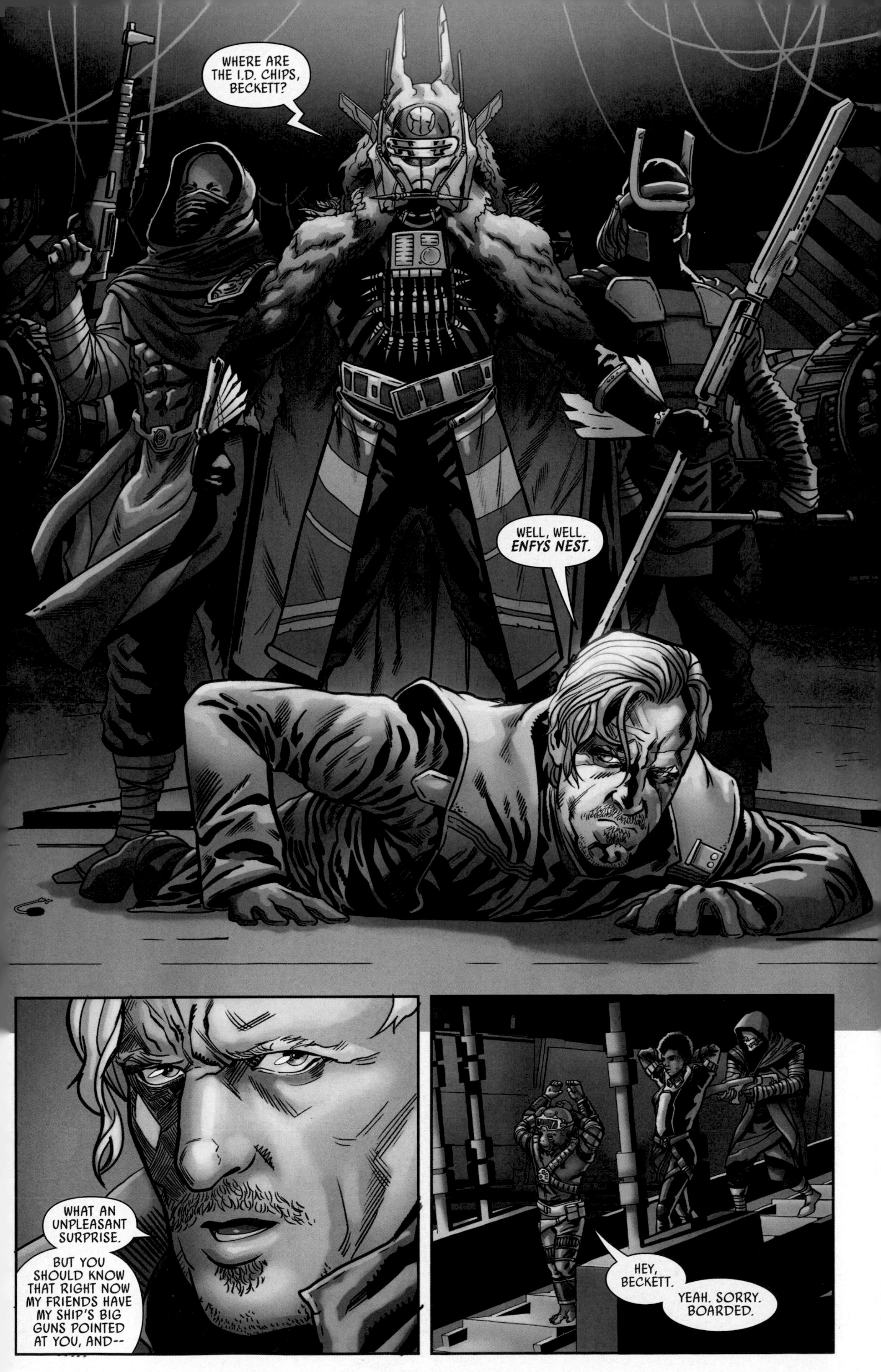
WHERE ARE THE I.D. CHIPS, BECKETT?
WELL, WELL. *ENFYS NEST.*
WHAT AN UNPLEASANT SURPRISE.
BUT YOU SHOULD KNOW THAT RIGHT NOW MY FRIENDS HAVE MY SHIP'S BIG GUNS POINTED AT YOU, AND--
HEY, BECKETT.
YEAH. SORRY. BOARDED.

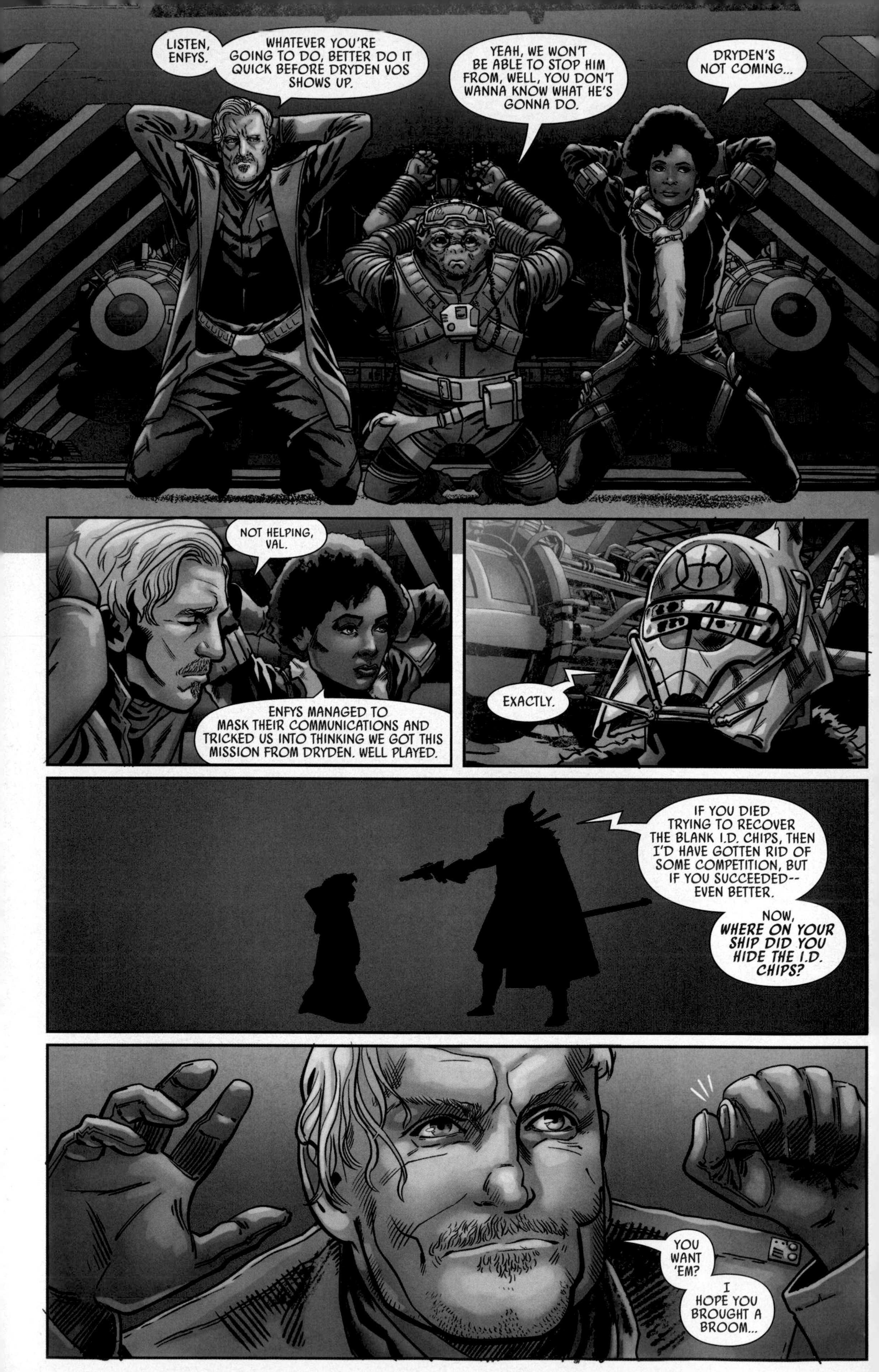
LISTEN, ENFYS.
WHATEVER YOU'RE GOING TO DO, BETTER DO IT QUICK BEFORE DRYDEN VOS SHOWS UP.
YEAH, WE WON'T BE ABLE TO STOP HIM FROM, WELL, YOU DON'T WANNA KNOW WHAT HE'S GONNA DO.
DRYDEN'S NOT COMING...
NOT HELPING, VAL.
ENFYS MANAGED TO MASK THEIR COMMUNICATIONS AND TRICKED US INTO THINKING WE GOT THIS MISSION FROM DRYDEN. WELL PLAYED.
EXACTLY.
IF YOU DIED TRYING TO RECOVER THE BLANK I.D. CHIPS, THEN I'D HAVE GOTTEN RID OF SOME COMPETITION, BUT IF YOU SUCCEEDED-- EVEN BETTER.
NOW, ***WHERE ON YOUR SHIP DID YOU HIDE THE I.D. CHIPS?***
YOU WANT 'EM?
I HOPE YOU BROUGHT A BROOM...

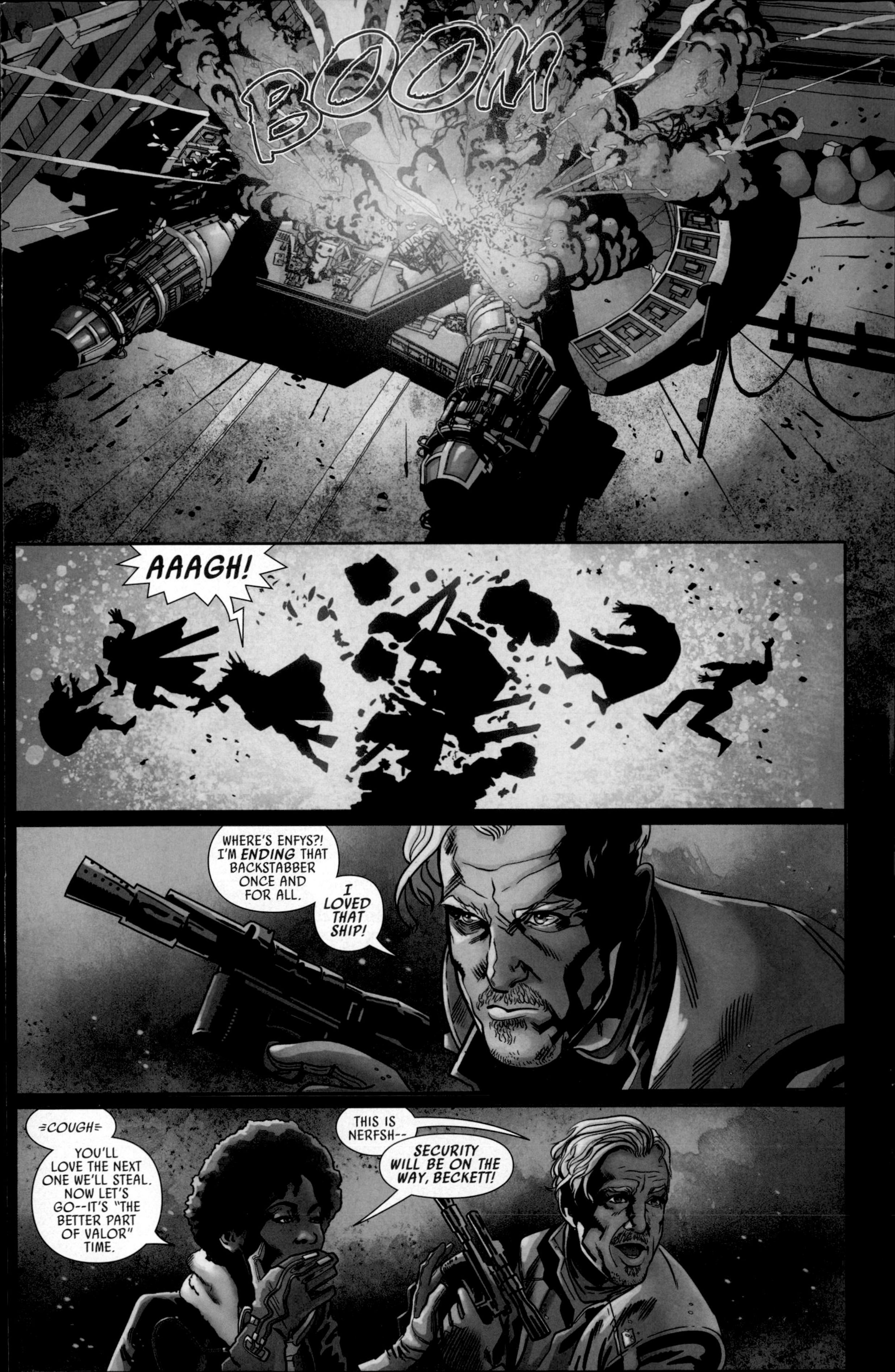
BOOM
AAAGH!
WHERE'S ENFYS?! I'M ENDING THAT BACKSTABBER ONCE AND FOR ALL.
I LOVED THAT SHIP!
=COUGH=
YOU'LL LOVE THE NEXT ONE WE'LL STEAL. NOW LET'S GO--IT'S "THE BETTER PART OF VALOR" TIME.
THIS IS NERFSH--
SECURITY WILL BE ON THE WAY, BECKETT!

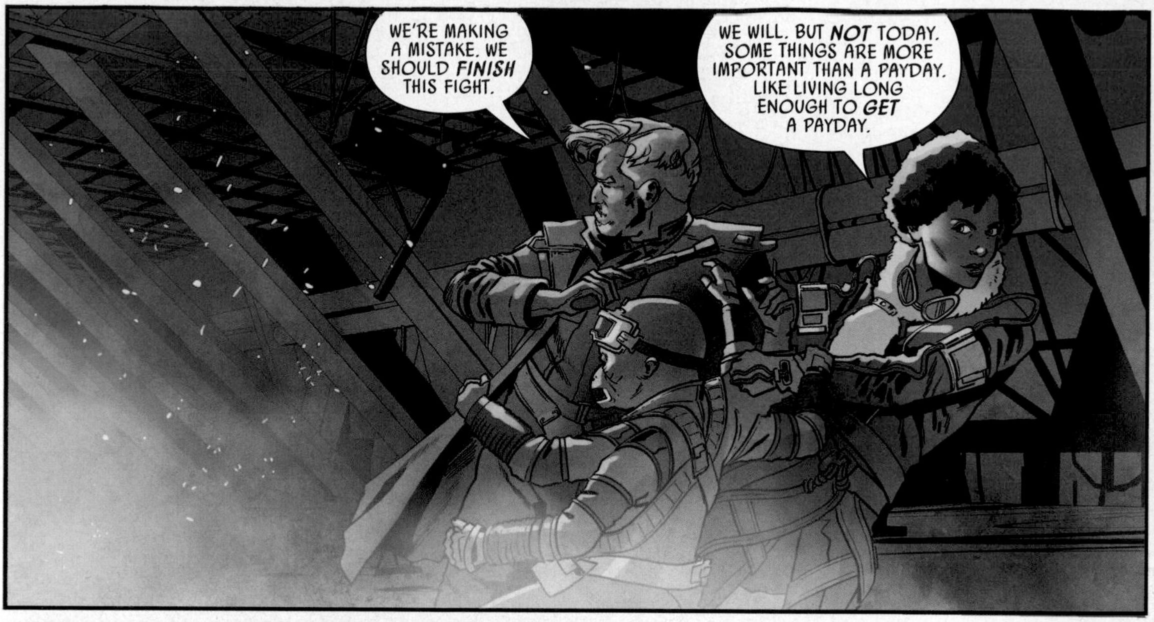
WE'RE MAKING A MISTAKE. WE SHOULD FINISH THIS FIGHT.
WE WILL. BUT NOT TODAY. SOME THINGS ARE MORE IMPORTANT THAN A PAYDAY. LIKE LIVING LONG ENOUGH TO GET A PAYDAY.

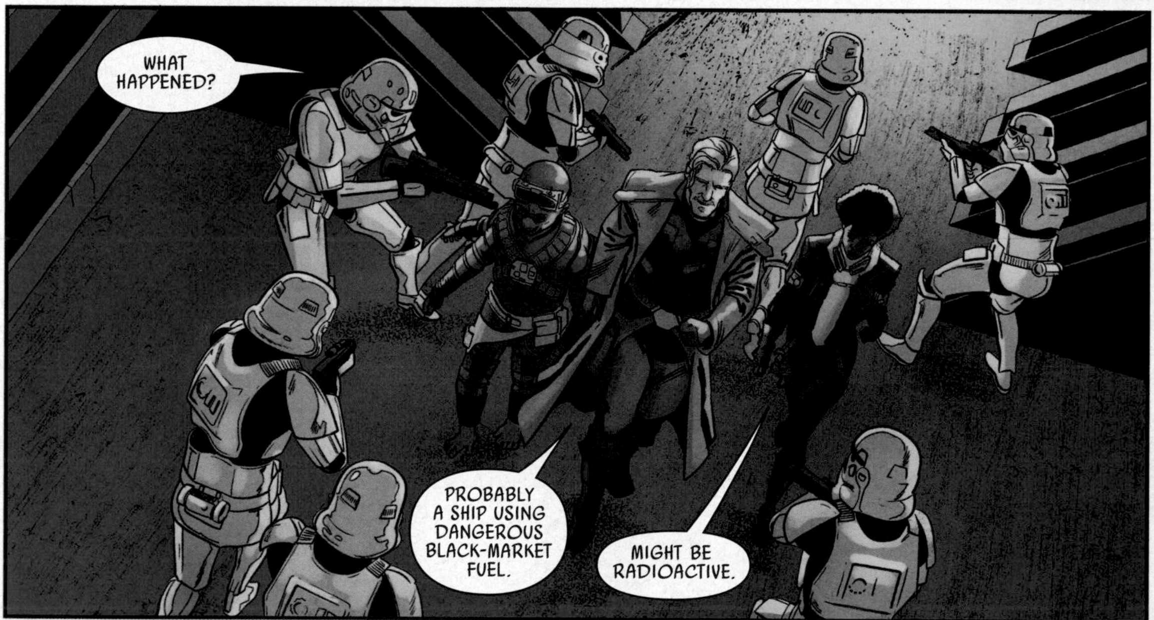
WHAT HAPPENED?
PROBABLY A SHIP USING DANGEROUS BLACK-MARKET FUEL.
MIGHT BE RADIOACTIVE.

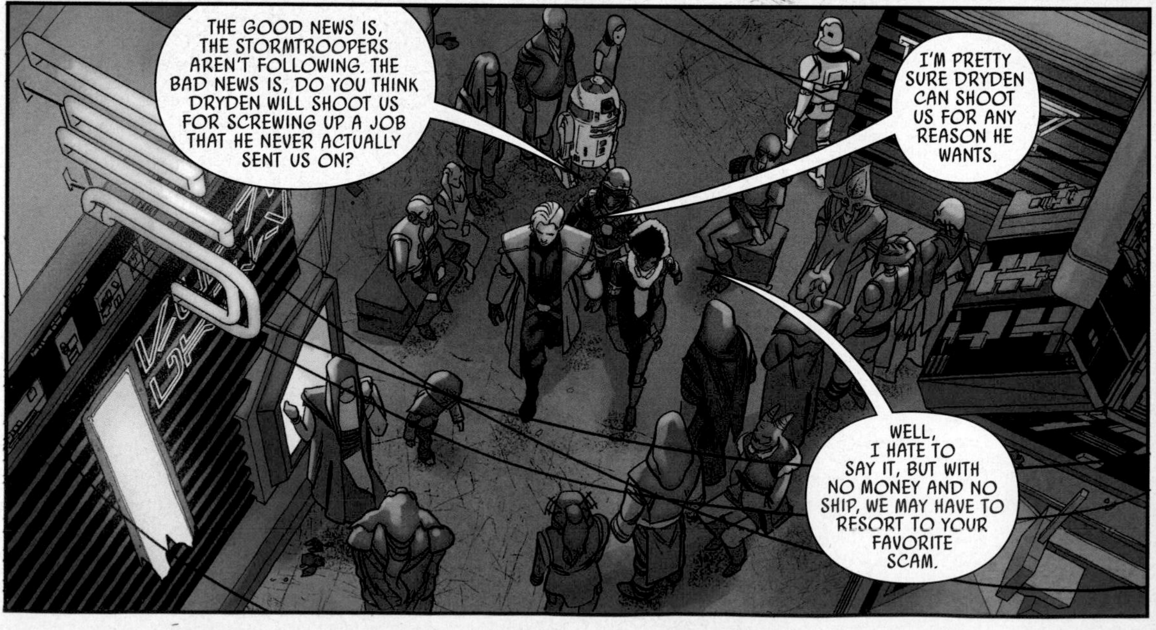
THE GOOD NEWS IS, THE STORMTROOPERS AREN'T FOLLOWING. THE BAD NEWS IS, DO YOU THINK DRYDEN WILL SHOOT US FOR SCREWING UP A JOB THAT HE NEVER ACTUALLY SENT US ON?
I'M PRETTY SURE DRYDEN CAN SHOOT US FOR ANY REASON HE WANTS.
WELL, I HATE TO SAY IT, BUT WITH NO MONEY AND NO SHIP, WE MAY HAVE TO RESORT TO YOUR FAVORITE SCAM.

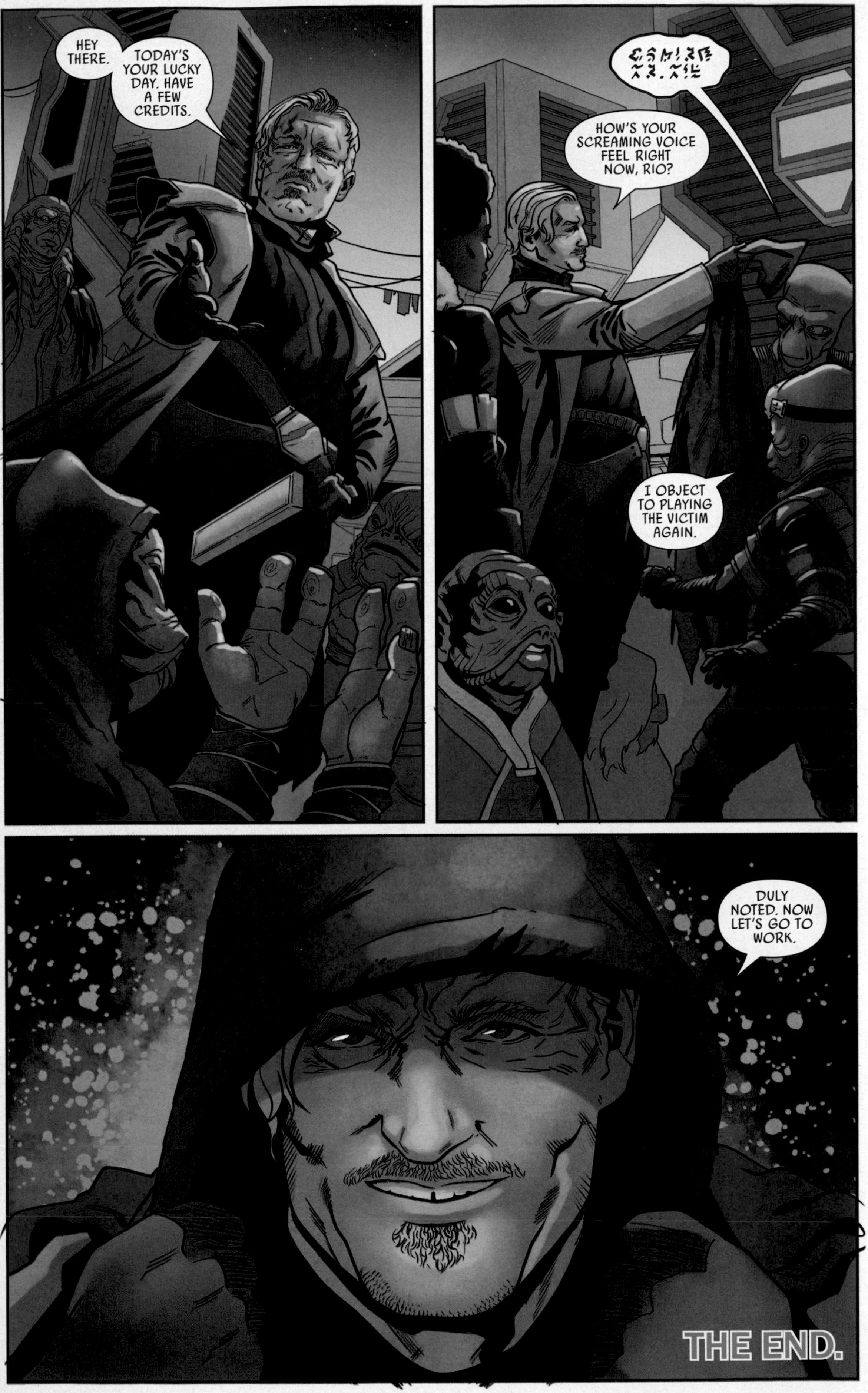
HEY THERE.
TODAY'S YOUR LUCKY DAY. HAVE A FEW CREDITS.
HOW'S YOUR SCREAMING VOICE FEEL RIGHT NOW, RIO?
I OBJECT TO PLAYING THE VICTIM AGAIN.
DULY NOTED. NOW LET'S GO TO WORK.
THE END.

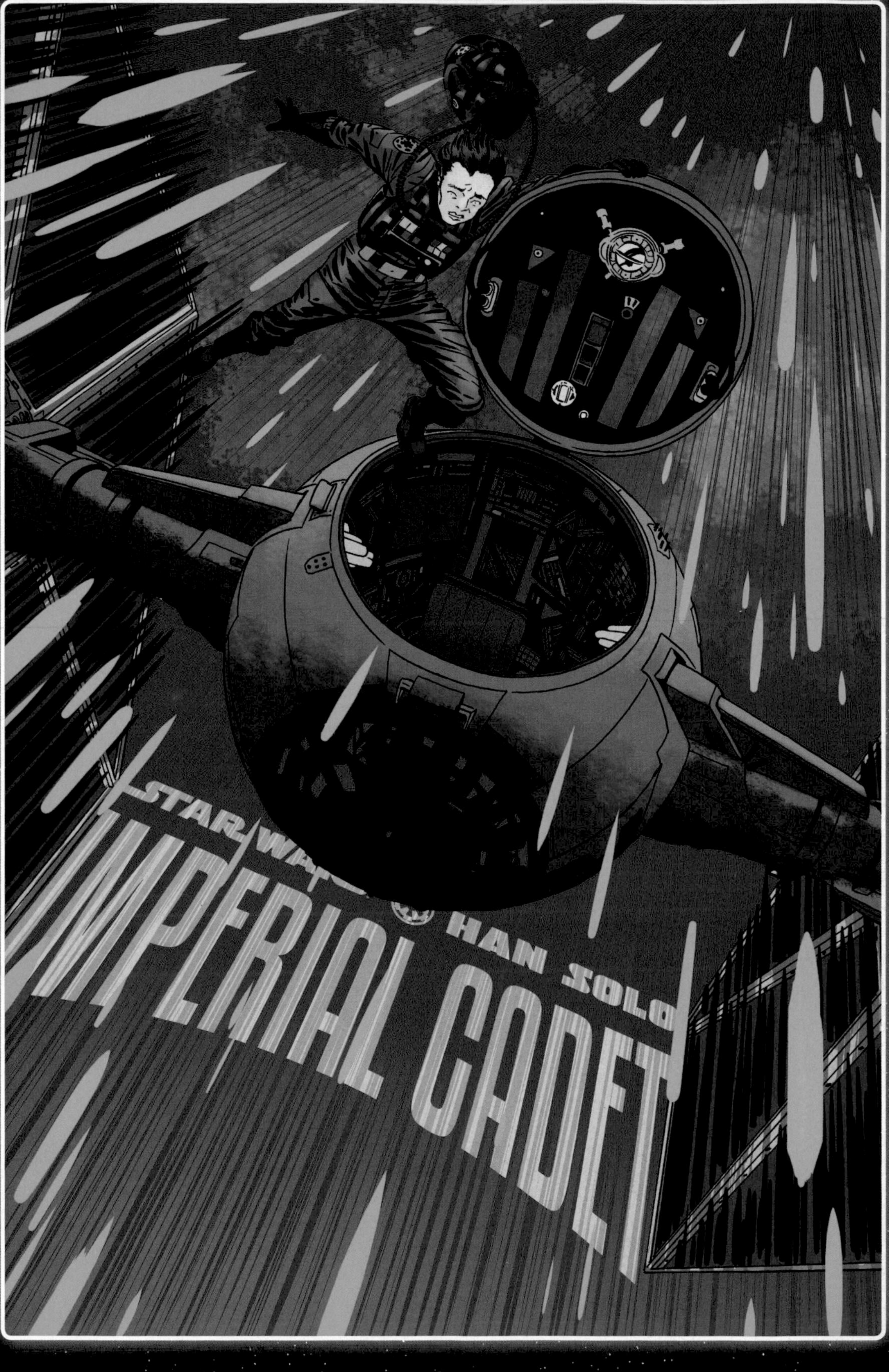
STAR WARS
HAN SOLO
IMPERIAL CADET

***STAR WARS: HAN SOLO — IMPERIAL CADET* 2 Variant by**
MARCOS MARTIN

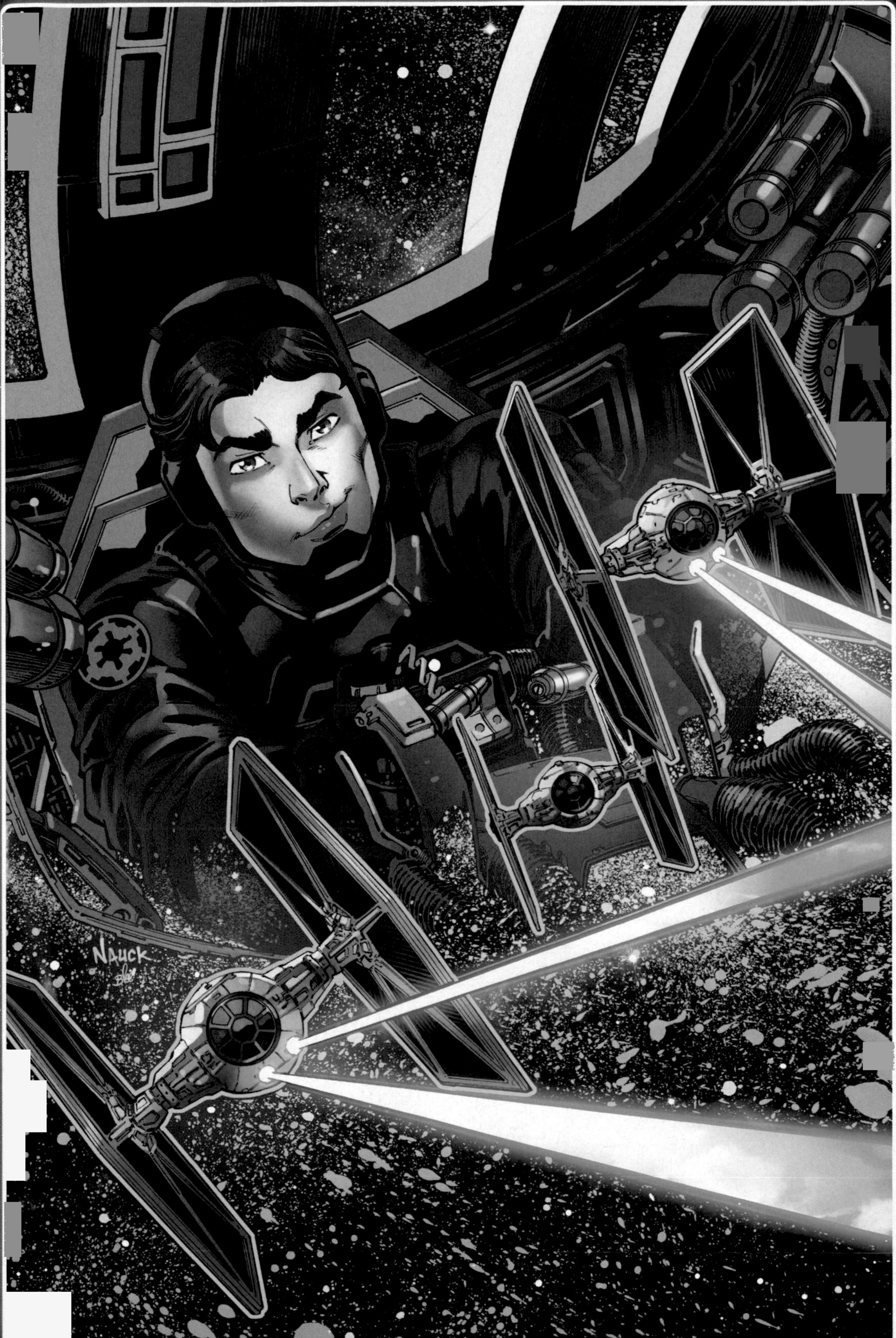
NAUCK
BLEE

***STAR WARS: HAN SOLO — IMPERIAL CADET* 3 Variant by**
TODD NAUCK & FEDERICO BLEE

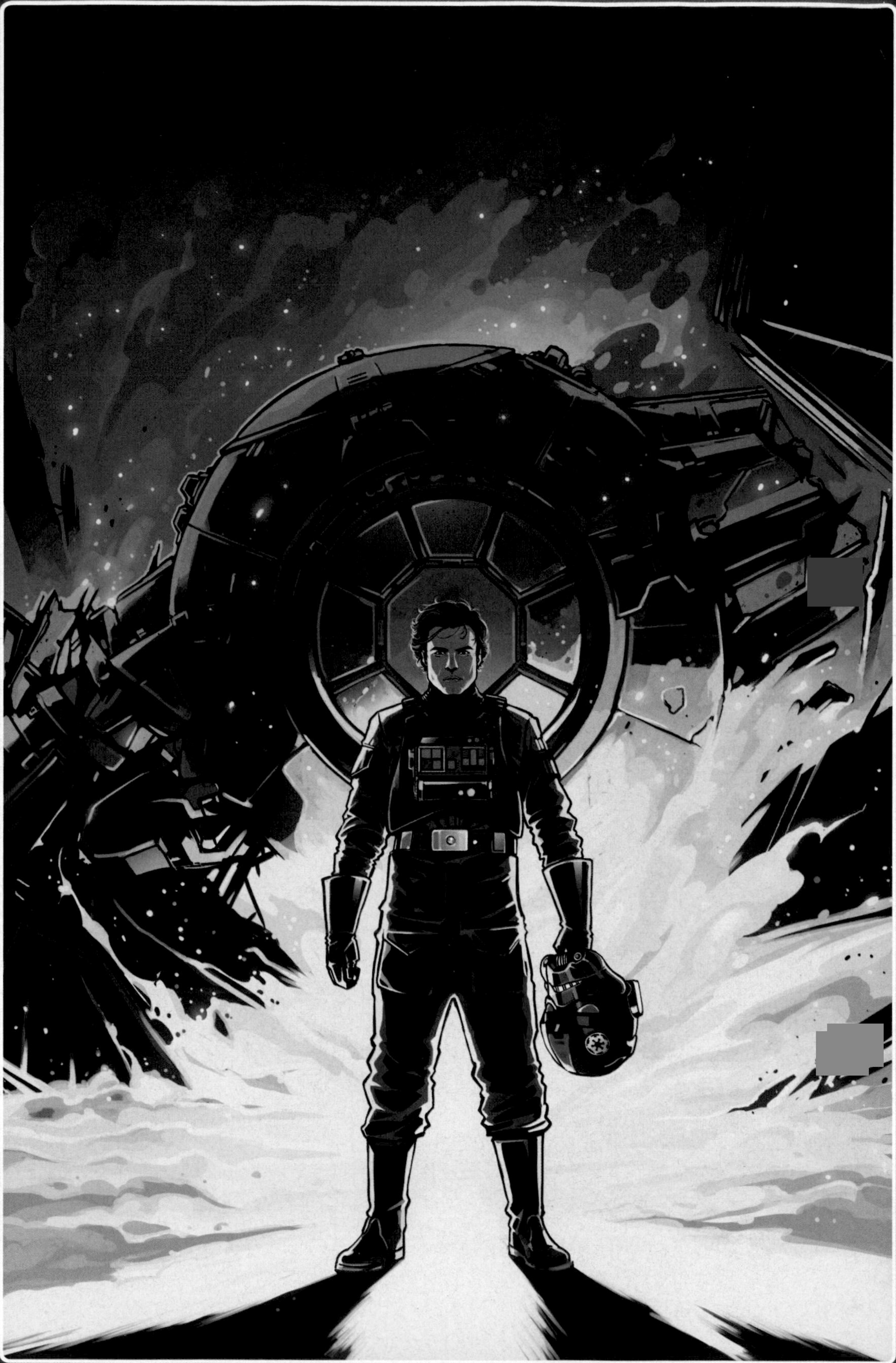

STAR WARS: HAN SOLO — IMPERIAL CADET 4 Variant by
CASPAR WIJNGAARD

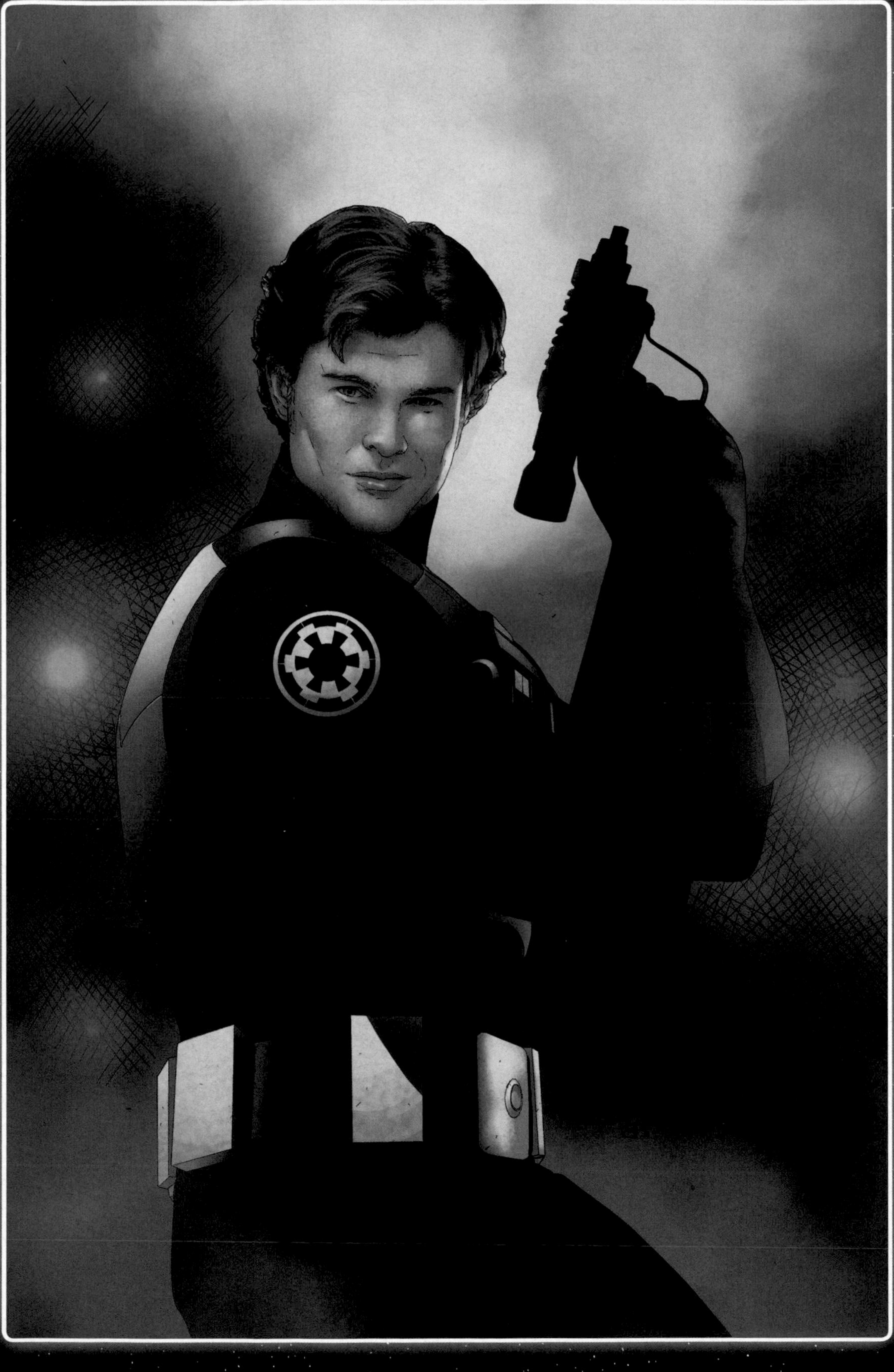

***STAR WARS: HAN SOLO — IMPERIAL CADET* 5 Variant by**
KHOI PHAM & BRIAN REBER

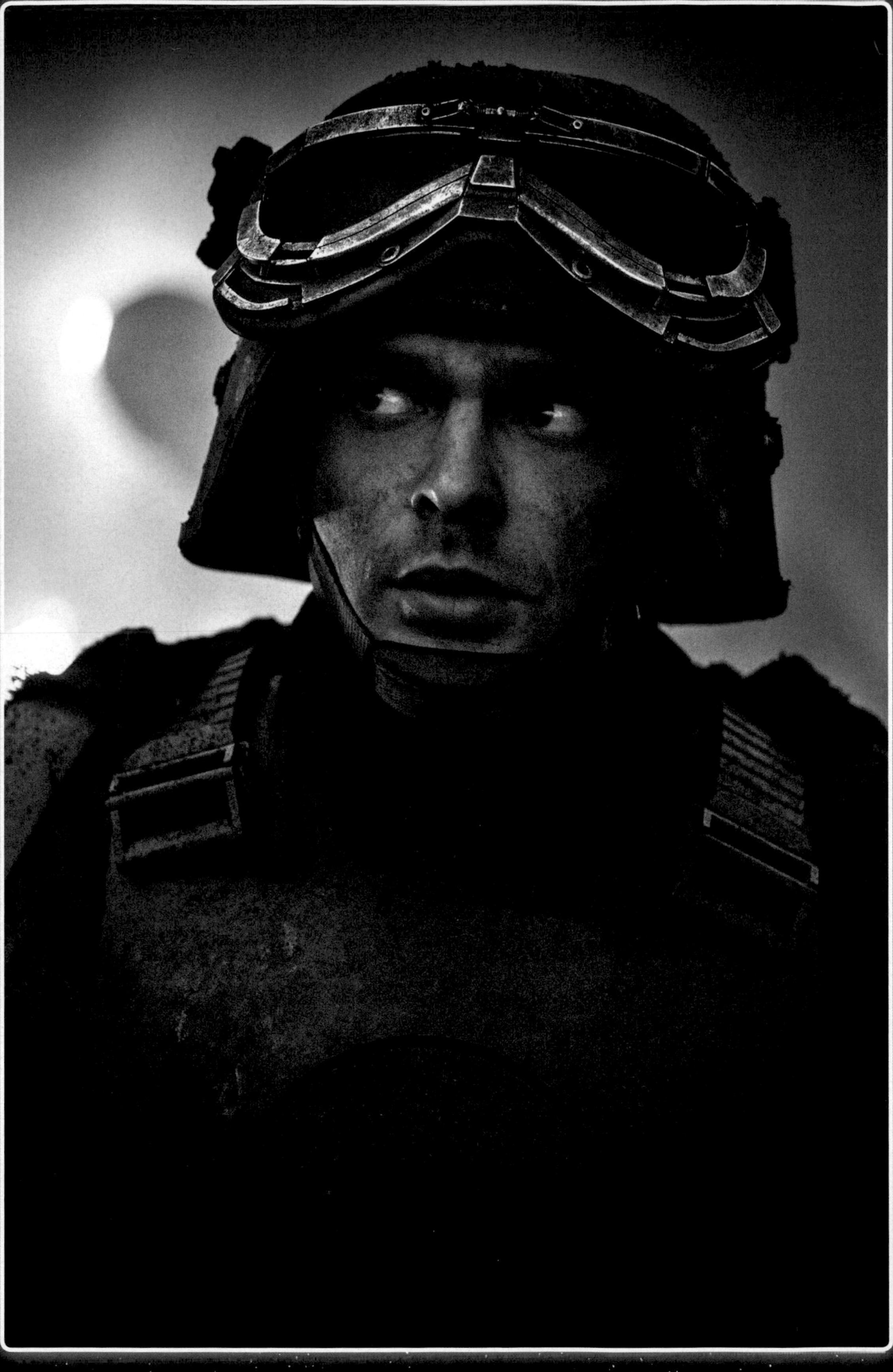

***STAR WARS: HAN SOLO — IMPERIAL CADET* 1 Movie Variant**

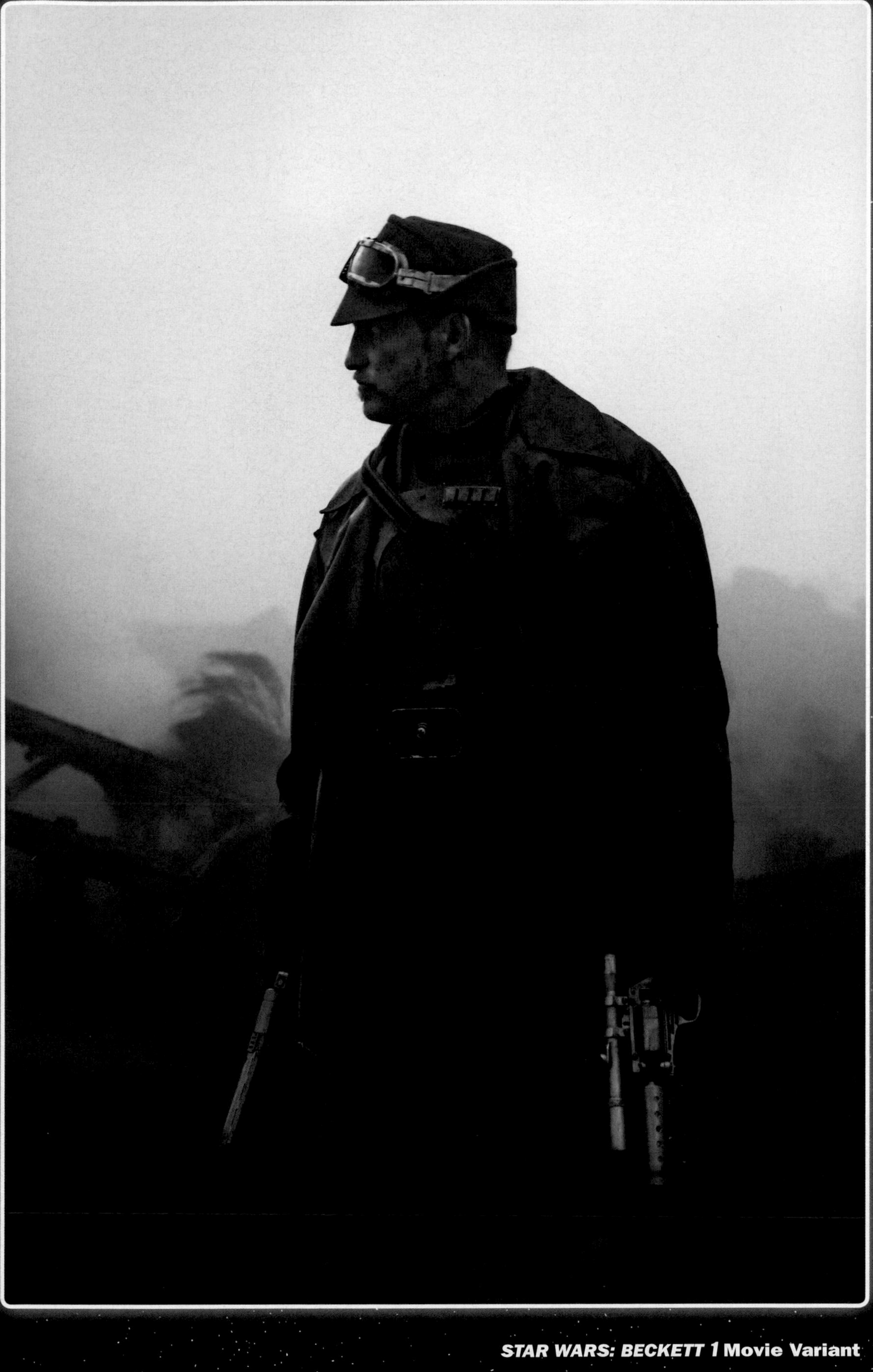

STAR WARS: BECKETT **1 Movie Variant**

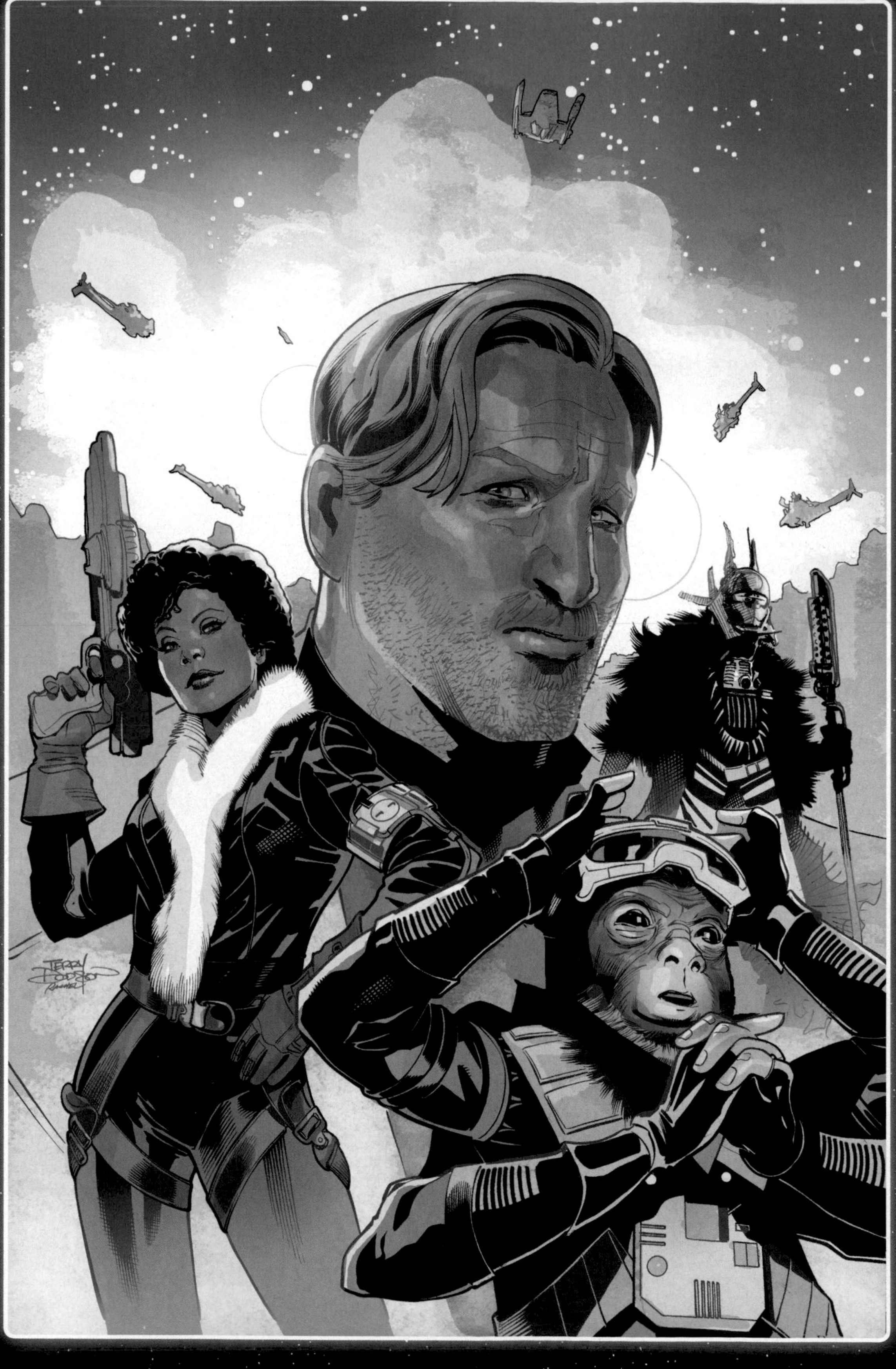
TERRY DODSON RACHEL

STAR WARS: BECKETT 1 **Variant by**

TERRY DODSON & RACHEL DODSON

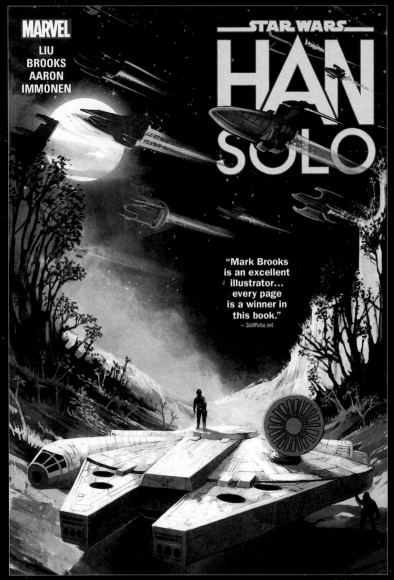

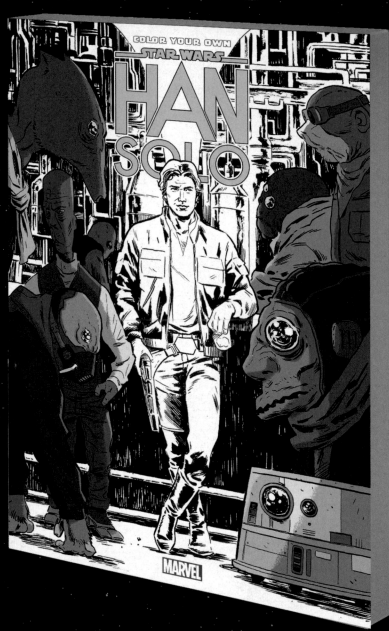

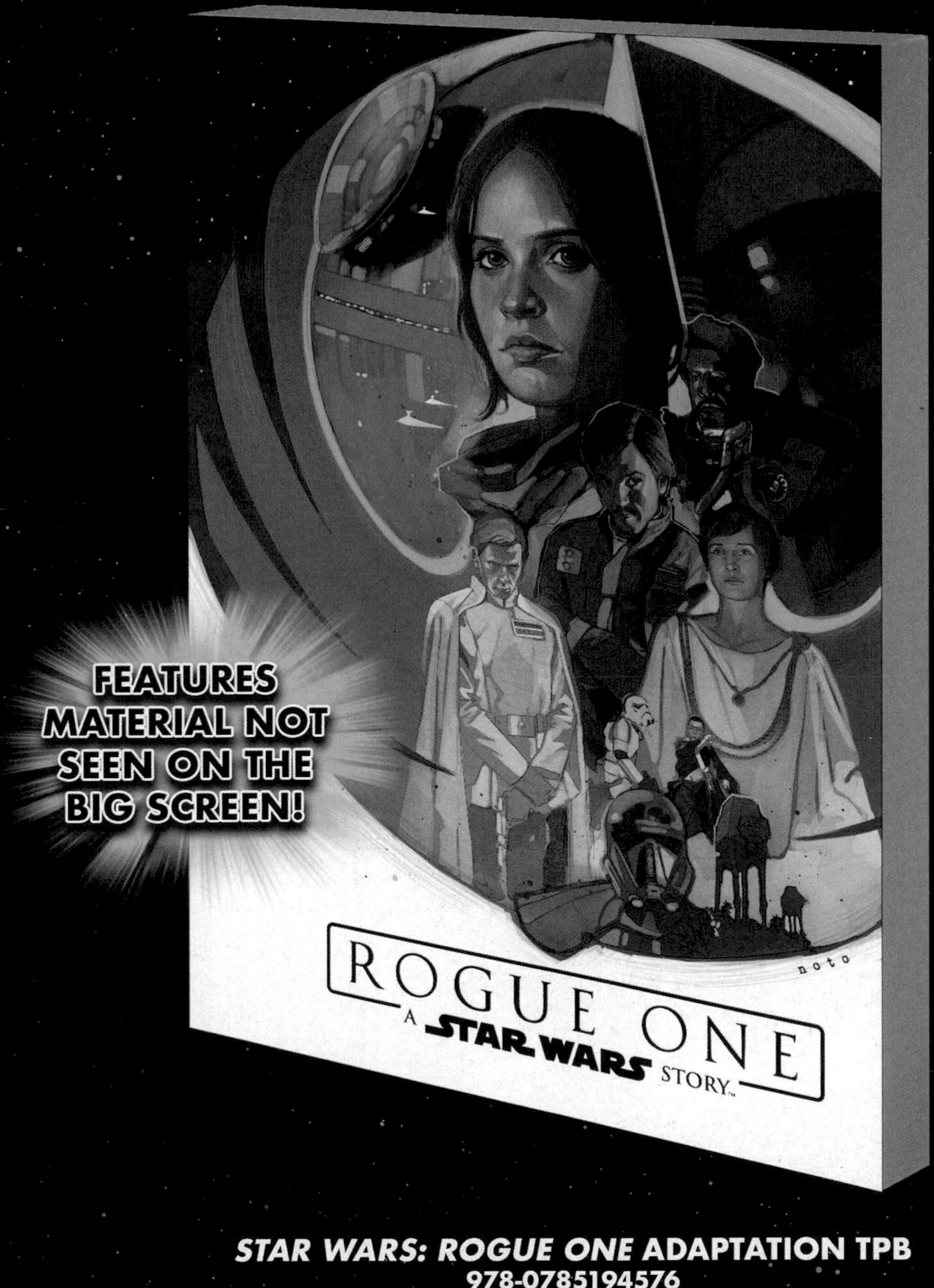
FEATURES MATERIAL NOT SEEN ON THE BIG SCREEN!
noto
ROGUE ONE
A STAR WARS STORY

AFTER BARELY ESCAPING DARTH VADER WITH HER LIFE, DOCTOR APHRA SETS OFF IN SEARCH OF RARE AND DEADLY ARTIFACTS!

MARVEL
GILLEN
WALKER
DEERING
FABELA
STAR WARS
DOCTOR APHRA
"If you're a fan of Star Wars, you gotta read this."
– AdventuresInPoorTaste.com
APHRA

STAR WARS: **DOCTOR APHRA VOL. 1 — APHRA TPB**

978-1302906771

ON SALE NOW

AVAILABLE IN PRINT AND DIGITAL WHEREVER BOOKS ARE SOLD

TO FIND A COM… MICSHOPLOCATOR.COM

MARVEL DISNEY LUCASFILM

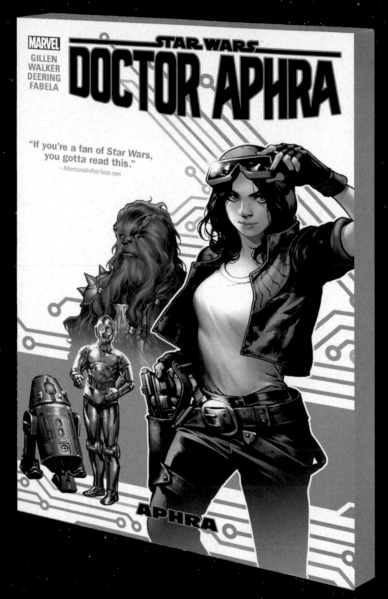